D1378313

# UNDERSTANDING EXCHANGE-TRADED FUNDS

Archie M. Richards, Jr.

## McGraw-Hill

New York Chicago San Francisco Lisbon London
Madrid Mexico City Milan New Delhi
San Juan Seoul Singapore
Sydney Toronto

1 2 3 4 5 6 7 8 9 0   FGR/FGR   0 9 8 7

ISBN-13: 978-0-07-148491-6
ISBN-10: 0-07-148491-4

This publication is designed to provide accurate and authoritative information in regard to the subject matter covered. It is sold with the understanding that the publisher is not engaged in rendering legal, accounting, or other professional service. If legal advice or other expert assistance is required, the services of a competent professional person should be sought.

> —*From a declaration of principles jointly adopted by a committee of the American Bar Association and a committee of publishers.*

McGraw-Hill books are available at special quantity discounts to use as premiums and sales promotions, or for use in corporate training programs. For more information, please write to the Director of Special Sales, Professional Publishing, McGraw-Hill, Two Penn Plaza, New York, NY 10121-2298. Or contact your local bookstore.

# Contents

## PART THREE
## GUIDELINES AND STRATEGIES

# Preface

**Exchange-traded funds (ETFs)** are extraordinary new investments, each one a cross between a mutual fund and a stock. They function like mutual funds but trade like stocks.

By my count, 318 exchange-traded funds are available in the United States, with more abroad. Only a few years after ETFs started trading, two of them have become the most actively traded securities in the world. ETF net assets currently stand at more than $350 billion. This pales in comparison with the $9.3 trillion held in mutual funds, but ETF assets are growing considerably faster.

This book explains how exchange-traded funds work, how you can use them, and why you should indeed use them. We begin from the bottom up:

- Stocks and bonds
- Mutual funds
- Exchange-traded funds
- Unsuccessful and successful ways of using ETFs
- A rundown of all ETFs currently available in the United States

Ironically, the person who invented exchange-traded funds intended them to be used by investment professionals for buying and selling over short periods. Short-term trading works fine for some professionals—we'll explore why. But it's highly unlikely that in-and-out trading will work well for you. ETFs work better for long-term investing—even better, in fact, than mutual funds.

The book contains an extensive glossary. Terms appearing in bold in the body of the work also appear in the glossary. A few words not otherwise mentioned in the book are explained in the glossary as well. Nearly a lifetime of learning is crammed into this book. But even for the novice, it's still an easy read. The book enables you to invest with more understanding, better returns, less worry, and less work. I wish you a fulfilling investment life and many happy returns.

## Acknowledgments

I am grateful to Dodd Kittsley of State Street Global Advisors for reviewing the entire manuscript. His assistance and advice were invaluable.

I appreciate the helpfulness of Vanguard's Gus Sauter, whose input added a great deal.

Many thanks to Scott Wentsel of Ibbotson Associates and Cindy Galiano of Morningstar for their kindness. Ryan Walker of Folio*fn* was very helpful. I appreciate the advice and encouragement of Tim Meyers of Rydex.

Thanks to Dr. Richard Geist and Kathleen M. Martin, CSW, for their insights.

I am very grateful to the five friends and colleagues who read and endorsed this book. They are Tom Lydon, proprietor of ETFtrends.com; Hunter Lewis, cofounder of CambridgeAssociates, LLC; Gary L. Gastineau, managing director of ETF Consultants, LLC; Steve and Annette Economides, authors of *America's Cheapest Family Gets You Right on the Money;* and Angele McQuade, book reviewer for *Better Investing* magazine.

And, as always, thanks to my wife Carolyn for her helpfulness, love, and care.

Archie Richards
Keene, New Hampshire

# PART ONE

# BUILDING BLOCKS

# 1

# Stocks

## Undivided Interest

You own a car, right? The title showing your ownership isn't the same thing as the car, of course. But it represents the car and proves that you own it.

The same goes for a **stock**. It represents your ownership of at least a portion of a business corporation. Unless you're a small-business owner, you don't own all of the company. You own only a "share" of it—hence the term **share** of stock.

Let's say that you and your spouse own your car jointly. You don't own the front seat and your spouse the back seat; you each own the whole thing. So it is with a stock. You don't own just a delivery truck or the front door of the headquarters. You have, as a lawyer would say, an "undivided interest" in the entire business.

What benefits you're entitled to depends on how many shares you own. Let's say the corporation has 1 million shares of stock owned by the public. If you own 100 shares, you have 1/10,000 (100 divided by 1 million) of the whole thing. Each share offers the same benefits as every other share; they're all interchangeable. The benefits you're entitled to are proportionate to the number of shares you own.

## Limited Liability

Let's say you buy shares of a company that overborrows or gets sued for a huge amount. The company goes broke. Even after selling off all its assets, it owes more money than it has.

Your liability, however, is limited. The price of your stock has already fallen to zero. That money is gone. But the company's creditors can't come after you for more. This is why millions of people all over the world are willing to buy stocks. Most stocks tend to rise and don't go to zero. But even when they do, investors can't lose more than they put in.

## Let's Vote on It

Your ownership of the shares gives you the right to vote on vital corporate matters. The election of members of the board of directors is generally the most important vote. You can approve or disapprove of the names proposed. The directors are key because they appoint the officers who run the company.

You don't have to attend the shareholder meeting to vote. You record your vote on a **proxy** form sent to you in advance by the corporation. If you fail to vote, the management votes your shares as it pleases.

Stocks that give their owners voting rights are referred to as **common stocks**; stocks that do not give their owners voting rights are referred to as **preferred stocks**. Preferred stocks generally pay higher dividends but offer less potential for gain. We'll pass on discussing the complex subject of preferred stocks, because few exchange-traded funds contain them.

## Certificates

Back to your automobile title: It was probably sent to you by the state in which you live—the state with which you registered the car.

With a stock, you can ask for a formal-looking piece of paper called a **certificate**, which demonstrates your ownership. It has your name on it and shows how many shares you own. If requested, the stock certificate is sent to you by a bank that's empowered by the corporation to keep track of the ownership of shares and to send out certificates.

Most people don't ask for certificates because they must be kept safe, and they're a pain when the stock is sold: A sale is delayed until you endorse the certificate, send it to the brokerage firm (preferably by registered mail), and wait for the shares to be transferred out of your name and into electronic form. (You may be charged to cover the expense.) No, most people hold their stock electronically in their brokerage account. The statements sent periodically by the brokerage firm are legal evidence that you own the shares.*

Issuing certificates is costly. You cannot obtain a certificate from an ETF. All ETF shares are held electronically in brokerage accounts. This is one reason why exchange-traded funds are inexpensive for investors.

## Dividends

Corporations are in business to make profits for their owners. After paying for raw materials, employees, taxes, and numerous other costs, companies don't always succeed in making money, but they try.

Let's say a company ends up with a profit for the year. It keeps some of it to help the business grow. If the company is relatively young, it probably reserves all of its profit for investment, in an effort to transform from a minor company to a major one. But many companies, especially more mature ones, also pay out some of the profit to shareholders in the form of **dividends**. To creditors who lent them money, companies pay interest. To shareholders, they pay dividends.

The dividends are generally paid quarterly, with the amount determined each quarter by the board of directors. With most companies most of the time, the dividends remain the same or go up over the years.

---

*The right to own property and the right to have that ownership supported and enforced by a court lie at the foundation of western civilization. Nations in which property rights are not enforced cannot help but be poor.

The amount of a stock's dividend is generally expressed in terms of the **yield**. To illustrate, let's say you have money in a savings account. For every dollar, the bank pays interest of 2 cents a year. To find the annual yield, you divide the $0.02 interest by $1.00, giving an interest rate of 2 percent.

Now assume you own a stock that's priced at $10 per share. Each quarter, the company pays a dividend of 5 cents a share—20 cents for the year. When you divide $0.20 by the $10 price, the annual dividend yield also comes to 2 percent.

Most companies change the amounts of their dividends every few years. But the stock price changes every few minutes. Both changes affect the dividend yield, but price fluctuations affect it much more often.

## Stock Classes

A few companies have different **classes** of common stock. In most cases, there are two classes, each offering different voting rights and different dividend yields. Let's say the founder of a company has done a good job at it, and his children look like they'll be on the ball as well. Even though a majority of the stock is now owned by the public, the founder still wants to run the show. But for tax reasons he prefers not to receive dividends. He therefore offers two classes of stock to the public—Classes A and B. (Why he offers *any* stock to the public we'll get to in Chapter 2.)

Class A stock pays a dividend and has one vote per share. The great majority of these shares are owned by the public. Class B stock pays no dividend and has, say, 10 votes per share. The majority of Class B shares are owned by the founder. When shareholder votes are cast, the founder holds sway. The members of the board of directors are the people he wants—perhaps members of his family and close associates—and they of course continue to appoint him as boss. He receives a salary, which is a tax-deductible expense to the corporation, but he receives no dividends, which are not tax-deductible expenses to the corporation. As the company grows, the stock price rises, probably hugely. That's the founder's big payoff.

# Splits

Let's say the stock you bought for $10 a share rises to $100 a share—a 10 bagger, you lucky dog. But many investors prefer low-priced stocks, enabling them to acquire at least 100 shares. To bring the price down, the company arranges a four-for-one **stock split**. For every share investors held before, the company issues three additional shares. On the date this becomes effective, the price drops by 75 percent. Instead of owning 100 shares at $100 (worth $10,000), you now own 400 shares at $25 (also worth $10,000). The value doesn't change. Slicing a pie into parts doesn't make it grow bigger. The sole purpose of the split is to bring the share price down to where investors are more willing to buy it.

Famous investor Warren Buffett doesn't believe in stock splits. At this writing, the Class A stock of his Berkshire Hathaway stock is priced at $91,300 per *share!* (The Class B stock is just a lousy $3,044 per share!)

# Markets

The sun never sets on stock trading. Stocks are traded almost everywhere. Even Iraq has an exchange.

The biggest stock markets are in the United States. Some are physical places, called **exchanges,** where the trading of stocks of a particular company occurs at a specific post on the exchange floor. The most prominent U.S. exchanges are the New York Stock Exchange (NYSE) and the American Stock Exchange (Amex or ASE).

A stock traded on an exchange is said to be **listed.** The 3,000 stocks trading on the New York Stock Exchange tend to be older and larger companies, like Goodyear, although quite a few NYSE stocks are closed-end funds. (This will be explained in more detail later.) The American Stock Exchange lists more exchange-traded funds than any other exchange and also favors new, technology companies. Several other U.S. cities, such as Los Angeles, Philadelphia, and Boston, have smaller exchanges.

Other markets have no physical place, except inside the computer room that links everyone together. Stocks traded this way are called **over-the-counter (OTC) stocks**. On the foremost electronic exchange, the Nasdaq (the National Association of Securities Dealers Automated Quotation System), over 5,000 stocks are traded. These include large technology companies like Microsoft. The stocks of many more smaller companies are also traded electronically; they're called **Bulletin Board** stocks.

The Amex recently merged with the Nasdaq, although the two continue to operate separately.

(I inform you about exchanges because you may hear about them from the media. But the knowledge makes no difference as far as your investing is concerned. Your broker obtains the best price he can for you, no matter where the trade is made.)

## Symbols

Listed stocks are traded with **symbols** containing no more than three letters, such as U.S. Steel (X), Proctor & Gamble (PG), and Spiders (SPY).

Nasdaq and other over-the-counter stocks have symbols containing four letters or more, such as Intel (INTC) and the Nasdaq 100 ETF (QQQQ).

## Who's in Control Here?

Most stock trades are arranged on behalf of financial institutions. But this doesn't mean that institutions "control" the market, as some people believe. Millions of participants the world over are simply too many to be controlled by anyone. Even financial institutions themselves generally don't conspire with one another, scheming to take control. On the contrary, there are thousands of financial institutions, most of whom don't know each other. They compete. Each group tries to scrape off a few bucks for themselves, not for the other guys. One institution may be trying to buy the stock that another is selling, with each striving for the best price. Stock markets are huge arenas for competition—nonviolent and generally honest competition. Do not think that you will be overpowered.

You probably cannot beat institutions at whatever games they may be playing. But you don't have to try. The stock market has room for you. Long periods of time are the right periods of time to be in the market. Get on board. Over the long pull, stock prices go up. Why this is so we'll explain later.

## The Costs of Trading

Getting on board can be expensive. In buying and selling stocks, there are two kinds of costs.

### Commissions

The first is brokerage **commissions**. These range widely, even for relatively small orders. As a general rule, the more you rely on a broker for advice, the higher the percentage of commission you should expect to pay. After reading this book, I hope you won't need a broker's advice and will place orders online at very modest cost—say, $10 a trade or less.

If you're investing $10,000, a commission of $10 is barely noticeable. But if you're investing only $100, a commission of $10 when you buy and another $10 when you sell means that right off the bat you lose 20 percent, which of course is prohibitive. On average, stock prices rise at about 12 percent a year. If you hit the average, you'd have to wait almost two years just to cover the commission costs—a bum deal. Later in this book, I'll suggest ways of cutting commission costs way down.

Some brokerage firms offer **wrap accounts** for which they charge a set annual fee of about 1 percent of the account's value. You can then trade all you like for no additional cost. But firms generally don't accept small wrap accounts.

### Spreads

The other cost of trading is the **spread**. As used here, the word doesn't apply to your waistband. To explain it, we return to our tried-and-true automobile market, which is similar to the stock market in many ways.

Suppose you want to sell your car. Not living on a busy street, you can't attract the attention of many potential buyers by setting your car out front with a for-sale sign. Neither do you know anyone who wants a car just like yours, right down to the model, mileage, color, condition, and year.

You therefore take the car to someone who makes it his business to buy and sell cars. We call him a "car dealer." If we were talking about stocks instead of cars, we'd call him a **market maker**.

Let's say the car dealer/market maker buys your car for $8,000 and places it on sale for $12,000. If this were a stock market instead of a car market, we would say that the dealer **bid** $8,000 to buy the car from you and puts it up for sale for the **ask** price of $12,000. The difference between the bid and ask—$4,000—is his spread.

The spread is 50 percent ($4,000 divided by the $8,000 bid), giving the dealer a nice piece of change. But he doesn't trade cars every other minute. He might have the darn thing on his lot for months, paying interest all along on the $8,000 he borrowed from the bank to buy the car from you. His ownership of the car is risky. If no one wanted to buy it, the dealer would have to sell the car for scrap at, say, $3,000, resulting in a loss.

## Lunch

Now consider the market makers of stocks. They *do* trade every other minute. On some days, there's hardly time to breathe, never mind eat lunch. Because of the volume, the spreads as a percentage of the price of the stock are very narrow, especially on stocks that trade in high volume. At this writing, for example, the bid price of General Electric is 32.58, and the ask is 32.59. (On securities prices, dollar signs are generally omitted.) The difference of 1 cent represents only a minuscule percentage of the price. But the market maker may trade 500,000 shares in a day. The pennies add up.

Market makers bear more risk in holding shakier stocks that trade in low volume. To compensate, they widen the spreads.

There are hundreds of market makers, most of whom specialize in a particular group of stocks. Each stock exchange has its own market makers; they're called **specialists**.

In standing ready to buy a stock at any time, market makers take risk. They may buy a stock for $20 a share. A few minutes later, the price might drop a half a dollar. Bingo, the market maker stands at a loss. In severe markets, some specialists and market makers lose almost everything. Some observers feel that market makers control the market. Now and again, they do, especially when the volume of trading is low. But most of the time, they don't. When they lose big money, the market controls them. Market making can be a hairy business.

In former years, market makers were individuals who had their own money at risk. Increasingly, the people on the firing line as market makers are employees of financial institutions.

· · · · · · · · · · · · · · · · · · · · · · · · · · · · · ·

In the next chapter we move on to how business owners and managers arrange for some of their stocks to be owned by the public, and why they want to.

2

# Secondary Trading

This is the last time with automobiles dealers, I promise. The analogy described here illustrates an important aspect of the stock market. It's especially important for exchange-traded funds.

When you buy a new car, you may well do so through a dealer. But the car wasn't manufactured by the dealer; it was assembled by an automobile manufacturer. The manufacturer sells the car to the public through a dealer. If this were the stock market, the sale would be called an **initial public offering**, or **IPO** for short.

Later, after you've used the car for a few years, you sell it, again through a dealer. But the car is not sold back to the manufacturer. It's sold by the dealer to another party who happens to want to buy a car like yours. Money passes, first from the dealer to you, and later from the new buyer to the dealer. The dealer retains the spread and accepts risk while he owns the car. (He also pays interest to the bank that finances his purchase of the car from you.)

We refer to all this as the *used-car market*. In the language of the stock market, the passing of stock from one party to another after the initial public offering is called the **secondary market**. The car is not sold back to the manufacturer. It's sold in the secondary market to someone who wants to own your car at a price the two parties agree to.*

All right already; that's it for the autos.

## Your Mama Would Be Proud

Companies engage in initial public offerings because they need money to grow. Let's say you're a budding **entrepreneur**. You've got an idea for making and selling a fancy widget. You also have the most important characteristics for an entrepreneur—gumption, ambition, and drive.

You need much more money than you have. Expensive equipment is needed to test your ideas and manufacture the widgets. You need employees, and, as it happens, they need money to eat. You need to rent a place of business and maybe even buy it. You're spending plenty of late nights working, and it helps when the lights and the heating system work. You need a lawyer and an accountant, and, heaven help you, you need to deal with the government for all kinds of things. You'll need to pay people to sell your product. And after all that, you have to wait a month or two for your invoices to be paid. In starting a business, you need a lot of money now, but you don't get paid until later.

Where does it come from? You spend every penny of your own savings, of course. Aunt Hattie, knowing that you have gumption, ambition, and drive, gives you a loan. Other acquaintances get excited about your widgets and provide money in return for a small **equity** interest in the corporation you've formed. (*Equity* is another word for

---

*Most people aren't aware that the used-car market is an important mechanism for "sharing the wealth." As a general rule, the people who buy new cars are prosperous, and the ones who buy used cars are less so. New cars tend to be overpriced, and used cars tend to be underpriced. The rich pay too much for their new cars, and the poor pay too little for their used cars. Through the used-car market, wealth is transferred down the income scale. It's not a "program." It's not intentional. It's certainly not government, but it works just fine. If government intervened less in real estate with zoning, tax advantages, and other measures, the transfer of wealth would have a greater effect in real estate markets as well.

"stock ownership in a business.") Recognizing the same qualities in you that Aunt Hattie did, your bank provides money in the form of a loan and other money in return for stock. All of these funds enable you to get your business going to make and sell your widgets. You've proven that your business ideas are viable and that you're the person to make it happen. You want to go big time, build a large factory, set up a substantial sales force, and sell your widgets throughout the world. For this you need $30 million.

## Investment Banker

Off you go to an **investment banker**, a broker who specializes in initial public offerings. Wall Street is where a lot of those guys hang out. Although your corporation had only a few thousand shares of stock before, your board of directors now authorizes the creation of 4 million shares. (The company remains the same. The board can divide the ownership into as many shares as it likes.)

You, your lawyer, and the investment banker prepare a prospectus, which explains to the investing public all about your business—its history, products, prospects, risks, management biographies, financial statements, and what the $30 million will be used for.

The investment banker organizes a group of brokers who call clients to tell them you have a terrific business idea and you have gumption, ambition, and drive. They sell 3.2 million shares of your company to the public at $10 each, raising $32 million. The investment banker keeps $2 million (it's high-paid work). You receive a check for $30 million, with which you construct a large factory, set up an international sales force, and otherwise build the business.

As mentioned, your company creates 4 million shares, and you sell only 3.2 million of them to the public. You and your early investors retain 800,000 shares. At the IPO price of $10 a share, they're worth $8 million. Before the IPO, you and your associates owned 100 percent of the company. Now you own only 20 percent. But the value of your equity has grown nevertheless, and your smaller portion is worth more than the much larger portion you owned before. You're getting up in the world.

## Sell to Whom?

Let's assume that I buy 100 shares of your stock at the $10 initial-public-offering price. Your company does well. A few years later, the price is $20. I want to sell my shares to build an add-on to my house. I can't sell the shares back to you because you don't have the money. The $30 million has already been spent constructing a factory, setting up an international sales force, and otherwise building the business.

I have to sell my shares through a broker, maybe to a market maker who deals in your stock or possibly to another member of the investing public who happens to enter an order to buy your stock at the very moment I enter my order to sell. The trade may take place on a physical exchange or an electronic exchange. But the point is, the trade is made after the initial public offering and takes place in the secondary market. The stock does not go back to you, just as the car in the used-car market doesn't go back to the manufacturer. (Whoops, sorry.) The stock in your company passes from one party to another, and money goes in the opposite direction. All these exchanges take place among members of the investing public.

## Where It's At

Most of the stock trading you hear about from the media is secondary trading. IPOs make up only a tiny portion of trading volume. From the point of view of the entire economy, IPOs are the absolutely vital. Without them, new businesses wouldn't receive the money they need, and the economy wouldn't grow. But secondary trading is essential too because no initial public offerings would succeed if investors weren't able to sell their shares on the secondary market. A stock market that's less **liquid** is less valuable to everyone.

From the point of view of most investors, secondary trading is more important than IPOs. Some new companies grow rapidly and make a lot of money for investors right after the IPO, attracting considerable attention. But many new companies do not make a lot of money for investors. Some fail altogether. Investing exclusively in IPOs is dicey. For most investors, the secondary market is safer.

## Stock Shares Last Indefinitely

Money obtained to develop a business is called **financing**. Once shares are created and sold to the public, they last indefinitely—probably long after the businesses they financed have gone by the boards. For example, Thomas Edison and his associates created the General Electric company to manufacture new-fangled electric motors. Over a century ago, Edison arranged for an initial public offering to sell GE stock to the public. Since then, General Electric has no doubt sold additional shares to the public, to build factories for the manufacture of refrigerators, for example. The point is that after being split many times, the original shares continue being owned and traded from one investor to another, even though the original electric motors they help build can now be found only in museums.

## Secondary Confusion

Let's say a company issues stock to the public in an initial public offering. It may later sell more new stock to the public to finance additional growth. This subsequent offering is called a **secondary offering**. A company has only one IPO, but it may have many secondary offerings.

The term "secondary offering" is uncomfortably close to the term "secondary trading." The two have entirely different meanings. A secondary *offering* is the sale of new stock to the public after the initial public offering. Secondary *trading* is the trading of stocks after they've been sold to the public by initial public offerings or secondary offerings.

Most companies arrange secondary offerings every few years. But exchange-traded funds arrange secondary offerings much more often, in some cases several times a day. With ETFs, secondary offerings and secondary trading occur at about the same time.

## Bonding

Although most ETFs hold stocks, a few hold bonds. I consider one of those bond ETFs to be an important part of a successful portfolio. We take up bonds next.

# 3

# Those Quirky Bonds

**Bonds** are IOUs given out in return for money borrowed. The borrowers can be the U.S. government, states, municipalities, or corporations. Financial institutions, mutual funds, and the public are the buyers of bonds. Insurance companies own billions of dollars of them. U.S. government bonds are owned by central banks all over the world.

Bonds are first sold by initial public offerings. Thereafter, they can be traded from one investor to another in the secondary market. Most bonds (not including U.S. savings bonds) are sold in units of $1,000 each. That's the price at which the bond pays off; it's called the **par value**. The minimum number of bonds one can acquire is generally 10 bonds.

Bond issues greatly outnumber stock issues. The amount of money invested in bonds also exceeds the amount invested in stocks. But except for U.S. Treasuries, bonds trade far less often than stocks. The bond market therefore receives less publicity. The market for U.S. Treasuries, however, is extremely active. Trades in the multimillions take place about once a second during the trading day.

The interest received by the owner of a federal bond is taxed by the federal government (the IRS) but not by the states. Interest received from most state or **municipal bonds** is taxed by other states but not by the state itself or by the federal government. Interest received from corporate bonds is taxed by both the feds and the states.

# What's the Price?

We dwell on a subject that many investors find confusing: As interest rates change, bond prices move in the opposite direction. Although bonds pay interest semiannually, for this illustration we'll assume they pay only once a year.

Let's say you invest $10,000 in 10 U.S. Treasury bonds that mature in 30 years. Every year, you receive $500 interest (a rate of 5 percent). In the thirtieth year, you receive the final year's interest ($500) plus the return of your loan ($10,000).

In the meantime, the interest rates on newly issued bonds change. What adjusts for this? The interest payments don't change; they remain at $500 a year. The par value doesn't change; the bonds pay off at $10,000. The maturity date doesn't change; your bonds pay off right on the button 30 years after they were issued.

What does adjust to the change in interest rates? Ah yes, the *price* of the bonds. As the interest rates on new bonds fluctuate, the price of your bonds goes up or down as well. But the price moves in the direction *opposite* to the change in interest rates.

Here's an illustration: As mentioned, you buy 10 bonds at the $10,000 par values. They pay off in 30 years at par, and in the meantime you receive $500 a year.

Five years later, your bond has become a 25-year bond. Assume that the interest rate on new 25-year bonds has risen from 5 to 7 percent. Ten *new*, 25-year bonds pay $700 a year. You decide to sell your bonds to pay the initiation fee to your local golf club. What price will you receive?

Let's see, the buyer of your bonds knows that she can acquire 10 new 25-year bonds, each of which pays $700 a year. Your bonds pay only $500 a year. Will she do you the favor of paying you the $10,000 par value? Not a chance. She'll pay you an amount that converts the **yield-to-maturity** of your bond from 5 to 7 percent a year. Not counting commissions and spreads, she pays you $7,669, which is a **discount** from the par value.

For 25 years, she receives $500 a year, plus $10,000 at the end. The profit of $2,331 at maturity converts the annual yield-to-maturity of your bonds from 5 to 7 percent.

You're on the opposite end of that deal. Having bought the bonds for $10,000, you sell them for a loss of $2,331. As interest rates rose, the value of your bonds went down. During the five years, you received $2,500 in interest. Whew, including interest, you just squeak by with a gain.

## If Interest Rates Fall

Now assume that interest rates on long bonds fall in five years from 5 to 3 percent. It's a happier story.

The buyer of your bond can acquire 10 new 25-year bonds that pay only $300 a year. From your bonds, he would receive $500 a year. To bring his yield-to-maturity down to 3 percent, you insist he pay you a **premium** over par.

The buyer pays you $13,483. He receives $500 a year for 25 years plus $10,000 at the end. His loss of $3,483 converts his yield-to-maturity from 5 down to 3 percent.

Look at it this way: As interest rates fall, the interest *payments*, which continue in level amounts, become more and more valuable. The price of the bond therefore has to rise. And as interest rates rise, the level interest payments become less valuable, causing the bond price to fall.

When interest rates change, bond prices move in the opposite direction.

## Longer-Term Bonds, Greater Price Volatility

The longer the maturity of a bond, the greater the price volatility. When a bond pays off in two or three decades, the impact of the inflow of money so far in the future is inconsequential today. The changes of interest rates therefore have maximum effect, causing the price to rise and fall a lot.

But if a bond pays off in only one day, the impact of that large, impending payment is dominating. Any changes of interest rates in the interim are hardly noticeable. The price remains basically the same.

## Quality

Bonds are promises to pay, and sometimes issuers don't keep their promises. The federal government always pays its bonds because it retains a monopoly over the money supply and can always create new money to pay its debts. Very rarely do municipalities fail to pay. More likely they just delay payments, although even this is rare. Defaults are more likely by corporations.

Bonds are rated for their likelihood to pay. The 10 ratings run from AAA (capacity to pay interest and principal is extremely strong) to D (in default, with payments of interest or principal in arrears).

## Calls

**Calls** are more important than many people think. The term means that the issuer of the bond, after 10 years or so (the exact terms are spelled out in the bond itself), has the right to buy back the bond from whoever holds it, often at a price that's 2 percent above par. Most state and municipal bonds can be called, and many corporate bonds can as well. U.S. Treasury bonds are not callable.

Assume you lend $10,000 to your city to build roads. In return, you receive 10 bonds that pay $400 a year for 30 years (4 percent) and pay off at maturity at the $10,000 par. But 10 years after the bonds are issued, they can be bought back at 2 percent over par ($10,200).

On the tenth anniversary, assume that interest rates on 20-year municipal bonds have moved up from 4 to 6 percent. Whoops, your bonds are worth only $7,706. The municipality doesn't call your bonds because it wants to continue paying you 4 percent rather than borrowing anew and paying 6 percent.

Alternatively, assume that interest rates on 20-year munis have moved down from 4 to 2 percent (which is about where I think they will be a decade from now—maybe lower). Without a call, your bonds would be worth $13,270.

Wait a minute! Because of the call, the bonds are worth only a lousy $10,200. The city knows a bargain when it sees it. It borrows *new* money, issuing a new set of bonds paying only 2 percent. It calls your bonds ("Heeere, bonds! Come to me, you little dears!") and uses the new money to buy back your bonds at the low call price.

If interest rates go up, the city allows you to lose. But if interest rates go down, the city doesn't allow you to win. Heads, the city wins. Tails, you lose. All's fair in love, war, and borrowing money.

I'd stick with ETFs of Treasury bonds. They have no risk of default and they're not callable.

## Municipal Bonds

The best way to save taxes on your investments is to hold all of them for at least a year and a day to gain the benefit of long-term capital gains tax rates.

The second best way to save taxes, providing your income is high, is to use municipal bonds. Many people describe municipal bonds as "tax free," which is not entirely accurate. True, the interest is federally tax free, as mentioned. And providing you acquire a bond from your state of residence (or one of its municipalities), the interest is state tax free as well. But if you sell the bond for a profit, the profit is indeed subject to capital gains taxes, long term or short, as the case may be. The same applies if you acquire the bond at a discount and it matures at par.

But be wary about those pesky calls. Almost all municipal bonds are callable, and many corporate bonds are as well. Heads, they win. Tails, you lose.

## A Tip

Let's say you want an investment that provides protection from inflation and complete safety of principal. You're also willing to receive relatively low investment returns. **TIPS** might be your answer—the short name for **Treasury Inflation-Protected Securities**. Unlike other Treasury bonds, neither the par value nor the interest payments for TIPS remains level. Both are continually adjusted for inflation.

The first TIPS bonds were issued in January 1997. The par value of each bond was $1,000. The interest rate was 3.375 percent. The first year's interest payment was $33.75 per bond (3.375 percent of $1,000). (Interest payments from TIPS are actually made twice a year, but for simplification, we assume they're paid only once a year.)

The par value is adjusted for inflation, based on the latest U.S. Bureau of Labor Statistics consumer price index for all urban consumers (CPI-U). The CPI-U is the best measurement available of the general consumer price level for U.S. urban dwellers.

Let's say we're now in the second year. Assume that rising prices cause the CPI-U to register inflation at the rate of 3 percent. The par value of the TIPS is therefore increased by 3 percent from $1,000 to $1,030.

The "real" return, after adjusting for inflation, remains at 3.375 percent. But because of inflation, the actual interest payment rises. The interest payment for the second year is 3.375 percent of $1,030, or $34.76—also an increase of 3 percent.

The increases in both the par value and the interest payments compensate for inflation. At maturity, the bond pays off at par value at its newly adjusted level.

You can buy or sell existing TIPS any time. The prices are also based on the adjusted par values.

If inflation reverses and prices fall instead of rise, the par values of TIPS will fall, although the federal government says they won't be allowed to fall below $1,000. (This promise is foolish. Should prices fall as much as I expect [see Chapter 15], the government will hemorrhage money if the promise is not revoked.)

## A Little Problem

For people who hold TIPS outright (not in an IRA or pension plan), there's a distinct tax disadvantage: The interest is federally taxable currently as ordinary income. But increases in the par value are *also* taxable currently as ordinary income. Yet the investor receives no cash from the par value increases until the TIPS is sold or redeemed, which may be many years later. This is called **phantom income**: Even though the income is not received and cannot be received, it's taxed currently anyway. A person is forced to come up with funds from other sources to pay the tax. Doing this for 20 years or more for a long-term TIPS could become tiresome.

Many people hold their TIPS in IRAs or qualified retirement programs. There, the phantom income factor makes no difference.

Both bonds and stocks are referred to with the generalized term **securities**. Neither bonds nor stocks are exactly secure, of course, because their prices can go down as well as up. But "securities" is an often-used term, and we'll use it too.

## Onward and Upward

We turn now to aggregations of securities, which are similar to exchange-traded funds. They're called mutual funds.

# Mutual Funds

Exchange-traded funds, as mentioned, are a cross between mutual funds and stocks. We've covered stocks; now comes **mutual funds**.

Mutual funds are portfolios of securities that can be bought and sold as a single unit. The securities can be stocks, bonds, or both. When the mutual fund owns stocks, don't get confused about the use of the word *shares*. The shares of the mutual fund you own are different from the shares of stocks owned by the mutual fund in its portfolio.

Mutual funds can issue a certificate showing how many shares you own. But most investors don't ask for certificates. The statements received from the mutual fund or the brokerage firm provide the necessary evidence of ownership.

There are three kinds of mutual funds. They're all quite different, although exchange-traded funds have similarities to each one:

- Open-end funds
- Closed-end funds
- Unit investment trusts

Open-end funds are by far the most popular type of mutual fund; we'll discuss that one first.

## Open-End Funds

The essential feature of **open-end mutual funds** is that the number of shares of the fund held by the public changes every day. The number is "open ended." The more money people invest in a fund, the more shares it has outstanding.

When you buy shares of the fund, the money goes to the fund. To reflect your ownership, the fund creates *new* shares for you. In effect, open-end funds engage in ongoing IPOs with no investment banker involved. If the portfolio manager approves, the fund uses the money to acquire additional shares of stock for its portfolio.

When you sell your shares of the fund, the shares are redeemed by the fund. The shares disappear and no longer exist. The fund sends you cash in return. If the portfolio manager approves, the fund sells some of the stocks in its portfolio to furnish the money. (If you're selling in panic at the bottom prices of a bear market, the fund may have to sell its stocks at low prices, increasing the losses for everyone. For your sake as well as that of all the other shareholders, try to avoid panic selling.)

Open-end funds value their portfolios once a day, as of the closing prices. They add up the values of all the securities and the cash held and deduct the liabilities. The net amount, called the **net asset value (NAV)**, is a multi-million-dollar number, in some cases multi-billion.

To arrive at the net price *per share*, the net asset value is divided by the number of fund shares held by investors that day. The net price per share is also called the net asset value. This can be confusing, but you can usually tell from the context whether NAV applies to the entire fund or whether it applies to the NAV per share. The NAV for the fund is an enormous number. The NAV per share is usually less than $100. The price of an open-end fund reported in the newspaper is the NAV per share.

All trades in open-end funds take place at market after the close. Here's what those terms mean:

- In the case of open-end mutual funds, *at market* means you buy or sell the shares at the net asset value. You can't specify that you want to buy a little below the NAV or sell a little higher. The trade is done *at* the NAV; that's it.

- *After the close* means after 4:00 p.m., New York time. The net asset values are computed on the basis of the closing prices. (Hedge funds do not disclose their net asset values on a daily basis. See Figure 4-1.)

In recent years, some mutual funds (a minority) engaged in *late trading*. To understand what this means, assume that a hedge fund acquires shares of a U.S. mutual fund that specializes in Japanese stocks. Trading

---

### Hedge Funds

**Hedge funds** are mutual funds for rich folks. You can't purchase an interest in a hedge fund unless you swear on a stack of Bibles that you have a ton of money. Oh, and in most cases, you have to invest $1 million or more in cash.

Hedge funds are regulated more lightly by the Securities and Exchange Commission than mutual funds. (The SEC is trying to pull in hedge funds completely under its wing, but hasn't succeeded so far.) Most hedge funds are active traders and use high-risk investment strategies, including futures and options. They can use margin and sell short. (All these terms will be explained in later chapters.)

Hedge funds do not disclose their net asset values on a daily basis. As an investor, you may not be able to determine the value of your interest at any given time. You also cannot sell your interest in a hedge fund on just any old day. You have to wait for the managers to open the exit gate, which may take place quarterly or in some cases even yearly.

The managers of hedge funds aren't shy about getting paid. Many of them charge 2 percent of the fund's value per year and also take 20 percent of the profits. But when the value of the fund falls, sorry, managers draw the line about sharing losses.

In recent years, hedge funds have proliferated, now numbering over 6,000 worldwide. Some hedge funds have performed magnificently. But many haven't, and some have gone broke.

One reason hedge funds have become popular is because there are a lot more rich folks than there were 20 years ago. Also, the rich prefer not to step their well-manicured toes into the investments used by the hoi polloi like the rest of us. They like to feel special, and they're willing to incur foolish risk to do so.

---

**Figure 4-1**

in U.S. funds is supposed to stop at 4:00 p.m. Eastern time. But the Singapore market, which lists Japanese stocks, opens at about the same time. Two hours later, at 6:00 p.m. Eastern time, the hedge fund is in a position to observe whether Japanese stocks in Singapore are up or down. If they're up, the hedge fund holds the shares of the U.S. fund and sells the next day at a profit. If the Japanese stocks are down, it sells *at the previous 4:00 p.m. price*, thereby preventing a loss for the hedge fund.

Late trading is illegal. It reduces profits and increases losses for the mutual fund's other shareholders. Compounding the violation, the hedge fund may pay the U.S. mutual fund or the fund manager for the right to engage in the late trading.

But do not assume that if you invest your hard-earned money, you will be sheared like sheep. You won't, especially if you use exchange-traded funds. Immoral behavior by mutual funds (I describe more such behavior later in the book) is made possible because mutual funds do not continually disclose what they own. This is not the case with ETFs. Every day, they disclose considerable information, including what they own.

Do not keep your money in the bank out of fear. The investments I recommend later in this book are especially law-abiding.

### Your Choice

Mutual funds generate cash when they receive dividends from their portfolio of stocks and when they sell stocks at a profit. In filling out the application for a fund account, you're asked to decide how you want this money to be treated. You can have it paid to your brokerage account or to another fund in the same fund family. (If you hold the certificate, the dividends and capital gains are paid directly to you.)

Alternatively, you can direct the fund to acquire more shares of the fund from which the money came at the net asset value pertaining at the time. These instructions can be changed at any time. Automatic reinvestment means no delay in getting the cash working again.

(With exchange-traded funds, dividends are not reinvested automatically in additional shares. They're paid to the brokerage account. You yourself can acquire more shares of the ETF, but you must place a separate order. Unless you make a special arrangement with the brokerage firm, it's not automatic.)

## A Word about Taxes

When dividends and capital gains are reinvested automatically at your direction, you don't see the money. But unfortunately, your friendly IRS agent says that since you have the right to receive it, the income *is* taxable in the year it becomes available.

Money earned by the mutual fund retains its character when it's passed on to you. Both qualified dividends and long-term capital gains, for example, are taxed at the maximum 15 percent federal rate. Unfortunately, mutual funds cannot pass out capital losses. Those are used by the fund to offset gains.

## Automatic Investing of New Money

One of the nice things about open-end funds is that periodic investments can be made automatic. Let's say you earn money that goes into your bank account. Each month, the bank wires whatever amount you specify directly to the fund. The additions help to build your fund account without your seeing the money first. What you don't see you won't spend. Automatic investments can be made monthly, quarterly, semiannually, or annually, as you please.

Later, perhaps in retirement, the automatic transfer of funds can go the other way. Periodically, the fund wires money to your bank account. *Then* you can spend it.

## Operating Costs

All funds have operating costs that are disclosed in the **prospectus**. The costs include very heavy money to the owners of the fund organization, heavy money to the manager who selects the securities, and pretty heavy money to the stock analysts who help decide which stocks are most attractive. The costs also include administration, custody of the assets, and other related costs, including, in some cases, marketing. All of this adds up to a hefty figure annually. A tiny portion is deducted from the fund every business day. This is one of the liabilities factored in before the net asset value is calculated. Annual operating costs are usually expressed as a percentage of net assets, called the **expense ratio**.

### Transaction Costs

When funds buy and sell the securities in their portfolio, they incur transaction costs. Like everyone else, they pay commissions and spreads (see Chapter 2). The commissions for financial institutions are generally lower on a percentage basis than they are for us regular folks. But because the amounts of money in institutional trades are usually larger, the spreads are generally wider.

Transaction costs, which reduce net asset values, are not included in operating costs and not disclosed in prospectuses. But prospectuses do disclose the rate at which the fund buys and sells its securities. On average, equity (stock) mutual funds of the open-end variety turn over something like 95 percent of their portfolios every year—a ridiculously high number. You should assume that the higher the rate of turnover, the higher the transaction costs. Stick to funds whose turnover rates are no greater than 25 percent—preferably lower. (Pssst, the turnover rates of the ETFs I favor are very low.)

Some open-end mutual funds charge fees of, say, 1 percent on redemptions that occur within a relatively short time, say, one year. The fees are paid to the fund, not the fund manager. Their purpose is to discourage investors from jumping from one fund to another, and to compensate the fund for the extra transaction costs.

### Sales Costs

When you buy a fund through a broker, the broker and the firm the person works for want to get paid. The broker may tell you, "No commissions are charged against the account." Or the broker may say, "The account has no front-end load." Such comments may technically be true, but they disguise the fact that the sales costs applying to your account are in fact paid entirely from your account. The charges may be called "expenses" and not "commissions." But no matter what term is used, no one pays for the sales costs on your account except you.

In some cases, the sales costs are deducted from your account up front. In this case, you're buying *Class A* shares. In other cases, you're assessed extra charges of various kinds. These may include extra costs for a certain number of years plus redemption charges (*Class B*) or extra costs indefinitely (*Class C*).

All funds that levy sales charges are referred to as **load funds**. Funds that do not levy sales charges are called **no-load funds**. With these, you have to take the initiative to contact the fund via the Internet or by phone. You have to read the prospectus, fill out the applications, and send in your check, all without a friendly salesperson looking over your shoulder, egging you on. Many funds assess modest extra charges to pay for marketing costs. With load funds, they pay the brokerage firm, say, 0.25 percent a year for servicing the account. With no-load funds, the extra charges may refund the manager for advertising. These marketing costs are referred to as **12(b)1 charges**, named after the section of SEC regulations that permit them.

With exchange-traded funds, you must pay commissions, as you do with stocks. But the fund itself incurs no sales costs, whether they be A, B, or C. ETFs may have tiny marketing costs, but these are included in the low operating costs.

Selling costs for mutual funds (not including transaction and tax costs) are spelled out in the firm's prospectus. (Check under "shareholder fees" and "annual fund operating expenses.")

*Minimums*

Mutual funds require minimum investments. At the Vanguard Group (my favorite mutual fund family), the minimums for non-IRA accounts are $3,000 per fund. On accounts with values of less than $10,000, Vanguard charges an extra $10 a year. The minimum for IRA accounts are lower, and so are the minimums for additions and the minimums from automatic electronic investments from bank accounts. As a general rule, the minimums for load funds are lower than those for no-load funds.

Some funds have minimums of $25,000, and a few that want to appear really special have minimums of $500,000.

# Closed-End Funds

The essential feature of **closed-end mutual funds** is this: The number of shares of the fund held by the public remain fixed. In other words, the number of shares is a "closed" matter. When you buy closed-end shares, you do not buy them from the fund, and the fund creates no new shares for you. Instead, you buy the shares on the secondary market from another investor who wishes to sell. Most trading of closed-end funds takes place on the New York Stock Exchange.

The price is the amount you and the seller agree to. This is seldom the same as the fund's net asset value. If the price is lower than the NAV, the fund is said to trade at a **discount**. If the price is higher than the NAV, it is said to trade at a **premium**. Most closed-end funds hold bonds, many of them at a fairly substantial discount averaging about 15 percent. (Never buy a closed-end bond fund at its IPO. The broker will proclaim that you can buy it without a commission. That's true, but as described in the prospectus, the broker-dealer is amply paid by the underwriter for selling the IPO. After the IPO, the price of the fund is likely to fall by at least that amount.)

Okay, you own shares of a closed-end fund, and now you want to sell it. Your broker must find another party who's willing to buy your shares. If no one's available at the moment, the market maker will buy it; the fund itself will not.

If the NAV has gone down, you take a whammy, of course. If the NAV has gone down *and* a 10 percent premium has turned into a 10 percent discount, you take a double whammy. Try to avoid this.

Dividends and net capital gains of closed-end funds are generally used by the fund manager to purchase additional securities in the portfolio. This cash is not paid out to investors, and the money is not made available for the automatic purchase of additional shares of the fund.

## Unit Investment Trusts

**Unit investment trusts (UITs)** are open-end but unmanaged mutual funds. The portfolio composition is determined at the beginning, and the fund is offered to the public via an IPO. Thereafter, the securities (usually bonds) remain unchanged. As bonds mature, they're generally not replaced. Interest, dividends, and net capital gains are paid to investors. No reinvestment in additional shares is permitted. Investors may redeem their interest at any time. To obtain the cash, the manager sells a portion of the portfolio. Termination of the fund occurs after a certain number of years specified at the beginning in the prospectus. Any securities then remaining are sold, and the proceeds are paid to shareholders. The regulatory burden on unit investment trusts is lower than on open-end mutual funds. To cut costs, the first few exchange-traded funds were organized as UITs. But after ETFs proved to be popular, most subsequent ETFs were organized as open-end mutual funds.

## Moving On

We forge on to a key element of ETFs: indexes and index funds.

# Indexes and the Funds That Track Them

## Indexes

**Indexes** are not investments. They're measurements of the performance of a particular group of securities. They serve as benchmarks.
Indexes that track the entire stock market answer the question, How's
the market doing?

While the market's open, indexes are recalculated and dissemi-
nated every 15 seconds.

Investors suffer from no lack of indexes. A few apply to bonds,
but most apply to stocks. Some indexes measure entire markets or
certain styles of stocks. Others measure particular industries, foreign
regions, or foreign nations. The preeminent global equity index, the
Morgan Stanley Capital International (MSCI) Europe, Australia,
and Far East (EAFE) Index, includes almost 1,000 securities from 21
countries.

Need an index? You got it.

### Market Conditions Don't Count

The designers of indexes follow a clearly defined set of rules that are held constant *regardless of market conditions*. Why? Because the ups and downs of the market are not predictable. They should therefore be disregarded.

I'm one of those fools who occasionally write market predictions in my newspaper columns that make me appear to know a little something. But my short-term predictions so far haven't made anyone rich.

Ms. Market specializes in surprises. Pardon my language, but in the short term, she goes out of her way to give each of us the shaft. Don't expect to sell when the market is high and buy when it's low. Index designers don't, and you shouldn't either. You'll probably succeed occasionally, but not consistently. Fail once and you'll never catch up. Market timing is a loser's game.

The long run is quite another story. Over long periods, stock prices rise. That little nugget you can take to the bank ... er, no, take the money *out* of the bank and invest it in stock investments that copy indexes. The reason why stock prices rise in the long run? Sorry, you'll have to hold your breath until a later chapter.

### First Out of the Gate and Still Leading

The Dow Jones Industrial Average (DJIA) was developed over a century ago, in 1896. Actually, it's not an index; as the name implies, it's an average. But we'll give it a pass anyway because it's so well known.

The Dow was started by Charles Dow for a newspaper that later became the *Wall Street Journal*. The market closed (and still closes) at 4:00 p.m. By the time Wall Streeters went home, Mr. Dow wanted to provide an idea of how the market had performed that day. Using hand calculations, the method had to be quick and easy, enabling the paper to be printed in time. He selected 12 successful and growing industrial companies, added up their prices, divided by 12, and, bingo! that was his average—40.94 on the first day. In effect, Mr. Dow created a hypothetical fund consisting of one share of each Dow stock.

Later, the number of companies was increased to 30. The components of the average are changed every few years. Of the 12 originally selected in 1896, only General Electric remains.

The 30 Dow stocks represent only about 2 percent of stocks listed on the NYSE. But the market values of these 30 constitute about 25 percent.

## Adjustment for Splits

Mr. Dow didn't want stock splits to affect his average because, as mentioned, splits leave the values unchanged; they're the equivalent of receiving two tens for a twenty. He wanted to treat splits so that they wouldn't affect the average.

To illustrate how he did this, assume that the Dow average has 30 stocks and stands at 100. Also assume that in one day, every single one of the companies splits its stock two-for-one. Without adjustment, this would pull down the average from 100 to 50. But Mr. Dow wanted the average to remain unchanged, since no value was lost. The denominator would therefore be reduced by half, from 30 to 15, keeping the average at 100.

As mentioned, the Dow's original level in 1896 was 40.94. Since then, the economy has grown a bit—man, has it ever! The Dow stocks have gone up and up and split over and over. The Dow divisor is nowhere near 30, or 15, or even 1. At this writing, it's only 0.12493117. (The number is disclosed every week in *Barron's*.)

Just for kicks, assume that the prices of the 30 Dow stocks average 46.72. If you multiply by 30 (1,401.60) and divide by 0.12493117, you get 11,219, which is where the Dow average stands at this writing.

The Dow divisor is not adjusted for stock dividends of less than 10 percent. The average is therefore slightly lower than it otherwise would be.

## Price Weighting

The Dow Jones Industrial Average is *price weighted*. To illustrate, take the member of the Dow 30 that currently has the highest price (Boeing at 79.75). If the price rises by 2 percent, the increase is 1.60 points. After dividing by 0.12493117, the average increases by almost 13 points.

This time, take the member of the Dow 30 that has the lowest price (Intel at 17.30). If that price rises by 2 percent, the increase is 0.35 points. After dividing by 0.12493117, the Dow Average rises by only about 3 points.

Both stocks go up by the same percentage. But the higher-priced stock affects the average far more than the other. The average, as I say, is price weighted.

Not that it matters in the long term. Boeing may split its stock, causing the price to drop back down into the pack. Intel may enjoy a spurt in earnings, causing the price to rise. In the long run, the price differences come out in the wash.

As you can tell from the above, the calculation of the Dow Jones average uses a clearly defined set of rules that are held constant regardless of market conditions. But how do Dow Jones editors select the 30 stocks in the first place? They don't say. I doubt that they use a clearly defined set of rules in making the selections. They just pick 30 companies representing American industry as best they can. That's okay with me; Dow Jones editors seem unbiased and knowledgeable.

Dow Jones has two other market averages: transportation and utilities. The only other market benchmark I know of that uses Dow Jones averaging techniques is the Nikkei 225 Stock Average, the principal measure of the Japanese stock market.

So much for price weighting. We turn now to *capitalization weighting*, which is what most indexes use.

## The S&P 500

In the 1940s, Standard & Poor's (a division of the McGraw-Hill Companies, publisher of this book) created a new kind of index. It is now the most widely followed index in the world.

Called the **S&P 500 Index**, it reflects the changes in value of the 500 U.S. companies that are generally the largest. To be included, a company must be a U.S. company, have a market cap in excess of $4 billion, possess financial viability, display adequate liquidity and reasonable price, have at least 50 percent of its stock available to the public for purchase, exhibit sector representation, and continue to operate. If a company violates one or more of the conditions or is involved in a merger, an acquisition, or a significant restructuring, it may be removed from the index.

Most indexes today use the method first introduced by Standard & Poor's. Most exchange-traded funds are based on this method as well.

Standard & Poor's started with fewer than 500 companies and later expanded the list to 500. Here's how the index was calculated: Standard & Poor's determined the capitalization of each company (the price times the number of shares outstanding) and added them together. To this large sum, it assigned an index value of 10. Thereafter, as the capitalization of all of the stocks changed from day to day, the index was adjusted by the same percentage. Standard & Poor's ran the numbers back to 1926, when the value was also about 10.

The index now stands at 1,275.77, which is a whole lot higher than 10. Yes, the U.S. economy has grown a tad. The higher the market value of a company, the greater its impact on the index.

## *Top Heavy*

The capitalizations of the 500 S&P Index stocks total about $9.75 trillion, which is about 75 percent of the nation's gross domestic product (GDP) of $13 trillion.

The economy is top heavy. The capitalizations of 10 of America's largest companies (just 2 percent of the 500 companies in the index) constitute about 25 percent of the capitalizations of all 500. The biggies count for a lot.

Like most indexes today, the S&P 500 Index is **capitalization weighted.** The price changes of a company that's 10 times larger than another have 10 times greater impact on the index. Since more money is invested in the big caps than in the small, the approach seems reasonable. (See Figure 5.1.)

---

### Caps Galore

The total market value of a company is its **capitalization**. For example, the price of Wal-Mart stock at this writing is 44.82. The company has 4,167,782,000 shares outstanding. Multiplying the two gives a total market value of $186.8 billion—no small piece of change. That's the company's capitalization.

Relatively large companies (which certainly includes Wal-Mart) are referred to as *big caps*. In-between companies are *mid caps*. Relatively small companies—surprise, surprise—are *small caps*, and very small companies are *micro caps*. Now you're in the know.

---

**Figure 5-1**

## Rebalancing

As circumstances change, Standard & Poor's adjusts the index. When a company in the index is absorbed by another, for example, Standard & Poor's chooses another company to fill the vacancy. When price changes cause a particular industry to bulk too large in the index, Standard & Poor's rebalances by removing one or two of those companies from the index, replacing them with companies from other industries.

With both of the early birds (the Dow Jones Industrials and the S&P 500 Index), dividends are assumed to be paid out and not "reinvested." In other words, the dividends received are not added back to the company's capitalization. Later indexes, developed with the aid of computers, do assume the reinvestment of dividends. This is a more realistic approach.

## Float

Most publishers of indexes adjust the capitalizations of companies whose stock is partially unavailable for purchase. The descendents of the founder of the company may have no intention of selling their shares. The members of Houghton family, for example, are unlikely to sell their 4 percent of the stock of Corning, Inc. anytime soon. The shares of other companies are held by company managements and financial institutions that have no intention of selling.

To determine how much of the capitalization of a company should be included in the index, most publishers exclude stock that is unavailable for purchase by the public. They multiply the current price only by the number of shares actually available. Those shares are referred to as the company's **float**. The adjustments reduce the impact of price changes of companies whose shares are partly illiquid.

## Equal Weighting

Other than price weighting and capitalization weighting, there's another type: equal weighting. Here, the number of shares are adjusted so that the capitalizations of every stock are the same. Value Line, for example, publishes several equal-weighted indexes. Indexes followed by certain ETFs do as well.

### *Cleanup on Indexes*

The following three indexes, published by the Frank Russell Company, give you an idea about the construction of indexes. They also illustrate how *big* the big-cap stocks are. These indexes were started in 1979. (This brief section contains a lot of numbers. Feel free to skip down to the last paragraph.)

- Russell 3000 Index
- Russell 1000 Index
- Russell 2000 Index

About 16,000 U.S. stocks are publicly traded in the United States. The Russell 3000 Index tracks the performance of the largest 3,000. These constitute about 98 percent of the capitalization of all 16,000. (The other 13,000 make up the other 2 percent.)

The Russell 1000 Index tracks the performance of the *largest* 1,000 stocks included in the 3,000 index. These 1,000 each have market capitalizations of at least $300 million. Together, they constitute 92 percent of the top 3,000.

The Russell 2000 Index tracks the performance of the *smallest* 2,000 stocks included in the 3,000 index. Their capitalizations run from $20 million to $300 million and constitute about 8 percent of the top 3,000. Russell adjusts for cross-ownership. For example, IBM owns 20 percent of Intel. The Russell 3000 and 1000 Indexes therefore include only 80 percent of Intel's outstanding shares.

Are you still with me? If not, you didn't miss much. Anyway, that's the end of our discussion about indexes. On we go to the mutual funds that track indexes, called, naturally, **index funds**. We're coming ever closer to exchange-traded funds. In effect, ETFs *are* index funds.

# Index Funds

Remember that indexes are not investments. They're hypothetical portfolios used to measure the performance of a specific group of stocks. Why not make real-time investments of them?

Indeed, this is what index funds do. They buy in the correct proportions the very same stocks included in an index. Generally, the higher a company's market value, the more shares of it are bought by the fund.

An index fund endeavors to equal the performance of the underlying index, except for costs. In effect, index funds are parasites, which is fine with me. Some index funds, including Vanguard's S&P 500 Index Fund, copy the index as exactly as possible. The index has 500 stocks. The fund has 500 stocks, in the correct proportions. These funds use the **replication method**.

Others funds, such as the Russell funds and Vanguard's Total Stock Market Index Fund, consider exact replication too unwieldy. They use **representative sampling**. Vanguard's Total Stock Market Index Fund, for example, tracks the MSCI US Broad Market Index, which currently contains 3,997 stocks. Some of these are small and illiquid, with wide spreads. Copying the index exactly would raise transaction costs. The fund holds only 3,772 stocks, which match the characteristics of the entire index in terms of performance, industry weights, and market capitalization. Funds using representative sampling do not track the underlying index as exactly as those using the replication method.

## Low Costs

Index fund costs are low. They have no need to pay a ton of money to managers and stock analysts for picking stocks that will supposedly outperform others stocks. Instead, the stock selection is undertaken by the publisher of the index. The fund pays a royalty for using the index. For all ETFs, annual royalties average about $600 per million dollars invested. This is considerably less costly than stock research.

Low costs are a big plus for index funds. Indeed, according to John Bogle, founder of Vanguard, index funds account for something like 10 percent of stock market values. But, probably to the dismay of the brokerage industry, they account for a mere 0.40 percent of trading.

## The First Index Fund

The first index fund was launched in 1976 by John Bogle. This fund, the Vanguard 500 Index Fund, tracks the S&P 500 Index. Other money managers greeted the launching with derision: One mutual fund executive commented that if you settle for matching the market instead of outperforming it, "you're conceding defeat."

Another said, "Indexing is a sure path to mediocrity." Some mediocrity! The Vanguard 500 Index Fund has outperformed most other funds. With $107 billion under management, it is now one of the largest mutual funds in the world.

## Bond Indexes

Bond indexes are difficult to compile and even more difficult to track. Bond issues greatly outnumber stock issues. A single company has only one common stock, but it may issue scores of bonds. Because of infrequent trading, many bond prices are impossible to determine accurately. Insurance companies, for example, often buy large portions of bond issues and hold them to maturity. Moreover, companies that offer lots of bonds may not exactly be leaders in corporate performance. Enron, WorldCom, and Global Crossing come to mind; those companies went broke.

## The Broad Picture

Some indexes are tracked by more than one index fund. Indeed, one study found that from 1996 to 2001, the S&P 500 Index was tracked by 52 funds. This is unfortunate. Although the S&P 500 is the most widely known index, it is also, for technical reasons, difficult to track.

Index funds do not try to outstrip the indexes they track. Except for minimal costs, they simply try to equal them. Nevertheless, index funds time and time again outperform the actively traded funds that do try to outstrip their benchmarks. There are three reasons for this:

- Index funds have lower costs.
- They have lower turnover, meaning that they do less buying and selling of the shares in their portfolios.
- They minimize the exercise of investment judgment. Regardless of what many investment professionals say, the less often you exercise investment judgment, the better the results.

All our ducks are in a row. We're ready for the big time—exchange-traded funds.

# PART TWO

# EXCHANGE-TRADED FUNDS

# The Basics of Exchange-Traded Funds

Ta-daahh! We've made it to the promised land.

## Peter's Purchase

Peter wants to diversify his investments and decides to place money in the S&P 500 Index. While the market is down a bit at lunch hour, he buys through his online brokerage firm 100 shares of Spiders (SPY), with a commission of only $10. He pays the ask price of 127.78.

Peter is amazed to discover that the bid price at that moment is 127.76—just 2 cents lower. He marvels that on such a high-priced stock, the spread is so narrow.

Peter's total costs are $12,788. He intends to hold for the long term. But if he were a short-timer, the price would have to rise only 23 cents for him to make a profit, including the 2-cent spread and two commissions. That's a lousy 0.18 percent. Golly, the price of Spiders fluctuates considerably more than that every day!

If Peter had the money to buy 5,000 shares of Spiders, the spread would probably be no wider. But as a percentage of the value of the ETF, the $10 commissions would become almost immaterial. The Spider price would have to rise only about 4 cents for him to profit.

Peter realizes that he's buying on a normal day when the market is not under stress. On the rare days when a flood of selling occurs, spreads widen. But he has no intention of selling on those occasions.

Furthermore, the annual operating cost of Spiders is only 0.10 percent a year. Peter knows that stock prices fluctuate all over the map. But on average, they've risen at about 12 percent a year. There are 250 trading days in the year. If Spiders gain at the average annual rate of 12 percent, the operating costs would be paid in less than three days. This is all hypothetical, Peter realizes, but in the other 247 days, the profits would be all his.

Moreover, unlike S&P 500 Index funds, Spiders are unlikely to pass out capital gains to investors. Peter will pay tax only on gains he chooses to take, not on the gains realized by others.

How could such an extraordinary investment have come into being?

## In at the Creation

Nathan Most had the original idea. For many years, Nate worked with commodities and futures markets in Chicago. He figured that, if warehouse receipts worked for wheat, why not for a index fund of stocks? The receipt wouldn't have to be exactly the same as the index's portfolio, but it would represent the portfolio, take on its approximate value, be negotiable, and pass easily from one party to another during the trading day. (See Figure 6-1.)

With significant help from the American Stock Exchange, Nate Most and members of the Wall Street community nailed down the details of the first exchange-traded fund. In three years, they obtained approval from the Securities and Exchange Commission to begin trading. (Government isn't lightening fast with new ideas.)

## Futures

On a pleasant spring day, Darryl, an Iowa farmer, seeds a field of wheat from which he expects to harvest 10,000 bushels. Darryl is an expert farmer, but he doesn't care to dabble in short-term price movements. He knows his farming costs, however, and realizes that the current price of wheat in the Chicago futures market is sufficient to make a comfortable profit. Today, while the seeds are germinating, Darryl calls his futures broker and sells 10,000 bushels of wheat, to be delivered in the fall.

Darryl has other risks, of course, some of which are insured. But he prefers not to take the risk of the wheat price plummeting during the summer. By selling in the futures market, he transfers the risk of adverse price movements to short-term speculators who are willing to accept that risk. Darryl forfeits the opportunity for extra profit if the price of wheat rises during the summer. But he doesn't care; a good profit in hand is sufficient.

In truth, most speculators in the futures markets lose money. They're buying and selling products that have yet to be delivered, usually with considerable leverage (or borrowing). Darryl wonders whether they're compulsive gamblers. But whatever they are, he's grateful to them for removing the price risk from his shoulders.

Come the fall, Darryl harvests the wheat and brings it to a nearby silo, called a warehouse. The warehouse gives him a **warehouse receipt**, a negotiable title of ownership that can be bought and sold like a stock. Whoever holds the receipt has the right to sell it.*

Darryl delivers the warehouse receipt to his broker, who delivers it to Chicago in satisfaction of the terms of the futures contract. Eventually, General Mills may buy the warehouse receipt and obtain the wheat from the warehouse to bake Wheaties.

---

*Warehouse receipts were the forerunners of paper money. In seventeenth-century England, goldsmiths issued warehouse receipts for the gold deposited with them by merchants. While the gold remained stationary, the receipts circulated as money.

**Figure 6-1**

# Spiders

The trading of Spiders began on January 29, 1993. The formal name was "Standard & Poor's Depositary Receipts." The first letters of those words spell "SPDR," but the developers stretched it to "Spiders," the informal name referred to in advertisements. The shares trade on the American Stock Exchange under the symbol SPY.

Based on the S&P 500 Index, the Spider ETF is in effect an index fund. The trustees and managers of the fund, the State Street Bank & Trust Company in Boston, exercise no discretion about the choice of stocks. The index is controlled by one organization (Standard & Poor's), and the ETF is controlled by another (State Street Bank & Trust). The S&P index is a hypothetical portfolio; the ETF is a real one.

As you recall, the stocks in the S&P index are apportioned by their capitalizations. Accordingly, the trustees buy and hold stocks in the same proportions, with more shares of the biggies and fewer shares of the small caps.

Spider shares can be owned by anyone. Each share represents an undivided interest in all 500 stocks in the correct proportions.

While the shares of the portfolio sit electronically in the trust in Boston, the Spider shares represent an ownership interest in the trust. The shares can be traded from one party to another at the prices agreed to. Spider owners vote the proxies sent by the fund, but they do not vote the proxies sent by the underlying stocks. (A good thing too, because voting the proxies on 500 stocks would consume too much of your valuable time.) The prices agreed to by the buyers and sellers of Spiders are often different from the net asset value of the portfolio. Yet the two prices are remarkably close, nothing like the 15 percent discount that often applies with closed-end mutual funds.

What makes this possible?

# Creation and Redemption of Spiders

When you buy Spider shares in the secondary market, they are not newly created just for you, as would be the case with open-end mutual funds. No, the shares already exist and are available for trading from one investor to another.

But neither are the shares of the Spider ETF created all at once in an initial public offering, as would be the case for individual stocks, closed-end funds, and unit investment trusts. Instead, shares are created and redeemed by the trustees nearly every day. (On less popular ETFs, creation and redemption occurs less often.) The shares are not created at the request of you and me, however. Creation and redemption of Spider shares are called for by third parties, called **authorized participants.** There are only about 30 authorized participants for Spiders, all of them financial institutions with plenty of money in the bank. Having big bucks for this purpose isn't a bad idea because authorized participants can request the creation or redemption of Spiders only in **creation units** of 50,000 Spider shares! At this writing, each creation unit has a value of $6.4 million.

## Back to Specialists and Market Makers

Many of the authorized participants are also specialists or market makers. Let's say you give an order to buy 1,000 shares. The order goes to the Amex specialist to execute it. (With an ETF trade, you're more likely to have a specialist on the other side of the transaction than you are with an individual stock.)

The specialist's computer may tell him, "Listen, man, your inventory is getting too low. In case some big buy orders come in, you'd better call for new Spider shares."

Well, computers don't talk like that, at least not yet. But you get the idea.

Following his computer's lead, the specialist digs into his employer's pocket and hauls out 6.4 million smackers. He purchases the shares of every one of the 500 stocks in the S&P 500 Index in the correct proportions. This is easier than it seems. Computers know the correct proportions; the purchases are executed in seconds.

Electronically, our authorized participant-specialist delivers these 500 stocks to the Spider trustees. If the shares of some of the S&P stocks can't be purchased immediately, the specialist delivers cash instead, enabling the managers to buy the shares as soon as possible.

In the final step, the Spider managers confirm the transmission and immediately create 50,000 new shares of Spiders, which are electronically delivered to the specialist. His inventory is replenished. The shares are available for trading in the secondary market, and the specialist's computer is happy.

## And Redemptions?

Alternatively, let's say you give an order to *sell* 1,000 shares of Spiders, and the party on the other side of the transaction is again the specialist. His computer tells him, "Wait a minute, we're getting overloaded with Spider shares. Better do a redemption."

The specialist therefore transmits to Boston 50,000 Spider shares acquired from the secondary market. After confirmation, the fund managers deliver to the specialist $6.4 million of the 500 S&P stocks in the correct proportions. The specialist immediately sells these in the secondary market.

These orders and transmissions usually occur in *multiples* of 50,000 shares. As Spiders are used more and more and the value of the underlying portfolio has grown, more creations than redemptions have occurred. At this writing, the trust is worth about $57 billion.

When calling for creation or redemption, the authorized participant pays the trustee a flat fee of $3,000. But if the authorized participant calls for the creation of 20 creation units, which is not uncommon, this covers 1 million shares with a value of $127 million. In comparison, a fee of only $3,000 is peanuts.

As mentioned before, exchange-traded funds are a cross between mutual funds and stocks. The mutual fund aspect pertains to the creation and redemption of shares. These are undertaken by the trust and authorized participants, who absorb all the costs. The stock aspect of ETFs pertains to the trading in the secondary market. With the help of market makers, this privilege is enjoyed by investors like you and me.

## Arbitrage

One reason authorized participants call for creations and redemptions is simply to manage their inventories, as described above. But there's another reason too, especially for authorized participants who are not specialists. The reason is **arbitrage**, which serves to bring ETF prices into alignment with their net asset values.

### Hot Tomatoes

Let's say you pass a roadside stand that's selling tomatoes at only 50 cents a pound. A nearby supermarket is selling tomatoes for $1 a pound. Being as sharp as a tack, you load up your SUV with every tomato the roadside stand offers at 50 cents a pound and sell them to the local supermarket at 90 cents a pound. You make a profit of 40 cents and enable the supermarket to make a few bucks as well.

Nice going; you've performed an arbitrage. You've bought a product in one market and sold it in another. You've also brought the prices of the two markets more into alignment. After learning about your success, the roadside stand is inclined to bring its prices up, and the supermarket may consider bringing its prices down. We refer to you as an *arbitrageur*. (Actually, the supermarket won't accept foodstuff on the spur of the moment from just any old person, for fear that the product may be spiked with cyanide.)

### Aligning Spiders

Okay, for ease of explanation, let's assume that Spiders are priced at 100. Also assume that you're an authorized participant. You see on your computer that the ask price of SPY is 100. You also note that the net asset value of the trust (symbol SXV) is only 99.90 a share. Time for action!*

You submit an order in the secondary market to buy all 500 S&P stocks in the correct proportions, equivalent to 1 creation unit. The NAV per Spider share, as mentioned, is 99.90. The NAV per creation unit is $4,995,000 ($99.90 times 50,000).

---

*Actually, net asset values of ETFs are computed only once a day, at the close. The asset values computed every 15 seconds have various names, including "indicative net asset value," "underlying trading value," "intraday proxy value," "intraday indicative index value," and "indicative optimized portfolio value." To avoid confusion, and since you're probably not hankering to *run* an exchange-traded fund, we'll continue using the tried-and-true "net asset value."

Although you hope to pay $4,995,000 for the S&P stocks, your purchases raise the prices a little. Your actual cost is $4,996,000. You've increased the NAV of the trust to 99.92.

You receive 50,000 shares of Spiders, which you immediately sell in the secondary market. You hope to receive the 100 ask price for Spiders, but your offer lowers the price from 100 to 99.98. On the sales, you receive $4,999,000.

Let's see, the purchase of the S&P stocks cost you $4,996,000, and the sale of 50,000 Spider shares brought you $4,999,000. Quick as a wink, you made three grand. Only you didn't do this with a single creation unit. You did it with 10 of them and made $30,000, which isn't a bad day's pay for you and your employer.

Your arbitrage brought the two markets closer together. Your purchase of the S&P stocks raised the NAV of the trust from 99.90 to 99.92, and your sale of the 50,000 shares of Spiders reduced the ask price from 100 to 99.98. You've reduced the premium from 10 to 6 cents. Even that is probably too large. Arbitrage generally keeps the difference between the NAV and the price of Spiders down to about a nickel. (The difference is called the *variance*.) Someone else may step in to perform another arbitrage.

The current price of Spiders is approximately $127. A premium or discount of only a nickel is peanuts—about 4/100 of 1 percent. This is nothing like the 15 percent discount usually prevailing with closed-end mutual funds.

## That's Basically It

After you finish reading this book, you may say to yourself, "Wait a minute! I thought this book was supposed to be about ETFs. Other than the references in the appendix, how come there's so little about ETFs and so much about investment strategy?"

The answer is, there's not much to describe about ETFs directly. If you know about stocks, IPOs, secondary markets, spreads, premiums, discounts, mutual funds, indexes, and warehouse receipts, you fuse them all together, add a few wrinkles, and you've got exchange-traded funds down pretty well.

Well, there's a little more—about taxes and costs and stuff. But the basic knowledge we've already covered. Knowing that, however, won't give you anything like a comfortable retirement unless you use ETFs correctly. The methods of losing money in the market greatly outnumber the methods of making money. I want you to end up a winner. This book lays out the best way to use ETFs to accomplish your financial goals.

## Hedging

Most market makers, specialists, and authorized participants don't make money by betting on which way the prices will move. They make their money from spreads and arbitrage profits. When they take positions, they hedge the risk of prices moving against them.

For example, the Spider specialist may call for the creation of two creation units and temporarily have 100,000 shares in inventory, worth almost $13 million. If the market should move down by 1 percent within a short time, which is not at all uncommon, the specialist would lose $130,000.

The specialist doesn't have time to watch the market. He certainly doesn't have time to watch the news about things investors might take into account in deciding what to buy or sell. He's busy; the pressure is constant. He's deciding which orders he'll fill himself, and at what price, and which ones he'll allow others to take care of.

He therefore hedges his potential market risk, constantly adjusting the hedge to accommodate his changing inventory. Actually, someone else does this hedging for him. Indeed, some professionals do nothing but set up hedges for other professionals (see Figure 6-2).

## Take Your Pick of Hedges

An investor hedges a position (reduces the risk of holding that position) by taking an opposing position in a related market. Here are ways that a long position in Spiders can be hedged:

- Sell an S&P 500 futures contract.
- Buy a Spider put or sell a Spider call (we'll explain these later).
- Short Spiders against the box.
- Short at least some of the 500 stocks included in the S&P 500 Index.

## Short Selling

To profit when a stock goes up, you buy it, wait, and sell at a higher price. To profit when a stock goes down, you sell it, wait, and buy it at a lower price.

Wait a minute! How can you sell a stock you don't already own?

You borrow it from the brokerage firm, sell, wait, buy the stock later at a lower price, and then return it to the brokerage firm. Take a bow; you've performed a **short sale**.

You can't sell short unique items like diamonds, houses, cars, and fur coats, because you can't repay to the lender the very same item he or she lent to you. But stocks (along with bonds and commodities) are homogeneous. Every share has exactly the same value as every other share. You don't have to buy the stock from the same person you originally sold it to. You sell it short to one person and buy it back from another. Neither party knows that you're engaged in short selling. (Buying a stock you hold short is called **covering** the short.)

Now, let's say you own 500 shares of XYZ, which you don't want to sell. But you do expect the market to fall temporarily. (If you expect to be able to anticipate the market's short-term trends consistently and accurately, you'd better think again, but that's neither here nor there.)

You borrow 500 *other* shares of XYZ and sell them short. This means you're long 500 shares and short 500 shares. No matter what happens to the price, you neither make nor lose (except for the commissions—those you always lose). After you cover the short, you're back on the long side, free and clear. This kind of a short sale is called a **short against the box**.

Where does the brokerage obtain the stock that's lent to you?

From someone who owns it. The firm may own it. But more likely, it obtains the stock from an institution, such as a mutual fund which owns a lot of the stock. A market maker who has plenty of inventory may also lend the stock. A short seller is not allowed to take the proceeds and spend it. Oh no, the proceeds are held on deposit as security that the short will eventually be covered and the loan repaid. If the stock was obtained from the firm's own customer, the firm keeps the interest earned on the cash balance. If the firm obtained the stock from another firm or from a market maker, it shares the interest with that party.

When you're long a stock, you receive the dividends. When you're short a stock, you pay the dividends. The party to whom you sold the stock short is the new owner, and the transfer agent pays the dividend to him or her.

But the party from whom you borrowed the stock is *also* entitled to the dividend. The transfer agent isn't aware that that party remains an owner. This dividend you must pay yourself.

The typical common stock has a short interest of 1 to 2 percent of its capitalization. But short interests of ETFs are usually 10 to 20 percent. Generally, ETF specialists hold more than 10 percent of the shares outstanding. Many of these are on loan for short selling.

No short selling occurs in futures markets. Nothing needs to be borrowed. In fact nothing *can* be borrowed because the underlying product has yet to be delivered. All of the buys and sells are bookkeeping entries, with the gains and losses tallied currently.

**Figure 6-2**

## Turnover

Spider trading in the last three months has averaged about 82 million shares a day (worth about $10.8 billion). The value of the Spider trust is $57 billion. This implies that the Spider trust turns over about every five days.

The implication is misleading. The average *investor* holds Spider shares for much longer. Oh, not all of them do, of course; some are day traders. But many investors and investment institutions hold Spiders for long periods. Indeed, one of the people who helped develop Spiders, an executive for a leading market maker and arbitrageur, told me that the Spiders held in his personal portfolio he never intends to sell.

Yet when those investors do step into the market to buy or sell Spiders, they're given great advantages. Even in volume, the premiums and discounts from the net asset values are remarkably close, and the spreads between bid and ask prices are remarkably narrow. This is made possible by the enormous flurry of trading by authorized participants, specialists, arbitrageurs, hedge funds, and brokerage firms. Without long-term investors, these professionals would have nothing to bother with. Without the professionals, investors would have unsatisfactory trading costs.

Everybody wins.

## ETF Prices in Relation to the Underlying Index

Spiders were originally priced at 1/10 the level of the S&P 500 Index. The 1-to-10 ratio doesn't hold over time, however. It slowly changes partly because of the accumulation and payouts of dividends and perhaps because the fund expenses may exceed the dividend income.

Diamonds were originally priced at 1/100 the level of the Dow Jones Industrial Average. Qubes were priced at 1/40 the Nasdaq 100. The original ratios vary from one ETF to another.

## How Are We Organized Around Here?

Back in the early 1990s, ETFs were a new kind of investment. The American Stock Exchange was uncertain of the demand and didn't want the infrastructure to be more costly than necessary. It therefore organized the initial ETFs (Spiders, Diamonds, and Qubes) as unit investment trusts.

Unit investment trusts are not required to have boards of directors. They're unmanaged and must follow the index exactly, using the replication method. UITs have finite lives. The Spider trust, for example, terminates on January 22, 2218. UITs must also keep their dividends in non-interest-bearing accounts until payout, which is a bummer.

But after the initial ETFs grew hugely, the Amex knew it had winners (see Figure 6-3). Most subsequent ETFs were organized as open-end mutual funds. They're required to have boards of directors. They have unlimited lives; they can invest dividends in money market funds or other cash equivalents before payout; and they can use representative sampling, meaning they can approximate the underlying index.

## Fiddling for Your Benefit

To benefit shareholders by cutting costs, the managers of open-end ETFs may fiddle with their selection of stocks. Here's an example

## A Visit to the American Stock Exchange

What was once the mezzanine visitors' platform overlooking the trading floor of the American Stock Exchange is now the trading area for exchange-traded funds. I had the pleasure of observing the proceedings.

All of the traders face computers and are equipped with head sets at the ready. With little space available, almost everyone is stationary. A family-sized television carries CNBC with the sound off, but with the spoken words spelled out in real time. Large black panels display the current quotes above.

Three metal counters, arranged end to end with walkways between, are the focus of trading for the three major ETFs: Qubes, Spiders, and Diamonds. Behind each counter, in front of a black partition, stand the specialist and his aids, each such group being employees of a major trading company.

The specialist faces a "crowd," numbering something like 25 people for the Qubes, and 20 each for Spiders and Diamonds. Crowd members remain standing, with laptops resting on wooden stands.

On one side of the mezzanine area is the entrance. Ringing the other three sides are two rows of brokers, market makers, hedging facilitators, and specialists for other ETFs, all seated.

Short-term positions are the rule here, mostly with borrowed money. The goal is to scalp a penny or two per trade. Most positions are hedged immediately. A purchase, for example, would be offset by one or more sales of futures, options, other ETFs, or the underlying stocks. When the position is exited, the hedge is undone.

It's a young person's game. Almost everybody I saw looked to be in their thirties. Many of them are in amicable competition with one another. If you plan to trade, they'll be in competition with you. Their reactions are quick. If you think you can beat them at what they do, I suggest you think again.

For the Qubes, Spiders, and Diamonds, small orders coming in to the AMEX floor are usually accommodated by the specialist. Big orders, whether buys or sells, elicit immediate shouts from members of the crowd, indicating their eagerness to fill the other side of the order. The specialist decides how much of the trade he wants, with the rest parceled out among members of the crowd. On a large order I overheard, one member of the crowd quickly took charge of allocating the order, calling out numbers

*(Continued)*

representing thousands of shares: "I'll take 15; Billy, you've got 20; Jimmy, 10, ..." On other orders, different members of the crowd would do the parceling. When working together helps, the traders work together. When it comes time to compete, they compete.

Qubes, as mentioned, are the most actively traded securities in the world—currently about 122 million shares a day. In dollar volume, Spiders are the largest, with net asset value of approximately $57 billion. Not bad for securities created only a few years ago. The trading of these ETFs takes place on various U.S. exchanges, electronic communications networks, and on both sides within a single brokerage firm. Less than 10 percent of this enormous volume is handled on the American Stock Exchange.

Still, we're not whistling Dixie here. By scraping off a penny or two per share, those 30-year-olds have plenty to shout about.

*Note:*    This excerpt is drawn from *All About Exchange-Traded Funds*, by Archie Richards, Jr., New York: McGraw-Hill, 2003. Some of the numbers have been updated.

**Figure 6-3**

having to do with Barclays Global Investors' management of the iShares Russell funds:

The Russell 3000 Index, as mentioned, includes all 3,000 of the largest public companies domiciled in the United States and its territories, weighted by capitalization.

The 3000 *Growth* Index measures the performance of the 3,000 index companies that have *higher* price-to-book ratios and higher forecasted growth. It represents approximately half of the market capitalization of the companies in the 3000 Index.

The 3000 *Value* Index measures the performance of the companies that have *lower* price-to-book ratios and lower forecasted growth. It represents the other half of the market capitalization of the companies in the 3000 Index.

As market values change from month to month, you can well imagine that stocks at the margin between growth and value might bounce from one fund to the other. To switch these stocks frequently would increase transaction and accounting costs unnecessarily.

Barclays therefore includes some of these marginal stocks in *both* its growth and value ETFs.

## Avoiding the Crunch

Let's say a company disappears from the market and no longer has a stock price. It may have gone out of business and liquidated. But more likely, it has merged or been bought out by another company. The publisher of the index must react to this without delay and cannot wait for its periodic rebalancing.

The Securities and Exchange Commission requires that index publishers announce to the world that at the close of business on such-and-such date, the pertinent stock will be removed from the index and, if necessary, another will be added. The SEC's requirement is unfortunate because at the close of business on that date, a flurry of trading occurs, not only by the index funds and ETFs that track the index but by other traders as well.

The pressure to trade is all in one direction. For example, if Standard & Poor's has announced that a certain stock will be removed from its 500 index and 50 index funds and ETFs are tracking the index, most of the 50 funds are placing sell orders at about the same time. This of course causes the price to fall, possibly quite a bit. If another stock is to be bought, the price of that stock rises. The performance of all of the funds suffer.

The iShares Russell 2000 Index Fund (IWM) is especially vulnerable to unfavorable prices during rebalancings because the fund is so large ($10.3 billion) and has 2,000 small stocks with relatively wide spreads.

Some fund families, including Vanguard, place rebalancing orders *before* the close or perhaps the next day. This is one of the reasons why the results of Vanguard index funds are sometimes better than the performance of the index, even after the reduction of operating and transaction costs.

The SEC rule is faulty. Index publishers should be permitted to notify the funds that follow the index about the impending changes in secret. Only after the sales and purchases are completed would the rest of the world be told. This would alleviate the crush of trading at the appointed time. It wouldn't do away with the problem, but it would help because the copycats would be less likely to trade at the same time.

· · · · · · · · · · · · · · · · · · · · · · · · · · · · · ·

We now turn to several chapters that compare ETFs with other investments in terms of costs, risks, and returns.

# Comparison of Costs

Collectively, investment institutions cannot outperform the market as a whole. Since they generate most of the trading, in effect they *are* the market. Some investment managers beat the averages for a while, of course. But studies have shown that the number of years in which they accomplish this is no greater than random. Here's an illustration.

## Oh Your Poor Thumb!

Say you flip a coin 1,000 times. On many occasions, the throws alternate between heads and tails. Once in a while, the throws come up heads 4 times in a row. Very seldom do they come up heads 15 times in a row.

The same goes for investment managers. They alternate many times between good years and bad years. Once in a while, managers have 4 good years in a row. Any manager who beats the market 15 good years in a row is a genuine rarity—and is much heralded in the press.

Studies have shown that investment managers don't have successive good years any more often than coin throws come up successive heads. In other words, good records by investment managers may be attributable to luck, not skill.

At the very least, you should assume that if you find a manager who's had a good record, other people will make the discovery at the same time. All will climb onboard, making the amount of money too large for the manager to continue the outstanding performance.

Do not strive to beat the averages by investing in funds that have lately had good records. Assume that they will eventually return to the mean. Instead, strive to hit the averages *with costs as low cost as possible.*

That's exactly what exchange-traded funds do. They endeavor to hit the averages with costs as low as possible. They fill the bill on both scores. In many respects, ETF costs are lower than those of conventional funds.

## Except for ...

Commissions. Ay, there's the rub. The purchase or sale of exchange-traded fund shares requires the payment of a brokerage commission. A no-load fund you can buy for nothing. Your purchase has a cost, all right, but it's paid by the existing shareholders.

Not so with exchange-traded funds. ETF shareholders pay their own costs of entry and exit. It costs more to trade ETFs than to trade conventional, no-load funds.

But it costs *less* to *hold* ETFs than conventional, no-load funds. I want you to be a long-time holder. The low costs of exchange-traded funds make them desirable for this purpose.

Brokerage commissions may be prohibitive for beginning investors who want to add small amounts to a fund on a periodic basis. Bear with me. In a later chapter, we will grab hold of this problem and wrestle it to the ground.

## Operating Costs

The operating costs of actively managed mutual funds average well above 1 percent a year, with index funds averaging only a little over 0.50 percent. ETF operating costs range from 0.09 percent to 0.95 percent, but the average is only 0.38 percent a year.

The principal savings stems from not having to perform stock research. No one needs to travel around asking questions of management and watching how their eyebrows move to judge whether they're lying. No one needs to pour over the footnotes in financial reports in an effort—usually a failed effort—to ferret out the real story.

The low costs ETFs are also due to the elimination of unnecessary shareholder accounting at the fund level. Instead of thousands of individual investors, the fund is required to keep track of relatively few authorized participants. ETFs have no need for extra 12(b)1 fees, and no need to keep track of salespersons who were responsible for placing orders. For low operating costs, you can't beat exchange-traded funds.

## Transaction Costs

When conventional mutual funds buy and sell individual stocks, they incur a variety of transaction costs, as follows:

- The funds pay heavy brokerage commissions.
- The spreads on individual stocks become considerably wider on large transactions.
- A large transaction can have a substantial impact on the price of the stock, always to the fund's disadvantage.
- Fund managers spend considerable time and effort trying to squeeze out good prices for their trades. To avoid making an excessive impact, they slowly feed out large orders. The delays cause them to miss opportunities they would otherwise take advantage of.

Seldom do any of these costs affect exchange-traded funds. When the ETF shares are redeemed by an authorized participant, for example, the individual stocks held by the fund are not sold; they're passed out to the authorized participant in a tax-free exchange. Only when a stock is removed from the underlying index is the fund required to make a sale in the market.

The flat fees paid by authorized participants when creating or redeeming cover the paperwork and other transaction costs. The authorized participants recover this cost from arbitrage profits or the spreads.

The key is, the transaction costs of short-term shareholders are incurred by those same short-term shareholders in the payment of commissions and spreads. The costs are not incurred by the ongoing shareholders. The long-termers are protected from the entry and exit costs of the short-termers.

## Spreads

The spreads between bid and ask prices on exchange-traded funds are remarkably narrow. This is true for most ETFs, but especially so for the major ones that trade in high volume. We've already seen the spread for Spiders. But the spreads of even the lesser ETFs aren't bad either. On the day of this writing, the market is acting normally and not under particular stress. The spreads of a few prominent ETFs are listed in Figure 7-1.

If you buy even Vanguard's Emerging Markets ETF (with the complexity and risks those numerous countries entail) but turn around and sell immediately before prices have changed, you're paying only 14/100 of 1 percent for the specialist's services. Pretty cheap, in my opinion.

| ETF | Symbol | Bid | Ask | Difference | Percent Difference |
|-----|--------|-----|-----|------------|--------------------|
| iShares Russell 2000 Value | IWN | 69.77 | 69.79 | 0.02 | 3/100 of 1% |
| Select Sector SPDR Health | XLV | 31.60 | 31.61 | 0.01 | 3/100 of 1% |
| Vanguard Emerging Markets | VWO | 63.39 | 63.48 | 0.09 | 14/100 of 1% |
| iShares MSCI Austria | EWO | 31.51 | 30.55 | 0.04 | 13/100 of 1% |

**Figure 7-1    The Spreads of a Few Prominent ETFs**

## *Why So Narrow?*

The spreads of exchange-traded funds remain narrow even for large transactions. Indeed, ETF spreads are usually lower than the average spreads of the underlying stocks. Here's why:

- The investor in ETFs (for large trades, more likely an institution) is in effect buying a substantial fraction of an entire market rather than the shares of a single company. The market impact of the trade is dispersed among many stocks.
- ETF market makers hedge their positions—more so than with individual stocks. Since they're protected from the risk of prices moving against them, they're willing to trade large positions with modest spreads.

Narrow spreads make exchange-traded funds highly suitable for investment by financial institutions as well as individual investors. Spreads are especially narrow for high-priced ETFs with high trading volumes.

## *ETFs of Foreign Stocks*

With the ETFs of foreign stocks, spreads may be modestly wider. Say the market maker takes a position in iShares MSCI South Korea. He probably can't hedge his position until South Korean stocks begin trading the next day. Since an unhedged position is a bigger risk for him, he must therefore maintain a wider spread, to compensate for the times when South Korean stocks move against him and he loses significantly on an unhedged position.

Foreign taxes may also increase the cost of hedging. Great Britain, for example, imposes a tax on purchases and sales of U.K. securities by foreigners. A U.S. market maker endeavoring to hedge a position in iShares MSCI United Kingdom must pay that pesky "stamp tax." His spread must widen as a result.

The economies of some nations are dominated by just a few companies—Austria, Switzerland, and Sweden are examples. The spreads on such nations tend to be wider because the lack of diversity increases the market maker's risk.

China is a special case because the Chinese government owns about two-thirds of Chinese companies. The spread of PowerShares Golden Dragon Halter USX China (PGJ) is somewhat wider than others because of the possibility that the Chinese government may sell its majority interests, causing the prices to plunge. But even this spread isn't bad: At this writing, the PGJ quote is 15.74 to 15.78, for a difference of 3/10 of 1 percent.

## Variance

As mentioned, the difference between the price of an ETF and the net asset value of the underlying index is called the *variance*. Because of arbitrage, ETF variances are remarkably small, as we've already seen with Spiders. Many times, in fact, the NAV falls between the bid and ask prices (although not when the spread is just a few pennies). But arbitrage keeps the premiums or discounts remarkably close.

## That Pesky Close

Unfortunately, variances are recorded and promulgated as of the day's closing prices—the very time when they're wider than normal. Here's the story:

I've mentioned that market makers hedge the risk of holding large positions in ETFs. But those who hold positions in other securities, such as stocks owned outright, use ETFs to hedge those risks. Exchange-traded fund developers intended ETFs to be widely used as hedges.

The stock market closes at 4:00 p.m. New York time. But futures markets continue trading until 4:15 p.m. Since ETFs are in competition with futures for hedging business, the developers arranged for ETFs to remain open as well.

During those final 15 minutes of trading, wide variances cannot be corrected by arbitrage because the underlying stocks are not trading. Variances therefore widen during this period, undeterred. It's not that ETFs become mispriced; they're properly priced on the basis of new information that becomes available during those 15 minutes. If Coca Cola should report surprising earnings at 4:08, for example, the prices of ETFs that include Coca Cola stock change accordingly, even though the price of the stock itself can't be adjusted until the next morning.

The closing 4:15 prices are the ones used to calculate and publish ETF variances. This is the very time of the day when they're likely to be the widest. The published numbers are misleading and should be disregarded. While the stock market is open for trading in individual stocks, variances are narrow and are kept so by arbitrage.

## Tracking Errors

In some cases, the portion of an ETF occupied by an individual company may exceed the limits imposed by the SEC. The government imposes no such limits on indexes because those are only hypothetical investments. But exchange-traded funds, which are real, are subject to the requirement that no more than a certain percentage of a fund may be occupied by a single company.

Back in the late 1990s and early 2000s, when Internet stocks soared, the market value of Nortel Networks exceeded the permitted percentage for iShares MSCI Canada. A substantial number of shares of Nortel had to be sold by the ETF, generating big capital gains to surprised shareholders and causing the tracking error to widen.

In Europe, the economies of Austria, Switzerland, and Sweden, as mentioned, are dominated by relatively few huge companies. SEC requirements force the tracking errors for the ETFs of those nations to be wider than is the case for a regional ETF such as iShares MSCI EMU. Rather than concentrating on single nations, you will parallel indexes more closely if you stick to regional ETFs.

Not that it matters much. Some professional managers care intensely how close their performance is to a benchmark because this determines how much they're paid. But you're just looking for a fulfilling retirement. If your fund follows its benchmark pretty closely, this seems satisfactory enough.

## Tax Costs—Mutual Fund Variety

When shareholders of conventional mutual funds redeem their shares, they sell, as mentioned previously, directly to the fund. In return, the fund pays out cash at the net asset value. If the fund doesn't have the cash, it must sell a portion of its portfolio in the market. This incurs transaction costs, which are shared by all the shareholders, especially the ones who aren't selling. In other words, the shareholders who are selling incur costs for those who are not. To reduce the current tax burden, the fund sells shares that have high costs. This leaves low-cost stocks in the portfolio. Any subsequent sales of these low-cost stocks realizes long- or short-term capital gains that are passed out to shareholders.

Let's say the fund is left with shares of a stock whose costs are relatively low. Also assume that the company is acquired by another at a premium, resulting in a taxable sale. A hefty gain results, which is passed out to the shareholders. The fund prefers not to sell its low-cost stock, but on a taxable buyout, it has no alternative.

Worse yet, the entire mutual fund may be bought by another fund organization. (This occurs more often than one might think.) Some or all of the stocks held by the fund may be sold, resulting in substantial gains being passed out to shareholders.

## Tax Costs—ETF Variety

In contrast, the managers of exchange-traded funds are seldom required to sell the stocks they hold. They make exchanges instead— in-kind exchanges that are not taxable transactions. Let's say an authorized participant is requesting the creation of Spiders. She delivers to the trustee all 500 of the S&P stocks in the proper proportions, and the trustee delivers Spider shares in return. No sales are made, and no taxes result.

It doesn't matter to the authorized participant that the fund passes out low-cost stock on redemptions. The stock takes on a new tax cost in her hands anyway, this being the stock's value at the time of the redemption.

The authorized participant herself makes sales, all right. The Spider shares she receives from the trustee she may sell a few minutes later. The value at the time of the exchange with the fund is her cost. If the Spider price has gone up in the interim, the authorized participant pays ordinary income on the gain. Authorized participants and specialists must usually treat their gains and loss as ordinary income, not capital gain. But the payment of tax by the authorized participant on her sales is her problem. The point is, the prior exchange with the trustee incurs no tax for the fund or for its shareholders.

When Spider shares are redeemed, the fund delivers stocks that have the lowest cost. This means the remaining stocks have high tax costs. Subsequently, when the fund is required to sell the stocks because it's acquired or otherwise removed from the index, no gain results. As a result, little or no capital gains are passed out to ETF shareholders.

Spiders are the oldest of the ETFs, having been established in 1993. In 13 years, Spiders have passed out a total of $0.12 in capital gains. That's 12 cents in 13 years on a fund currently priced at 127! And even those gains occurred in just the first three years. During the last decade, the capital gains have been zero.

## Big Brother

The SEC requires that no single stock may constitute more than 25 percent of the assets of a fund or ETF. It also requires that the stocks that individually constitute 5 percent or more of the portfolio cannot, as a group, exceed 50 percent of the portfolio.

Many ETFs adjust their portfolios to meet these requirements. But occasionally, small-sector funds with relatively few holdings may contain a stock whose price soars in value to the point where the fund no longer complies with SEC requirements. The managers must then sell enough of the stock to bring the fund into compliance. The price having risen, the sale generates capital gains that must be passed out to shareholders.

## Global, *Schmobal*

I love foreign stocks. But I suggest buying ETFs that hold only foreign stocks. Do not acquire global funds that hold a majority of domestic stocks and a minority of foreign stocks. (Since U.S. companies tend to be large, they usually constitute more than half the value of global funds.) A minority of foreign stocks creates a disadvantage in U.S. federal taxes. Here's why: The dividends of foreign stocks are commonly taxed by the nation in which the company resides. Only the net amount of the dividends, after payment of the tax, is received by the ETF. This means that the ETF's shareholders in effect pay the foreign tax.

Foreign taxes paid by U.S. shareholders are compensated for in the shareholder's U.S. return. If the fund holds a *majority* of foreign stocks, the foreign tax is treated as a credit, which reduces the U.S. tax itself. If the fund holds a *minority* of foreign stocks, the foreign tax is treated as a deduction, which reduces the income to which the tax rate is applied.

For reducing taxes, credits have more impact than deductions. Therefore, avoid global funds that hold just a minority of foreign stocks. Instead, to take advantage of credits, acquire ETFs that concentrate exclusively on foreign stocks. (The distinction between deductions and credits in this case is one of the many ways that the government has "simplified" income taxes.)

# Comparison of Risks

Most people aren't aware how much risk they take when they buy the stocks of just a few individual companies. You take on risk for which you are not compensated in market returns. For any number of reasons, the stocks you own might hit the skids while the entire market is performing well.

Buying too few securities introduces what's called **specific** (or **unsystematic**) **risk**. The market, in a way, is the system, while the stocks you own may go their own way by a wide margin. The stock *market* is rewarding in the long run, all right, but it rewards only for **market** (or **systematic**) risk.

*Specific risk* doesn't necessarily mean the risk that the company will fail altogether and go out of business. Not many listed companies do that. *Specific risk* is more likely to mean that the price of the few stocks in your portfolio will be more volatile than that of the market as a whole. The stock of the average individual company is considerably more volatile than the market as a whole.

It's vital to reduce volatility. For one thing, the mathematics are poor: A stock that falls by 50 percent requires an increase of 100 percent just to get back to even. Also, the more your stocks move up and down, the more intense your emotional reactions. You're riding high when they're up, and you're likely to buy more. You're in a funk when they're down, and you're likely to sell. Buying high and selling low is not exactly the way to go. (My Pulitzer Prize for poetry is assured.)

# How You Get Paid

The entire market of stocks pays well—very well. But only if you avoid jumping in and out. You have to stay in for the long pull. Here's why: Over time, the creation of wealth by the people of world, unhindered by government, causes stock prices to rise.

Since 1926, the S&P 500 stocks, not adjusted for inflation, have gained in excess of 12 percent a year. 12 percent! This beats savings accounts by a bunch. Bear in mind that the period since 1926 included the Great Depression, a massive, all-consuming world war, the cold war, and terrible economic policies in the 1970s.

Yes, the market's performance has been remarkable for a long time. But from month to month and even year to year, it jumps all over the place. In a later chapter, we'll discuss how to use exchange-traded funds to reduce market risk. But you cannot reduce market volatility to zero. Learn to live with reasonable market risk. Over time, your payoff will be highly rewarding.

# Back to Individual Stocks

You get paid well for tolerating market swings. But you don't get paid at all for the extra volatility of individual stocks. You may luck out and jump on the next Microsoft when it's just a pup. But you're just as likely—actually much more likely—to jump on the next loser. Why? Because stock prices are remarkably efficient. It's called the *efficient-market theory* or the *random-walk theory*. There are several degrees of belief in the efficient-market theory:

- Some people think that historic price and volume patterns predict nothing about the future.
- Others believe that the price of a security also reflects all of the information that's publicly available, including the firm's product line, accounting practices, earnings forecasts, and the quality of its managers.
- Still others believe that the price of a security also reflects all of the above information, plus the knowledge available even to company insiders.

I share in all those beliefs, but I take it one step further. I believe that the price of a security reflects information that won't become known to anyone, even company insiders, for four to six months in the future.

## Stock Prices Are Smarter Than You Think

How do investors know the information that won't become available to anyone for several months?

They don't know. They just guess. But it's not just one or two of us that are guessing; it's millions of people. Every publicly held company has managers, employees, vendors, customers, government regulators, bankers, advertisers, stock analysts, TV viewers, neighbors, observers, and just hangers-on. Some people know more about the company than others, of course. But everyone has an opinion.

Actually, more likely, they have only intuitions, and the only way they can express them is by buying or selling the stock. Those who don't like the company avoid the stock, making the price lower. Those who like it buy the stock, making it higher. At every moment, the price is perched halfway between the optimists and pessimists—halfway between the bulls and the bears. The stock market is a giant voting machine, which anticipates the future with remarkable accuracy. Sometimes, investors are surprised, of course, and the price adjusts immediately. If the surprise is negative, the price moves down. But here's the key: If the negative news is in accord with bad news that won't become known for several more months, the price continues down. But if the current bad news is *not* in accord with primarily good news that will be revealed in several months, the current decline doesn't persist, and the price resumes its upward course.

### *The Bookie's Line*

To be successful in buying individual stocks, you have to be smarter and more knowledgeable than everyone else who has any awareness of the company.

To illustrate, let's say it's the day a Super Bowl. The Pittsburgh Steelers again face the Seattle Seahawks. Most people think that Pittsburgh will win, and you do too. You bet on the Steelers.

They win, but unfortunately, you also had to guess by how *much* they'd win. The bookie's "line" required that the Steelers had to win by at least 12 points. They win by only 10. Sorry, you lose.

Until game time, the bookie adjusts the line according to how the bets come in. The more bettors that expect the Steelers to win, the higher he raises the line. The line doesn't reflect the bookie's opinion; it reflects the collective knowledge and intuition of every bettor. The only way to know the collective intuition of everyone betting is to know the line. (If you bet the line itself and the margin of victory comes in at that level, no one wins; the bookie takes all the money.)

If you bet on football often, naturally you're going to win some of the time. But to win consistently, time after time, you have to guess the future *more accurately than everyone else put together*. As you can well imagine, that's a tall order.

### *Tough Row to Hoe*

It's the same in purchasing individual stocks or in trying to outwit the market as a whole. To win consistently, you have to predict the future better than everyone else put together. Are you that good? Hotshot Wall Street analysts aren't. They're good at selling to customers, sure. But when it comes to beating the market, they're just normal folks. Oh, one of them may have a good record for a year. He or she is considered a guru and is interviewed on television. But the next year, Lady Luck touches another fellow, and the last one slinks back into the pack, unnoticed.

There are only two ways you can beat the market:

- You can consistently buy individual stocks that outperform their peers.
- You can consistently buy when the entire market is low and sell when it's high. (This approach we discuss in the next chapter.)

No matter which approach you take, or even if you adopt both, the chances of your making a succession of investment judgments that beat the market over a long period of time are very slim indeed. We're far better off in the long run letting the market do the work. Doing this properly requires relatively little worry and remarkably little effort.

You want to try your hand at purchasing a few individual stocks? Fine, if you have a bunch of money, take 5 percent of it and have a ball. But for your serious money, don't even think of individual stocks unless you acquire a lot of them, of different types and industries.

How many? Studies show that holding a single stock instead of a well-diversified portfolio increases the annual volatility by about 30 percent. (**Volatility** means the average amount by which a portfolio's return differs from that of the long-term market.) Let's say the market's average volatility is 15 percent. The single-stock investor is likely to suffer volatility of 45 percent, this being the *market's* volatility of 15 percent plus *extra* volatility of 30 percent from holding a single stock.

Rising and falling 45 percent a year! Maybe you like roller coasters. But you're better off sticking to the amusement park variety. High volatility ruins long-term investment results.

Investing in 25 stocks cuts diversifiable risk by about 80 percent. Investing in 100 stocks cuts it about 90 percent; 400 stocks about 95 percent. But why bother with even 400 stocks when you can do away with diversifiable risk altogether by buying a few ETFs that collectively hold over *1,000 stocks*. With iShares Russell 3000 Index Fund, for example, you'd participate in the fortunes of 3,000 stocks. With an investment like that, you're buying America!

## How's Your Aim?

Here's an approach that will give you better results than doing stock research: Pin stock pages on the wall and throw a dart at them, oh, say, 40 times. Buy whatever stock the dart lands on, providing it's a common stock and not a closed-end mutual fund. Once the portfolio is assembled, don't change it for 10 years or so. You'll probably leave most mutual funds far behind you.

*Forbes* Magazine did this in 1967. Throwing a dart at the stock page, the editors chose 28 common stocks. They assumed an investment of $1,000 in each and created a hypothetical portfolio of $28,000, the components of which were published at the time. By 1984, 17 years later, so many buyouts and mergers had occurred that the test had to be discontinued. The portfolio was then worth $131,697. The 1970s, as mentioned, were very difficult ones for the stock market. Despite that, during the 17 years from 1967 to 1984, the compound annual return was 9.5 percent. This beat the broad market and was exceeded by only a tiny percentage of professional money managers.

The dart idea subjects your portfolio to pure chance, which means you're not exercising investment judgment. The market goes out of its way to surprise. The more often you exercise investment judgment, the more likely you'll commit error. This is not an insult to you personally. As a reader of this book, you're *way* above average. The generality applies to all of us.

### A Cagey Approach

In the short term, Ms. Market goes out of her way to make us wrong. Here's how to deal with her:

Assume that if you buy something, it will fall, short term. If you don't buy it, it'll rise. Assume that in the short run, you'll be wrong no matter what you do. This minimizes feelings of guilt, which can do heavy damage to an investment program. The goal is to get past the short term, to enjoy the benefits of the long term.

The more often you exercise investment judgment, the more often you face short-term consequences. If you exercise investment judgment most of the time, you face short-term consequences most of the time. This means you'll be wrong most of the time.

## More ETFs; Less Judgment

Which brings us back to exchange-traded funds. They minimize investment judgment. In the first place, each ETF holds a lot of stocks. Bingo, specific risk is much reduced. If you buy *several* ETFs, specific risk is cut to zero, which is where you want it. Actually, the managers of ETFs don't need to exercise much investment judgment either. For the most part, they simply follow along behind the publisher of an index. The publisher chooses the stocks constituting an entire market, and the ETF manager copies.

Certainly you're better off buying an ETF of an industry rather than selecting an individual company in that industry. But I myself do not try to guess which industry will outperform the others. Even this involves specific risk. You're better off choosing different *types* of securities—different asset classes, such as big stocks, small stocks, growth stocks, value stocks, stocks of foreign regions, REITs, and bonds. We'll get to all that later in the book.

In some cases, ETF managers design their own index. The design involves the exercise of investment judgment, certainly. But it's a one-shot deal. The manager creates a clearly defined set of rules. Thereafter, she exercises no judgment; she just follows the rules. Now, the manager may not share the rules with us. She doesn't want other people to follow her rules. When buyouts, mergers, or other changes make it necessary to sell a stock from her portfolio, she doesn't want third parties jumping into the market ahead of her, putting her at a price disadvantage. She just tells us, "We follow rules. Trust us." Whether you choose to do so is up to you. But the point is, investment judgment is minimized—that's the main thing.

In Chapters 16 and 17, I suggest an ETF portfolio and exercise judgment in making the choices. I also create a set of rules for annual rebalancing. You don't have to accept my judgments, of course. But if you do, it's pretty much a one-shot deal. If you read my columns in your local newspaper or on the Web (www.archierichards.com), you may find that I adjust the allocations modestly every few years. If you follow along, that's fine. If you don't, that's fine, too.

Here's the point: Judgment is required to set up the portfolio and set the rules for rebalancing. Judgment is also needed to change the allocations modestly from time to time, but I'm talking about from year to year, mind you, or even half decade to half decade. Other than these occasional judgments, no creative thought is required. But if you change your judgments from day to day, you're walking in quicksand.

C H A P T E R

# Comparison with Actively Managed Mutual Funds

You don't want to bother with purchasing individual stocks, right? Good; I don't either. Specific risk is not only undesirable, it's unnecessary. To get rid of it altogether, acquire mutual funds or ETFs, preferably ETFs.

But first let's knock off the idea of buying actively managed funds. They offer less than we're led to believe. To begin with, actively managed funds beat their heads against the proposition that everything about a stock—even the things that won't become known about it for several months—is already discounted by the current price. They generally fail to surmount this burden, but they incur heavy costs in the effort. In some cases they also engage in skullduggery.

## Big Difference

Dr. Jeremy J. Siegel has found that over the 35-year period from 1971 to 2004, the average annual return of all actively managed equity mutual funds trailed the broad-based Wilshire 5000 Index by 105 basis points a year. (A **basis point** is 1/100 of 1 percent; 105 basis points are a little over 1 percent.)

Here's a comparison: Assume you invest $10,000, leaving the earnings in the fund to compound at 10 percent a year. After 25 years, the account is worth $108,300.

Now assume that the return drops to only 9 percent a year. After 25 years, the account is worth $86,200.

Although the annual return drops by only 10 percent (10 to 9 percent), the final value falls by 20 percent ($108,300 to $86,200). After a period of years, a relatively small difference in the rate of return makes a much greater difference in the ending value.

Index funds significantly outpace managed funds. Indeed, John Bogle, founder of Vanguard, found that after taking into account management expenses, brokerage costs, and sales charges, the difference is 2 to 2.5 percent a year. Add in the higher taxes on managed funds, and you're probably looking at a difference of 3 to 3.5 percent a year.

I suggest that you not acquire actively managed mutual funds at all. The odds are against you. Over two or three decades, the difference between a return of 10 and 6.5 percent is huge. As mentioned above, $10,000 compounds at 10 percent a year in 25 years to $108,300. At 6.5 percent, the ending balance is only $48,300, a difference of 55 percent.

## Conflicts of Interest

Much of the research concerning the active management of securities comes from companies that have a stake in active management. This includes brokerage firms, of course, who benefit from rapid trading. It includes newspapers and television programs that want to feed us the latest news. It also includes investment publications that promulgate up-to-date information. Morningstar, for example, assigns "stars" to mutual funds. Five-star funds are expected to have superior records, and the assignment of five stars attracts a great many investors. Alas, studies have found that five-star funds do not have superior records after all. Once all those new investors attracted by the stars come onboard, the fund slinks back into the pack.

Actively managed funds attract far more investor dollars than index funds and exchange-traded funds. Do not fall prey to their sales efforts. The chances of your attaining an outstanding record with an actively managed fund is slim. Instead, buy funds that endeavor to equal the market and incur low costs.

With mutual funds, you get what you *don't* pay for.

## Market Timing

Actively managed mutual funds have two ways of trying to beat the market. One way is to select individual stocks that outperform others. The other way is to *time* the market—to hold cash when the market seems likely to fall and be fully invested when the market seems ready to climb.

We've already seen that picking stocks that outperform doesn't work. The same thing goes for market timing; this doesn't work either. Indeed, the percentage of cash held by mutual funds tends to be the lowest at market tops and highest at market bottoms. Here, we have to give actively managed funds a bit of a pass because the fund shareholders are active too. The funds must hold plenty of cash to meet redemption requests at market bottoms, when shareholders are most inclined to sell.

But we don't give actively managed mutual funds much of a pass. They certainly don't resist shareholder inclination to buy at market tops, when the news is good. No, the mutual fund managers are bullish too. Their competitors are fully invested. No one knows how far the stocks will rise. No one wants to be behind the eight ball, and everyone wants to be fully invested.

Actively managed mutual funds tend to hold the largest percentage of cash at market bottoms and the smallest percentage of cash at market tops—the very opposite of what they should. In the effort to beat the street, market timing doesn't work any better than stock selection.

Oh sure, market timing may work for a few hardy, and perhaps lucky, fund managers. Stock selection may work too. But doing either one of these things consistently is impossible. All the stocks in the market must be held by someone. Collectively, all of us *are* the market. As a group, we hit the average right on the nose (after the collective costs).

For everyone who beats the market, others must lose; it's a zero-sum game.

After costs, all of us, collectively, do worse than the market. How well we perform individually depends on how well we keep our costs down. Since actively managed mutual funds incur so many heavy costs, they are not appropriate vehicles for investing one's hard-earned cash. Here are some of those costs.

## Sky-High Operating Costs

In most industries, prices decline as the volume increases. In the last 25 years, for example, the number of calculations per second performed by personal computers has risen by millions of times. The costs have fallen accordingly, close to zero.

Mutual fund costs have moved in the other direction. Since 1980, the market value of mutual funds grew nearly 70 times, from less than $100 million to $6.5 trillion. During the same period, the average annual costs as a percentage of assets did not go down. Oh no, they almost doubled from 0.75 to 1.5 percent of assets invested.

## Transaction Costs

Transaction costs are also high. Actively managed funds are constantly jumping in and out of stocks, trying to take advantage of the latest dope before anyone else. They pay commissions, of course, and since the amounts of money are considerable, they pay wide spreads.

But rather than trying to avoid these costs, actively managed mutual funds are trading more rapidly then ever. Since 1980, the rate of turnover of mutual fund portfolios has risen from 20 to nearly 100 percent a year. Almost 100 percent! This means the funds change almost their entire portfolios nearly every year! The Plexus Group (now part of the Investment Technology Group) has estimated that the transaction costs for a fund with 100 percent turnover come to about 2.3 percent. With small-cap trading, the costs are higher.

With turnover so rapid, more and more proceeds are taxed as short-term capital gains, subject to high tax rates of up to 35 percent. If funds cut back on trading, most proceeds would instead be subjected to long-term rates at a maximum of only 15 percent.

## Sales Costs

Buying a mutual fund through a brokerage firm also adds sales costs. As discussed earlier, the sales charge might be paid by (1) a deduction from your account up front, (2) a deduction from your account when you redeem within a certain number of years, (3) extra operating and marketing costs, or (4) a combination of deductions 2 and 3.

With mutual funds, you get what you don't pay for. Even though the costs of index funds and ETFs are less, they consistently outperform their actively managed cousins.

# Not Always on the Up-and-Up

Some actively managed funds also engage in skullduggery. A fund, you see, attracts new investors when it outperforms its peers. Once onboard, investors tend to stay with the fund after the performance deteriorates. Funds therefore jump through hoops to outperform their peers, even for a limited time. Let me count the ways:

One way to outdo the competition is to engage in **style shift**. Unlike ETFs, actively managed mutual funds don't tell us what they own. Only in semiannual or quarterly financial statements do they do so.

Let's say that an actively managed mutual fund, according to its prospectus, is supposed to concentrate on big value stocks. But during a particular period, assume that big value stocks haven't gone anywhere. In between the reporting statements, the fund therefore sells some of its big value stocks and buys small growth stocks that are "moving"—the ones that seem to have upside momentum. Then, before the next statement, the manager, like a mischievous altar boy, reverts back to the big value stocks he was supposed to hold all along. If the small growth stocks continue their upside momentum in the interim, the fund beats the competing funds that stick to their proper, big-value style.

### Limiting the Competition

Here's another way mutual funds outperform their peers for a limited time, or at least give the appearance of doing so: They restrict the apparent competition. For example, you might have heard or seen an advertisement in which a mutual fund boasted that, among big value mutual funds whose assets ranged from $250 million to $500 million, it had the best record for 2006. Although the advertisement was a stretch, it was in fact true. There are hundreds of big value funds overall, but the mutual fund marketers work around this by restricting the time period and the size of the funds being compared with, all of which limits the apparent number of competing funds. New investors pour in, and the new money tends to stick around, at least for a while, after the fund's performance slinks back into the pack.

### The Quick Push

Another trick: Just prior to the date of the public statement, the fund buys more of the stocks it already owns. This beefs up the price of those stocks, making the performance for that period all the more appealing. So far, I've given three examples of skullduggery. It's my impression that only a minority of actively managed funds engage in them. But the next two examples of wrongdoing are widespread:

### Incubation

Say a mutual fund family starts four new funds. None of them are offered to the public; the investors are private individuals, some of whom may work for the fund.

The four funds are invested differently. The organization doesn't know which one will outdo the others. But after a year or two, it can see the records and knows which one has had the best performance.

The fund then closes the three inferior funds and offers only the best one to the public. It promulgates the fine record the fund had *from the beginning.* Investors pile onboard, not knowing that the good record resulted simply from good luck and after-the-fact selection.

### Scandalous Soft Dollars

You'd think that fund managers would pay for the normal costs of doing business out of their operating fees. I'm talking about magazines, online services, accounting services, proxy services, office administration, computers, printers, cables, software, maintenance, and entrance fees for resort conferences. Some managers do pay for these things, of course, but not all of them. They'd rather *you* paid, enabling the managers to keep more of the operating fees for themselves.

How to legally accomplish this? Simple. The fund arranges for a broker to pay the costs. In return, the broker charges 5 to 10 times the normal commission amounts. These are called *soft dollars*. Ultimately, you pay, of course. The published performance of a fund is net of transaction costs, and transaction costs include soft dollars.

This practice is widespread among actively managed mutual funds. It's been estimated that soft dollars have increased fund transaction costs by something like 70 basis points (7/10 of 1 percent) for all funds.

Operating costs are reported in prospectuses, but transaction costs are not, and transaction costs are where the soft dollars are hidden.

This all started because Congress authorized funds to pay soft dollars for investment research and other "investment-related services." But the mutual fund industry has carried this far beyond its intended purposes.

Some 95 percent of institutional brokers receive soft dollars. In the late 1990s, the Securities and Exchange Commission itself found that about a third of these brokers provided services to fund managers well beyond the scope of investment-related costs.

Why hasn't the SEC treated this as a scandal? Because, like other government regulatory bodies, it eventually takes on the point of view of the major companies in the industry it regulates.

### *Dropouts*

Funds whose performance has been inferior for several years lose the ability to attract investors. They tend to be bought out by funds with better records. The records of the bought-out funds disappear, while the records of the funds doing the acquisitions continue to be published.

To illustrate, assume that over a period of five years, Fund A has a lousy record and Fund B has a good one. Fund B acquires Fund A, lock, stock, and barrel.

Fund B continues to tell the world about its good record. But the shareholders of the former Fund A know that that record didn't apply to them. They wonder where Fund A's poor record is published. Little do they realize that it has simply disappeared, like a rainbow when the angle of the sun changes.

The performance record of mutual funds includes only the *surviving* funds. If the record of the dropouts were included, the collective records of all actively managed funds would be significantly lower than the published records.

## Best to Avoid

The total costs of actively managed funds, including sales charges, operating expenses, transaction costs, and taxes now amount to something like 3.3 percent a year—if the market gains at 12 percent a year, more than a quarter of it goes out the window in costs, much of it unnecessary costs.

Like everyone else, the managers of actively managed funds can't beat the market consistently either by selecting outstanding stocks or by timing the market. Their costs are excessive. And some of them engage in skullduggery. Overall, I'd stay away from actively managed funds. They're bum deals.

. . . . . . . . . . . . . . . . . . . . . . . . . . . . . .

We next compare ETFs to index funds. It's a far closer comparison, but even here, ETFs win the day.

# 10

# Comparison with Index Funds

Both index funds and exchange-traded funds are inexpensive for all the reasons actively managed funds are not. The principal reason for the savings, of course, is that index funds and ETFs don't have to pay the whopping costs of stock research. They simply follow the index by buying and holding its stocks. Nevertheless, for long-term holders, exchange-traded funds are the best deal of all.

## Operating Costs

Like index funds, ETFs have no need for stock research. But their operating costs are even lower than index funds because of reduced accounting costs. Instead of keeping track of thousands of individual investors, they need account to only a few authorized participants. The owners of ETF shares receive statements, all right, but they receive those from the brokerage firm, not the ETF itself. In addition, ETFs are rarely required to pass out capital gains to shareholders—another savings in accounting costs.

ETF buyers incur commissions, but they never have to pay the Class A, B, or C sales charges incurred by some index funds.

## Transaction and Tax Costs

When the owner of an index fund redeems, he or she receives cash. The fund may have to sell stock to provide it. This incurs transaction and tax costs that are borne by all shareholders, not just the one who's selling. The fund also tends to sell its high-cost assets, leaving behind low-cost assets that create a potential tax burden—another disadvantage to long-term holders.

With exchange-traded funds, an authorized participant who redeems receives stock in exchange. Sales of stock by the ETF fund itself are necessary only when a stock is removed from the underlying index, perhaps because of a merger or acquisition. But the exchanges ETFs have with authorized participants are tax-free, enabling the fund to pass out its low-cost assets and leaving behind little or no potential tax burden. In every respect, transaction costs are borne by the shareholders who choose to sell, not by those who don't.

## Flexibility

An index fund can be bought and sold only after the close, at market. At the time you place the order, the price is unknown. You may enter an order to sell an index fund at 10 o'clock in the morning and then turn your attention to other things. Unknown to you, the market plummets during the day. The sale goes through at the close at a price much lower than you expected.

ETFs, on the other hand, can be bought and sold during the trading day, when you can be more certain of the price. Limit orders, stop orders, short sales—any kind of order available for stocks—can be used for ETFs. (Explanations of these orders are found in Chapter 14.)

## Opportunity Costs

When the market has risen strongly during the day, unsophisticated investors of mutual funds and even index funds are inclined to make last-minute purchases at the close. The fund manager doesn't have time to put the money to work until the next morning, when momentum may carry prices even higher.

The buyers get credit for the 4:00 p.m. prices, but the cash isn't invested by the fund until the next day, presumably at higher prices. The buyers get a deal, but the other investors lose the opportunity to benefit from purchases at the previous night's close.

To solve this problem, mutual funds should close the door on new orders at 2:30 p.m., giving time for the managers to adjust the portfolio before the day's end. Orders received after 2:30 would be executed at the next day's close. This would put new investors on a par with previous investors and not disadvantage the latter.

Some mutual funds impose the 2:30 cutoff; others don't. But with exchange-traded funds, no such cutoff is necessary. Investors can trade ETF shares at any time during the trading day.

## Potential for Misdoing

Both index funds and ETFs are clean of skullduggery. ETFs are especially so. Not only do ETFs disclose their portfolio after the close every day, their net asset values are disclosed every 15 seconds. The more available the information, the less opportunity for wrongdoing.

## Tax Management

Exchange-traded funds enable better tax management than index funds. ETFs make it convenient to identify tax lots and sell shares with the highest cost bases, reducing capital gains taxes. ETF investors can conveniently donate low-cost shares to charity.

HOLDRs, which are quasi-ETFs, offer especially good opportunities for tax management. How they do so is described in Appendix B.

Shareholders of index funds have less flexibility for tax purposes. Regarding gains realized by the fund, the shareholders have no flexibility at all. They must accept the gains passed out by the fund. (Most index funds and actively managed funds use average purchase prices for their tax costs.)

## Asset Allocation and Rebalancing

Within a single brokerage account, you can allocate your money among any number and any type of exchange-traded funds. Later, to rebalance the portfolio, you can easily move funds from one ETF to another. But unless you use a single mutual fund family, no such flexibility is available with index funds. Moving funds from one mutual fund family to another is unwieldy, and while the money is in transfer the prices may move against you.

Through fund "supermarkets," you can acquire index funds from different mutual fund families in the same brokerage account. The idea was pioneered by Schwab; its "OneSource" supermarket is the largest. But there's a hook. Schwab charges the fund a hefty annual fee, currently 0.4 percent. Schwab also prohibits funds that participate in OneSource from offering shares to other retail investors or other brokerage supermarkets at lower fees than it charges when marketed by Schwab. In other words, if a fund wants to be sold by Schwab, it must charge higher fees to everyone. Most funds feel the fee is too high for the fund to absorb, and they pass it along to customers.

Avoid funds offered by OneSource. But why even bother researching which ones are marketed by OneSource and which ones aren't? Just acquire exchange-traded funds and avoid the problem altogether.

## The Risky Stuff

You can acquire ETFs on margin, meaning you acquire additional shares with money borrowed from the brokerage firm. You can also sell ETFs short and buy options on ETFs. You can't do any of these things with index funds.

But you're well advised to avoid using those high-risk techniques even with exchange-traded funds. Oh, you might sell ETFs short or use options on them for hedging purposes. But why trouble yourself? In many cases, these measures simply increase your transaction costs. Just get in the market with ETFs, unhedged, and hold for the long term. Once you get past the discomfort of being wrong in the short term, you'll enjoy remarkable long-term gains.

Figure 10-1 summarizes the comparison of no-load funds with exchange-traded funds.

We're done with what exchange-traded funds are and how they compare with other investments. On we go to how (and how not) to use them.

| | No-Load Funds | | | Exchange-Traded Funds |
|---|---|---|---|---|
| | **Individual Stocks** | **Mutual Funds** | **Index Funds** | |
| Operating costs | n/a | High | Low | Very low |
| Transaction costs to trader | n/a | No | No | Yes |
| Transaction costs to long-term holder | n/a | High | Low | No |
| Unwanted short-term capital gains | No | High | Low | Almost zero |
| Trading flexibility | Yes | No | No | Yes |
| Minimum purchase | 1 share | Varies | Varies | 1 share |
| Tax efficiency | Yes | Difficult | Difficult | Yes |
| Potential for misdoing | No | High | Low | Almost zero |
| Automatic reinvestments | No | Yes | Yes | No |
| Short sales | Yes | No | No | Yes |
| Use of margin | Yes | No | No | Yes |

**Figure 10-1    Comparison of No-Load Funds and Exchange-Traded Funds**

# PART THREE

# GUIDELINES AND STRATEGIES

# 11

# General Financial Guidelines

Before you begin taking on specific strategies involving ETFs or other kinds of investments, become familiar with the financial guidelines and strategies described here. Strategies to avoid greatly outnumber the ones that work. If you can just knock off the baddies, you'll be way ahead of most people.

## Pay off High-Interest Debt First

Before starting to invest, pay off your high-interest debt. Credit cards are handy, of course, but unless you're able to wipe them clean every month, give them the heave-ho. Even better, don't use credit cards at all. Postpone any purchases for which you have not already saved.

If you have significant funds in a savings account paying 3 percent, and you also have a revolving credit card account costing 19 percent interest ... well, check whether you're a glutton for punishment. Use the savings money to pay off the credit card debt. Remember that the interest you receive from the savings account is taxable while the interest you pay on the credit cards is not deductible—another example of heads they win, tails you lose.

## Cut Your Mortgage Costs

Here are a couple of ideas to provide more money for investing.

- Pay more attention to the interest rate of a mortgage than to the points. Let's say a bank offers two mortgage arrangements: One has more points but a lower interest rate. The other has fewer points but a higher interest rate. You're better off with the former, because points are a one-time expense while the interest-rate effect is continuous. Ask for illustrations of both plans.
- Let's say your monthly payments come to $1,000 a month. Instead of paying this amount monthly, pay $500 every two weeks. To handle the payments, search in your browser for "Paymap, Inc.," and call the number provided in contact information. It's amazing how many fewer years it'll take to own your house free and clear.

## Make Saving a Game

The rate at which your investment portfolio grows is less important than the rate at which you add money to it on a regular basis. Set aside 10 percent of your earnings for investing. Can't spare that much, you say? Consider the following:

- Do you skip breakfast at home and spend $3 on coffee and a muffin in the morning?
- Are you a regular for bottled water? Gallon for gallon, it costs more than gasoline.
- How about sodas on hot afternoons?
- You're already gorgeous. Why go overboard at the tanning studio?
- Do you spend a couple of bucks a day on a lottery in which your chance of winning is less than a meteorite landing harmlessly in your back yard?
- Cars look great and run great even though they're used.

- After taking into account the excise taxes and the danger to your health, cigarettes cost an arm and a lung.
- Live in a neighborhood where people have a standard of living you can readily afford.
- Rent your movies.
- Buy nothing at the grocery store except what you list in advance.
- No matter what you buy, look for bargains.
- Buy a how-to book on savings. Make saving a game.

## *Need Help?*

Many people spend right up to their income and feel just as broke with $250,000 income as others do with $40,000 income. Knock off that ridiculous overspending! Your sense of self-worth comes from inside, not from how much money you spend. If you don't know what's inside, see a shrink. You don't have to be a nutcake. Readers of this book are certified non-nutcakes. If the counselor has good judgment, the results could be wonderful. If the counselor has poor judgment, find another.

To help control your spending, buy *America's Cheapest Family Gets You Right on the Money: Your Guide to Living Better, Spending Less, and Cashing in on Your Dreams.* I had the pleasure of reading an advance copy. Steve and Annette Economides, the authors, are a terrific couple. Their last name just happens to match what they do so well: They economize, and they do it with joy.

## *A Lousy $10 a Day*

Say you earn $16 an hour. That's $640 gross a week, $33,000 a year. How about parting with just one hour of gross pay a day? That's $16. You won't know how much small stuff you can get along without until you try.

All right, all right, make it a lousy $10 a day. That's $300 a month, which you invest every month for 30 years. At 10 percent annual growth, you'll be worth $678,000.

In 40 years, make that $1,900,000—a little more than you expected, right?

Forget budgets. They're supposed to control normal human impulses. But they're no fun, which is why they don't work. Instead, invest a percentage of your pay automatically in an amount that's equivalent at the beginning to $10 a day. Then adjust your lifestyle to fit. As your pay rises, the amount automatically goes up. Later on, when you're wealthier, also raise the percentage.

## Get Rich Automatically

Automate the investments and grow rich. Arrange for the brokerage firm to dip into your bank account each month and withdraw the amount you specify. Set this up when you open the account. Brokerage firms can handle automatic investing just as well as mutual funds.

The money comes off the top. Money you don't see you won't spend. Get the money working for the future before you touch it in the present. If your employer offers matching, take maximum advantage. That's like picking up gold coins off the street.

## Known and Unknown Expenses

You may have expenses you know you'll have to pay within five years. These might include tuition payments, a summer home, or assisted-living costs. Set that short-term money aside in a money market fund.

But large, *unknown* expenses are a different story. Most people call them "emergencies." This money should be invested for the long term. I'm not talking about the cash balances you need to keep the family going. (If you avoid credit cards and buy only what you've saved for, you'll be reserving a *lot* of cash to keep the family going.)

Maintenance on your home is not an emergency; it's a known expense. You just don't know when you'll have to dole out the money. Reserve for such maintenance, adding a bit to savings every month.

Anticipate all of the expenses you'll eventually have to pay and reserve for them outside of an IRA or qualified retirement program.

But unknown expenses, such as an accident or losing your job? Don't go overboard reserving for those. Get as much money as you can working in long-term investments. When an emergency occurs, that's when a credit card comes in handy. But immediately sell some of your investments and repay the card.

Stock prices stay the same or go up about two-thirds of the time. Take advantage.

## When's the Best Time to Buy?

In the long run, the market goes up. In the short run, it's unpredictable. Therefore, the best time to buy is when you get the money.

Even if it's a big amount, invest it all. As mentioned, the market stays level or goes up about two-thirds of the time. If you postpone your investing to buy at lower prices, the chances are you'll wait in vain and end up feeling foolish buying at higher prices. The worse the news, the faster you should hurry to buy.

Investment professionals suggest putting in the money a portion at a time. It's in their interest to say this. An investment professional's major objective is to not lose you as a customer. He doesn't know where the market will go any better than you do. If he tells you to invest gradually and he's wrong, he can't be blamed because he was just being prudent with your money. If he tells you to invest all at once and he's wrong, he will indeed be blamed because he was supposed to know about those things.

Investment professionals favor **dollar cost averaging**, meaning that you invest a given amount of money periodically—usually every month—on the assumption that when prices fall, you can afford to buy more shares. The assumption is faulty; the market rises more often than it falls. You're better off buying when you get the money.

It's a different story if you don't *have* the money. Ah yes, then you invest the money as you earn it, in automatic monthly or semimonthly investments. Professionals call this "dollar cost averaging." I don't. I call it investing when you get the money. Investing automatically as you earn the money is your path to riches.

## IRAs and Other Qualified Retirement Plans Aren't All That Hot

Deductible retirement plans and traditional IRAs aren't as great as most people think. Assume you put $4,000 a year, pretax, into both an IRA and an outside investment. Both accounts compound at 10 percent a year, with the tax brackets remaining at 25 percent throughout. Using reasonable assumptions, I calculate that after 25 years, you're better off with the IRA by about 25 percent after tax. (For the details, see www. archierichards.com for the column dated May 8, 2006.)

Better by 25 percent is an improvement, certainly, but it's a long way from being twice as good. The comparison, however, doesn't take the following into account:

- The operating costs of many 401(k) plans are something like 2 percent higher than the costs of outside investments. Right there, the tax advantages of 401(k) plans with no employer matching disappear altogether.
- Many individuals and institutions trade too rapidly in retirement plans because the rapid trading has no tax disadvantage. But commission costs, spreads, and trading losses reduce the returns substantially.
- Retirement plans are not entitled to a stepped-up basis at death. The beneficiaries must pay tax at ordinary rates on all withdrawals. In nonretirement accounts, however, the tax costs are "stepped up" at the owner's death to the date-of-death values. The capital gains on securities held at death are never taxed to anyone. If the assets are subsequently sold at the date-of-death prices, no gains or losses result.
- IRAs are complicated. IRS rules regarding their inheritance are particularly onerous. All too often, people with substantial IRAs make serious errors that result in significant and unnecessary tax payments. Okay, you can pay advisors to help you avoid the errors. But advisors who know complex tax rules are no dummies; they cost pretty heavy money themselves.

After factoring in all these elements, traditional IRAs and retirement plans are likely to come out worse than an outside account.

However, under the following circumstances, use a retirement plan anyway:

- If having your money in a retirement plan is the only way to avoid spending it, go with the retirement plan. But don't *trade* the investments.
- If your employer matches your contributions to a retirement plan, take advantage.

Except for those two conditions, deductible retirement plans and traditional IRAs are hardly worth it. Roth IRAs are fine, sure. But the deductible plans are a royal pain in the neck.

## Don't Go Overboard Saving Taxes

Don't let taxes control your financial life. Saving taxes usually means giving up control. The most effective way to pay no income tax is to have no income. Who wants that?

The next most effective way to save taxes—a far more desirable way—is to hold profitable investments for at least a year and a day. Avoid short-term capital gains like the plague. Long-term capital gains are federally taxed at a maximum of 15 percent, very likely lower than the rate applying to your earned income.

In general, choose investments because they're good investments, not because they save taxes. (As it happens, most exchange-traded funds do both.)

## Avoid Sales Charges

With ETFs and the stocks of individual companies, you pay commissions, of course. But how about mutual funds? Should you buy them through a broker and pay extra sales charges? I feel that if a person wouldn't buy a fund except for a broker's persuasion, the broker has performed a real service and deserves ample compensation.

But this doesn't apply to you. You have curiosity and gumption enough to read this book. After finishing it, you'll know far more about investing than most people. You won't need someone at your shoulder urging you to make investments and telling you what to buy. You already have the initiative to do it yourself, and you will soon have the knowledge to know how. Later, I will recommend using the brokerage firm Folio*fn* to acquire exchange-traded funds. No representative of Folio*fn* will be looking over your shoulder urging you on. The firm pays no one to do any such thing.

## Don't Chase Recent Performance

Just because a stock or fund has performed well of late doesn't mean it will continue doing so in the future. More likely, the performance will return to the mean, and you'll be left holding the bag. Don't chase recent performance.

## Stocks Outperform Bonds

Be willing to accept reasonable downside volatility in the short term to enjoy wonderful upside volatility in the long term. The best way to achieve big growth is to buy stocks. Put something like 60 percent of your money into them, with only 20 percent in bonds (and the remaining 20 percent in real estate investment trusts).

Remember, you don't need the money now. Consider a decline in market value as just fluctuation.

From 1802 to 2006 (204 years), there were 194 10-year periods. To illustrate, the first 10-year period is from 1802 to 1812; the second 10-year period is from 1803 to 1813, and so on.

In every one of those periods, stocks performed better than bonds, after adjusting for inflation. In a few of the periods, both stocks and bonds lost, but stocks lost less. In every 10-year period, you were better off with stocks than bonds.

From 1802 to 2006 (the same 204-year period), there were 184 20-year periods (1802 to 1822, 1803 to 1823, etc.).

In every one of those 20-year periods, stocks gained, after adjusting for inflation. In a few of those periods, bonds lost, but stocks did not.

For the 30-year periods (there were 174 of those), the differential between stocks and bonds was even greater.

Buy stocks. Buy them as soon as you can and hold them for as long as you can (with annual rebalancing, as described in Chapter 16).

## Assume the Worst

The long term is all very well, but we don't live in the long term. We live now. Our minds, our ideas, and our emotions all change from second to second. When we buy stocks, we can't help but notice when things are going wrong in the short term, which they often do. To gain long-term benefits, we have to deal with short-term disappointments.

Here's what I suggest: Assume that, no matter what you do, you're going to be wrong in the short term. If you buy a stock, it will fall. If you *don't* buy the stock, it will rise. Assume you have no control over the short term. The fact is, you don't. Assume that the near term is going to be disappointing.

Whatever happens, it's *not your fault.* This helps relieve you of a sense of guilt. Shame causes investment mistakes. The less of it you feel, the better your investment results.

## The Magic of Compounding

Get started with your investments as soon as you can. Let time and compounding do the work. Here's an illustration.

Go Gettum and Donny Delay, both 25 years old, each invest $4,000 a year in IRAs. (They don't take my advice about avoiding IRAs.) The funds grow at 10 percent a year.

Gettum begins right away, at age 25. He invests for only 8 years until he reaches age 32. At $4,000 a year, his contributions total $32,000. He then stops contributing and lets his IRA continue growing. (This is called *freezing* the IRA.)

Delay waits. Instead of beginning his contributions at age 25, he starts at age 33. For 33 years he adds money to his IRA, retiring at the end of his sixty-fifth year. At $4,000 a year for 33 years, Delay contributes $132,000.

Let's see, Gettum invests $32,000 over 8 years. Delay invests $132,000 over 33 years. At retirement, Delay has more, right?

Wrong! At 65, Gettum has $1,168,641, while Delay has only $977,907. That's $191,000 less.

Gettum ends up with more because he started earlier. Even after Gettum stops his contributions and Delay begins, Gettum's account still gains more every year. Delay's account falls further and further behind.

In the final year, Gettum's account grows by a whopping $106,000—three times more than the total he contributed in the first place. Gettum doesn't even have to do anything except move his eyeballs to review the brokerage statements. He simply takes advantage of the people of the world working hard for his benefit.

Each year, the current year's growth adds on to the previous year's balance. The longer the money remains at work, the better. After 25 years, compounding begins paying off big (see Figure 11-1).

### Why Compounding Works

Compounding works its magic because you leave the dividends, interest, and capital earnings in the account to compound. To illustrate, here's an exaggerated example:

Right after Columbus discovered America, you put $1,000 in an investment that pays 2 percent a year, or $20. Every year, you take out the $20 interest and spend it. At the end of 500 years, the account is worth ... you've got it, the same amount you started with: $1,000.

Alternatively, you leave the $20 interest in the account to compound. Each year, the investment earns 2 percent not only on the original $1,000 but also on the accumulated interest left in from prior years. In the second year, for example, the earnings are not $20; they're $20.40 because the previous year's $20 left in the account earns an extra 40 cents.

For the first few decades, the compounding effect is minimal. But after about 25 or 30 years, the accumulated interest becomes significant, and the compounding effect becomes astonishing. In this case, after 500 years, your $1,000 turns into about $20 million. If the earnings compounded at 3 percent a year, you'd have $2.6 billion.

| Go Gettum | | | Donny Delay | | |
|---|---|---|---|---|---|
| Age | Amount Invested | Year-End Value at 10 Percent | Age | Amount Invested | Year-End Value at 10 Percent |
| 25 | $4,000 | $4,400 | 25 | | |
| 26 | $4,000 | $9,240 | 26 | | |
| 27 | $4,000 | $14,564 | 27 | | |
| 28 | $4,000 | $20,420 | 28 | | |
| 29 | $4,000 | $26,862 | 29 | | |
| 30 | $4,000 | $33,949 | 30 | | |
| 31 | $4,000 | $41,744 | 31 | | |
| 32 | $4,000 | $50,318 | 32 | | |
| 33 | | $55,350 | 33 | $4,000 | $4,400 |
| 34 | | $60,885 | 34 | $4,000 | $9,240 |
| 35 | | $66,973 | 35 | $4,000 | $14,564 |
| 36 | | $73,670 | 36 | $4,000 | $20,420 |
| 37 | | $81,037 | 37 | $4,000 | $26,862 |
| 38 | | $89,141 | 38 | $4,000 | $33,949 |
| 39 | | $98,055 | 39 | $4,000 | $41,744 |
| 40 | | $107,861 | 40 | $4,000 | $50,318 |
| 41 | | $118,647 | 41 | $4,000 | $59,750 |
| 42 | | $130,512 | 42 | $4,000 | $70,125 |
| 43 | | $143,563 | 43 | $4,000 | $81,537 |
| 44 | | $157,919 | 44 | $4,000 | $94,091 |
| 45 | | $173,711 | 45 | $4,000 | $107,900 |
| 46 | | $191,082 | 46 | $4,000 | $123,090 |
| 47 | | $210,190 | 47 | $4,000 | $139,799 |

**Figure 11-1   The Magic of Compounding**                    (*Continued*)

(*Continued*)

| | Go Gettum | | | Donny Delay | |
|---|---|---|---|---|---|
| Age | Amount Invested | Year-End Value at 10 Percent | Age | Amount Invested | Year-End Value at 10 Percent |
| 48 | | $231,209 | 48 | $4,000 | $158,179 |
| 49 | | $254,330 | 49 | $4,000 | $178,397 |
| 50 | | $279,763 | 50 | $4,000 | $200,636 |
| 51 | | $307,740 | 51 | $4,000 | $225,100 |
| 52 | | $338,514 | 52 | $4,000 | $252,010 |
| 53 | | $372,365 | 53 | $4,000 | $281,611 |
| 54 | | $409,602 | 54 | $4,000 | $314,172 |
| 55 | | $450,562 | 55 | $4,000 | $349,989 |
| 56 | | $495,618 | 56 | $4,000 | $389,388 |
| 57 | | $545,180 | 57 | $4,000 | $432,727 |
| 58 | | $599,698 | 58 | $4,000 | $480,400 |
| 59 | | $659,667 | 59 | $4,000 | $532,840 |
| 60 | | $725,634 | 60 | $4,000 | $590,524 |
| 61 | | $798,198 | 61 | $4,000 | $653,976 |
| 62 | | $878,017 | 62 | $4,000 | $723,774 |
| 63 | | $965,819 | 63 | $4,000 | $800,551 |
| 64 | | $1,062,401 | 64 | $4,000 | $885,006 |
| 65 | | $1,168,641 | 65 | $4,000 | $977,907 |
| | Years invested | 8 | | Years invested | 33 |
| | Total invested | $32,000 | | Total invested | $132,000 |
| | Ending balance | $1,168,641 | | Ending balance | $977,907 |

Let time and the market provide their magic. Until retirement, leave the earnings to compound.

### Woodwork

When a carpenter saws wood, he doesn't press on the saw. He just keeps the saw in contact with the wood and lets the saw do the work.

Don't work too hard at your investments. Let the market do the work. Never mind moving your money hither and yon in an effort to catch big short-term profits. Just buy different types of index mutual funds or exchange-traded funds and hold. Give time for compounding to cast its magic.

Now, some people are in no position to invest at age 25. Even though their income is on the low side, they're nevertheless starting families and buying big-budget items like houses and cars. If you're treading water as fast as you can to keep your nose above the financial waterline, do whatever's necessary to keep breathing.

But as soon as you can, let compounding start working for you. Make regular investments and keep reinvesting the earnings. The earnings for each period will add to the balance for the previous period. Over many years, you'll come out a huge winner.

## Television News

Television news is likely to hurt your investment returns more than it helps. After all, it's not the television producer's job to make money for you. It's her job to make money for herself and her employer. To attract viewers in a competitive environment, she puts out the latest news, especially the latest bad news. If you're being fed a steady diet of ominous news, it's hard to resist selling stocks.

But in bear markets you're not selling when prices are high. Oh no, the prices have already declined because of the unfavorable news. You're selling near the bottom. You bought high, and now you're selling low. Feeling like a fool, you stay out, until the news is really good. *Then* you feel comfortable buying again. But whoops, that's the very time that the prices may start moving down. With your confidence completely shot, you sell and stay out altogether (until the next market top, when everyone you know is completely confident about the future).

Well, I exaggerate, but not by much. This scenario has happened to millions—literally millions—of people.

## Economic News

Do not be concerned about off-cited economic "problems." The federal deficit, for example. It's only about 3.2 percent of our $12 trillion gross domestic product (GDP). Twenty years ago, the deficit was 6 percent, yet the market rose substantially thereafter.

The same for the federal debt. At the end of World War II, the debt amounted to *more* than the GDP (108 percent, to be exact), and the stock market rose nevertheless. In 1993, the federal debt was nearly 50 percent of the GDP, and the stock market rose. Now, the debt is only about 39 percent of the GDP. The market will rise this time as well. The debt doesn't have to be paid off. As long as the economy grows faster, it becomes insignificant.

Also disregard currency fluctuations. In 1978, the dollar's *weakness* was headline news, and the stock market rose big. In 1985, the dollar's *strength* was headline news, and the stock market rose big. In 1995, the dollar's *weakness* was headline news, and the stock market rose big. Currency fluctuations don't affect long-term stock market trends. Forget about them.

Pay no attention to the statements made by the chairman of the Federal Reserve. Creating confusion is part of his job. Since the fed directly influences the economy, the chairman can't reveal his intentions in detail because speculators would jump on the information and become the major beneficiaries. But even if you figure out what the fed intends to do, lots of other people have figured it out too. Stock prices react immediately. There isn't time for you to profit from the chairman's statement—not in the short term.

Be aware of something the press consistently gets wrong. You may hear about the government "cutting taxes." That's an impossibility. The government has no control over its tax revenues. It controls only the tax *rates.* Lower rates cause taxpayers to work harder, stop reducing their income with uneconomic tax gimmicks, and stop hiding their income illegally. Time and time again, the reduction of tax rates causes faster economic growth, higher government revenues, and higher stock prices. In the twentieth century, tax rates have been cut by four administrations: Presidents Harding and Coolidge,

Kennedy and Johnson, Ronald Reagan, and George W. Bush. In every case, the results were beneficial. The blame heaped on President Reagan for the big government deficits in the 1980s is misdirected. Because of his tax-rate cuts, federal revenues *doubled*. But Congress tripled expenditures, causing the deficit to increase.

In recent years, tax rates have been cut significantly in Russia and many Eastern European nations, such as Estonia. Dynamic economic growth has resulted.

### Investment Sentiment

On the days when the market falls a lot, remind yourself that pessimistic sentiment about stock prices does not cause prices to fall further. People do not turn bearish and then sell. Some do, but for the market as a whole, they don't.

Pessimism does not lead to falling prices; it *accompanies* falling prices. When prices are on the bottom, pessimism is greatest. The prices can always fall further, making people even more bearish. But a panic sell-off, with heavy selling on big volume, is as good a signal as any that pessimism has reached an extreme and that prices are near their lows.

Never say to yourself, "I'm bearish, and so is everyone else. Prices will therefore fall more." You'll lose opportunities for profit because prices often rise fastest after bouncing off panic bottoms. When you sense intense pessimism (and you happen to have investment cash on hand, which I don't recommend), be inclined to buy, not sell.

### Stay off Bandwagons

Too many investors find out what's been moving up in the recent past and hop onboard. It doesn't work; at least not often enough to make the effort worthwhile. Far too many investment professionals jump on bandwagons, only they give it a fancy name: A stock that's been moving up is said to have "momentum," which they expect to continue. Sometimes it does. More people climb on until, right out of nowhere, upside momentum stops working, and downside momentum starts working big time. Plenty of people bought high-tech mutual funds in 1999 and early 2000. Oh, they had momentum, all right, until they crashed, carrying those foolhardy investors with them.

If the media frequently points out that prices of a certain kind of investment have gone up a lot, be wary. They're talking about an investment that, for the present, has momentum. Unexpectedly, it will lose that momentum and gain all too much of it in the other direction.

## It's Only Natural

Research has shown that investors suffer 2½ times the pain from losing money than the pleasure they feel from making money. Newspaper and television producers, for example, know that good news is generally ho-hum, whereas bad news attracts our attention.

The attitude is probably built right into our genes. Every one of us is descended from an unbroken line of survivors. Ancient hominids who didn't consider it bad news when they detected a sabre-toothed tiger eyeing them from behind a bush didn't make it to become one of our forebears.

Be aware that the discomfort from a 20 percent decline in your investment portfolio is probably about 2½ times more intense than the comfort you feel from a 20 percent increase. What should you do about this?

Absolutely nothing, except to be aware of your feelings. When the value of your portfolio falls, don't allow yourself to get caught up in the widespread pessimism. Be aware of your bad feelings, so that you may avoid acting on them.

Let's say the market goes down 20 percent, and you sell. It then falls another 5 percent, making the pessimism all the more intense. Your bad feelings caused you to sell before. You're relieved you're out. Will you buy now while the prices are even lower?

Are you kidding? Not on your life! You're attune to the bad news. No way are you thinking that now is the time to buy in anticipation of good news to come. You're not reminding yourself that there's a pendulum effect in all human affairs. You're just glad you're out.

But the prices surprise you: They rise. It's just a fluke, you figure, and you wait for the final plunge.

There is no final plunge.

Finally, the news gets a lot better and eventually becomes extremely promising. You buy in again. The trouble is, you buy at prices way above the ones at which you sold. Feeling sheepish about this, you're less confident about investing than you were before. When things next go badly, the shame you feel will be even more intense. Then your investing results will really deteriorate. Shame kills investment success.

None of this is an exaggeration. When prices go down, acknowledge your bad feelings, but do not act on them. Do not go to cash when the market falls.

## Boring Is Better

You'll probably have better investment results if investing is not a serious hobby. But let's say you have the talent for investing in individual stocks, you study books on how to buy them, you just love reading company reports, and you don't trade rapidly. Fine. Have at it, but with only a portion of your money.

Most of us, however, don't have that talent or interest or, possibly, that luck. We're better off allocating our money to various ETFs and rebalancing every year and a day. In between, unless we're adding or withdrawing money regularly, we don't even have to look at what's happening. The less often we exercise investment judgment, the better the results. When it comes to investing, boring is better.

As Jack Brennan, CEO of Vanguard, put it, "To make a small fortune in the market, start with a big fortune and trade a lot."

Richard Roll, an academic economist who also manages billions of dollars of investment funds, stated the following:

> I have personally tried to invest money—my clients' money and my own—in every single anomaly and predictive device that academics have dreamed up.... I have attempted to exploit the so-called year-end anomalies and a whole variety of strategies supposedly documented by academic research. And I have yet to make a nickel on any of these supposed market inefficiencies.... Real money investment strategies don't produce the results that academic papers say they should.*

---

*From Burton G. Malkiel, *A Random Walk Down Wall Street* (New York: W.W.Norton, 1999 edition). Reprinted by permission.

## Expect a Long Retirement

Medical technology is already fabulous, and it's advancing ever faster. Before many years, the major killers of today, such as cancer and heart disease, will be licked. You should anticipate living far longer than your parents. Make the assumption that the younger of you and your spouse will survive to at least age 100.

Do not, therefore, sell your stocks when you retire. Just because you retire doesn't mean you no longer need growth. Quite the contrary.

Unless you're already in your sixties, you probably can't rely on Social Security. Don't believe the people who proclaim that Social Security has reserves. It doesn't. All of the government's Social Security tax revenues not needed for current retirees and expenses are immediately spent on whatever Congress favors that day. Nothing is reserved.

Oh, Social Security files away notes from the Treasury for the money that's supposedly being borrowed. But those notes won't be paid off—not a chance. Social Security is an intergenerational transfer program; money is paid from young to old. In 1945, when many people didn't live past 65, over 40 workers stood behind every living retiree. Now, about 3 workers strain to support each retiree. By 2030, fewer than 2 workers will stand behind each retiree.

Do you think those two workers will allow their FICA taxes to be raised high enough to support one retiree between them? No way! Any congressman who favors raising taxes this high will be thrown out on his ear. Those special Treasury notes to the Social Security system will remain unpaid. Unless you're approaching retirement already, you should assume that the Social Security taxes you've paid will be lost. Social Security is the grandest Ponzi scheme the world has ever known.

Don't get rid of the growth in your portfolio. Hold on to your stocks when you retire. You're going to need them.

But don't retire too soon.

## Be Wary about Your Employer's Stock

If your employer gives you the company's stock on a matching basis, great; that's found money. But otherwise, be very careful. The employees of Enron certainly wish they'd been more careful. Tying both your current and your retirement income to the success of a single company is too much risk. The key to successful investing is diversification.

## Are You Special?

You probably are. Everyone is, in some way. And in your purchases of tangible goods and services, by all means, be as special as you can reasonably afford. But do not say to yourself, "An investment return of only 10 percent a year isn't good enough for me. I'm special; 20 percent a year is more like it."

If a statement of that nature applies to you, you're heading for big trouble. To Ms. Market, you're not special at all. If you start acting uppity by taking big risks or trading often, she'll knock you off your pedestal, and you'll end up flat on your financial back. Instead, accept what Ms. Market gives you over the long pull. This will far outdo what most people achieve.

## A Big Potential Investment Problem: Your Emotions

People commonly fail in their investment life not because of bear markets or lousy stockbrokers; they fail because of their own emotions. You can't stop emotions, of course; they come up whether you want them or not. But by being *aware* of them, you can limit the harm they cause. Here are some of the ways emotions can hurt a person's investments:

- When investments become profitable, we feel omnipotent. We're on a high. We feel that anything we touch will turn to gold. But when losses subsequently occur, we're set up for an emotional fall. We try to overcome the feelings of shame and depression by increasing excitement, by investing in high-risk ventures, or engaging in short-term trading. We think short-term trading gives us greater control. It doesn't; it gives us less.
- No matter how good any investment system, we're likely to stop using it when anxiety becomes intense. Our reactions then become controlled by our emotions. Let those emotions come to the surface and become aware of them, by all means. But then stick to the system.

- The anniversary of an agonizing divorce or the death of a loved one can cause more investment mistakes than you might think. Be careful about making investment changes at times of unhappy anniversaries.
- We allow our self-esteem to depend on the success or failure of our investments. Bad move. Get a life outside of your investing.

Here are a few other behavior patterns that can also hurt results:

- The money we earn we tend to spend and invest more carefully than "found" money, such as tax refunds and inheritances. A dollar's a dollar. Treat every one of those little beauties with care.
- The money matched by our employers is every bit as valuable as our salary income. Take maximum advantage of employer matching.
- We're more careful about what we spend when we pay with cash rather than with a credit card. Money is money. If you're loosey-goosey with the credit cards, heave them out and pay cash for everything.
- When a stock you decide *not* to buy goes up, do not think of it as a loss. It's not a loss. It's completely irrelevant.
- If you insist on buying the stocks of individual companies, be inclined to hold the good ones and sell the losers. Many people hate to sell at a loss because it brings up the pain of failure. Remember that when stocks go down, it's not your fault. The market couldn't care less about your costs. The only thing it cares about is the future.

## The Emotionally Healthy Investor

Therapist Kathleen M. Martin, CSW, of Rochester, New York, describes the characteristics of an emotionally healthy investor as follows:

- You have confidence you'll succeed.
- You adopt an investment style, write it down, and stick to it.

- You stay with what you know and trust that knowledge.
- You're aware of your irrational thoughts and work around them.
- You tolerate anxiety rather than act on it.
- You disregard short-term price fluctuations.
- You learn from others but rely on your own judgment.
- You know that when prices go against you, it's not your fault.
- You welcome the prospect of growing rich.

# 12

# Mostly Bum Strategies

Enough with the guidelines. We're on to various investment strategies. Most of the ones discussed in this chapter are unlikely to work well. Poor investment strategies outnumber the good ones.

Successful investors in individual stocks find that the stocks they sell at losses outnumber the ones they sell with gains. But here's the key: They keep their losses small and let the profits run. The many losses are just part of the business. They don't allow the resulting sense of shame to cloud their judgment.

If you knew in advance which stocks would be very profitable, why of course you'd just buy those. But when you make the purchases, you don't know. If you buy 10 well-chosen stocks, expect 2 to go down a lot, 6 to have moderate gains and losses, and 2 to be very profitable. Limiting the damage from the bad ones and letting the good ones run is vital. (I repeat: This applies to individual stocks. As we'll consider later, it does not apply to ETFs acquired in an asset allocation program with rebalancing.)

## Pretty Pictures

**Technicians,** also known as **chartists,** study the price and volume patterns of stocks in an effort to predict future prices. There are so many uncertainties about the stock market that it's comforting to look at those nice patterns to determine what the future holds. About 85 percent of our brain functions in terms of patterns. Stock charts are nothing but.

Yes, relying on stock charts is tantalizing. They're islands in a stormy sea. You might notice that a stock price has bounced up from a certain price several times, for example. You could conclude that buyers will continue to support the stock at that price and feel comfortable about buying it at that "support" level.

Alternatively, seeing a stock fall several times from a particular price might make you inclined to sell the stock at that area of "resistance."

And who can resist taking action on seeing a reverse head and shoulder, showing a person with his arms at his side standing on his head? The price moves down the left arm, levels off at the left shoulder, falls to a new low (the head), and again levels off at the right shoulder. The price will move back up the right arm, right?

Wrong! None of these patterns predicts anything. Historic price and volume trends have no predictive value. They look like they ought to work, but they don't. They certainly don't predict enough to pay for all the transaction costs and the short-term capital gains (if any) and still enable you to make a worthwhile profit.

When you buy a house, you don't care what the house sold for in the past, do you? Stocks work the same way. Investors focus on the future.

Bear in mind that when you see a price pattern you think is predictive, several thousand other people see it as well. Are you going to be a step ahead of all the others? You're plenty smart, I know, but no one can consistently and reliably get to the market ahead of the crowd.

Chartists say that we should use technical analysis only in combination with fundamental analysis. Baloney! If an investment method doesn't work on its own, it won't work in combination with any other.

Technical analysts don't make the lists of millionaires unless they've inherited the money.

## An Exception

There is one type of price and volume that often does have predictive value. When prices fall hugely in a single day on enormous volume—probably record volume—you can be reasonably certain that prices are somewhere near the bottom. These are called "panic sell-offs," and they don't happen often—something like once a year.

But don't wait in cash for these occasions because you'll miss too much on the upside. If a panic sell-off does occur, do not ... I repeat, do not ... allow yourself to become swept up in the widespread pessimism. Disregard the accompanying, horrible news, and be more inclined to buy than sell.

Remember that there's a pendulum effect in human affairs. The market bounces off the level of a panic bottom (not necessarily immediately) in anticipation of good news to come.

## Little Margin for Error

In a **margin account**, you borrow money from a brokerage firm and buy additional securities. Every dollar of the loan must be repaid, of course, and interest is charged.

The amount borrowed is called the **margin**. The current market value of all the assets held less the debit balance equals the **equity**. This would be the amount available to you if the securities were sold and the account closed. (Margin is not the equity; it's the amount borrowed.)

The brokerage firm can't lend more than half the market value of the securities purchased. Let's say you open an account with $10,000. You borrow an additional $10,000 (with interest at 8 percent) and buy $20,000 of stocks.

The stocks rise—you lucky dog—by 25 percent in a year. You sell for $25,000, repay the $10,000 margin plus $800 interest, leaving you with $14,200, for a profit of 42 percent. Nice going.

### Well, They Could Go Down

This time, the stocks fall by 25 percent. It has happened.

You sell for $15,000, repay $10,800, leaving you with $4,200. Whoops, you lost 58 percent. (On the upside, the gain was only 42 percent.)

The next investment you acquire after the 58 percent loss would have to rise by 137 percent just to bring you back to $10,000! Never, ever, will any investments perform well enough to catch up to what you'd have had if you'd continued holding during the downturns.

The brokerage firm keeps track of the values—a procedure called **mark to market**. If the equity falls below a certain level in relation to the amount borrowed, the brokerage firm issues a **margin call**, requesting that additional cash or marginable securities be added to the account. If you don't come up with the additional money, the firm sells some or all of the securities, with or without your consent. The terms of the margin loan are set forth in a **margin agreement** you're required to sign before embarking on this hazardous procedure.

Borrowing to increase buying power and risk is called **adding leverage**. It means accepting the price risk in an amount that exceeds the equity. If you buy a house with 25 percent down, you've leveraged the purchase three to one (one part your money; three parts other people's money). People are less concerned about heavy real estate leverage for several reasons: (1) Real estate prices aren't as volatile as stocks; (2) no one can look up the price of a particular property from day to day; and (3) no one marks to market.

### Unhealthy

If you have an overpowering urge to use margin, you're better off to do so with exchange-traded funds than individual stocks because ETFs represent entire markets and are less volatile.

But even with ETFs, owning stocks on margin is a poor idea. You have to be right about the short term, which is beyond most of us. Plus, stock prices generally fall faster than they rise. All in all, the use of margin makes anxiety shoot sky high. It forces us to become short-term traders; it makes bear markets impossible to endure; and it ruins good judgment. If I think of something good about margin, I'll let you know.

Brokers love margin, with good reason. Their commissions are based on the total amount of stock acquired, including the stock bought with the margin. It's a huge conflict of interest to which you should not fall prey. (Folio*fn* does not accept margin accounts—one reason to favor the company.)

# Short Selling

Short selling, as explained in Chapter 6, is a method of profiting when prices go down. You borrow stock, sell it, and later buy it back, you hope at a profit.

Most stocks (but not ETFs) are subject to the **uptick rule**. An *uptick* is a price that is higher than the last different price. If successive trades occur at 20.05, 20, and 20.05, for example, the third price is an uptick; it's higher than the last different price. The same goes if the trades occur at 20, 20.05, and 20.05. A *downtick* would be 20, 20.05, and 20. Every trade is either an uptick or a downtick.

The uptick rule requires that short sales may be executed only on an uptick. This supposedly prevents short sellers from driving the prices down. But since ETFs represent entire markets, they're exempt from the rule.

I recommend not going short, for the following reasons:

- Two-thirds of the time, stocks stay the same or go up. You're fighting the odds.
- The mathematics are against you. If you buy a stock at 20 and sell it at 40, you've profited by 100 percent. But if you sell short at 40 and cover at 20, you've made only 50 percent. To make 100 percent, the stock has to go to zero (providing you don't borrow extra money to increase the number of shares sold short). The employees of that company are fighting tooth and nail to prevent the company from going out of business. As I say, you're fighting the odds.
- When the price goes against you after selling short, there's no limit on how high it can go. Having your gains limited and your losses unlimited is not the ideal path to retirement nirvana.

# Options

Options are available on exchange-traded funds. Professionals use them for hedging. For nonhedging purposes, options are very speculative. They're best explained with a series of illustrations that contain many small numbers. If numbers don't appeal to you and you know you'll never use anything as speculative as options, skip to the "Hedging, Smedging" section below.

Here we go: Let's say a stock is priced at 20. You expect it to rise within six months. You buy a **call** that gives you the right (not the obligation) to buy the underlying stock at a price of 20 a share at any time in the next six months. The contract costs 2.

The 20 is the **strike price**. The 2 is the **premium**. Since the strike price and the actual price are the same, the option is **on-the-money**. The premium has **time value** only and no **intrinsic value**. (The meaning of those two terms will become clear.)

If the stock price rises to 22 within six months, you buy the stock (you "call" it) and pay the 20 strike price. You then sell the stock for 22, making 2. But since the contract cost 2, you break even.

If the price goes to 24 before expiration, you buy the stock for 20 and sell it for 24, doubling your money. Lotsa luck. Making several times your money sounds like fun. But remember, it's hard enough to be right in the short term about the direction of an individual stock. Banking on the price's also moving significantly in the right direction *within a short time* is too much to ask. Most people who buy call options lose.

If the price fails to rise above 20 before expiration, the option expires worthless, and the entire premium is lost.

There's a redeeming feature: Buyers of options cannot lose *more* than the premium.

## *In*

Okay, back to the beginning. The stock is again priced at 20. You buy a six-month call option with a strike price of only 18. The option is **in-the-money** by 2. You pay a premium of 3. The premium has 2 intrinsic value and 1 time value.

If the price rises by 5 percent to 21, you call the stock at 18 and sell it for 21, making 3. But since the contract cost 3, you break even.

If the price rises by 10 percent from 20 to 22, you call the stock at 18 and sell it for 22. You take in 4 on an option that cost 3, making a profit of 33 percent. If the price rises to 30, you make four times your money (30 less 18, divided by 3).

In-the-money options are safer than on-the-money options, but they're still highly speculative. Stocks usually don't make big moves in the right direction in a short time.

### Out

Once more, the stock is priced at 20. You buy a six-month call with a strike price of 22. The option is **out-of-the-money** by 2. The premium is 1—all time value.

If the price rises to 21, you break even. If it rises to 22; you double your money. If it rises to 30; you make 10 times your money. But out-of-the-money calls are the riskiest of all.

Options are available on most exchange-traded funds, with various strike prices and expiration dates.

### Upside Down

The buyer of a **put option** has the right but not the obligation to *sell* a stock by a certain date at a specified price. The put acts like a short sale. The holder of the put sells the stock at what is now a high price (he "puts" the stock to the option writer). He later buys the stock at the current low price and pockets the difference.

Everything about puts is pretty much the reverse of calls. Take the above description of calls and read them with the book upside down. That should do it.

### Other Characteristics

Additional characteristics of options are as follows:

- Minimum option purchases are for 100 shares. On 100 shares, a premium of 2 would cost 200.
- It's easy to lose all the money you place in options premiums—no trouble at all.
- Premiums have a natural tendency to decline. When expiration is months away, the time value shrinks slowly. As expiration draws near, it shrinks rapidly. At expiration, time value falls to zero.

If you acquire options often enough, eventually your portfolio will do the same.

- Expiration times vary in length from one day to several years. The options expiring in three months and six months trade most actively. Options expiring in a year or more in the future are called **leaps (long-term anticipation securities)**. When you *call* a stock, it's bought from the person from whom you bought the option. That person is called the *writer*.

- You're not required to hold an option until maturity. Most people don't. The exercise of options is often undertaken by market makers.

- An option that's exercised in America can be exercised at any time, up to and including the expiration date. An option that's exercised in Europe can be exercised only on the expiration date.

- Options commissions are high, and the spreads between the bid and ask prices are wide. Options are not only risky, they're expensive.

Buying options is perilous. If you buy them at all, acquire leaps. The premiums are higher, but at least the leaps will give you a little time to be wrong about the short term.

### Writing

The writer of a call assumes the risk of delivering the stock when the buyer exercises. The call writer wants the price to fall below the strike price. This makes delivery of the stock unnecessary and enables the writer to keep the entire premium.

The writer of a put assumes the risk of purchasing the stock when the buyer exercises. The writer wants the price to rise above the strike price. This makes purchasing the stock unnecessary and enables the writer to keep the entire premium.

### It's All Covered

Say you own shares of Diamonds (an ETF based on the Dow Jones Industrial Average). You don't want to sell them, especially not before a year has passed. But meanwhile, you're bearish about the market for the next six months.

You write an on-the-money call on Diamonds that expires in six months. If your prediction is correct, the market falls, and the option expires worthless. The option expires worthless even if the price remains the same. In either event, you keep all of the premium you received up front. To some extent, at least, the premium offsets any loss in value of the Diamond shares you own. You've written a **covered call** because you own the stock against which you wrote the call.

The more the option is in-the-money when you write it, the larger the premium. But the risk is greater that the stock will be called. If it is called, you simply deliver the stock you already own. You prefer not to do so, but that's the breaks. Naturally, you can purchase additional shares of Diamonds to deliver on the contract and continue holding the shares you previously owned until they attain long-term status.

If the option is out-of-the-money when you write it, the premium is smaller, but the risk of the option being called is lower.

If you're short Diamonds but fear the market is going to rise temporarily, you could write a put. That of course is a covered put. (Some of this stuff makes my head spin.)

### Watch Your Language!

If you write a call and do *not* own the underlying stock, you've written a naked call. If the price falls, great, you keep the premium. If the price rises, you must buy (or go short) the stock to comply with the call. If the price rises a lot, you lose a lot.

The writing of a put without being short the underlying stock is a naked put.

There is no shortage of options strategies. This chapter has barely scratched the surface. The problem is, if you use options a lot, you'll eventually be scratching for money. Some strategies are riskier than others. But all of them involve wide spreads and relatively heavy commissions, both of which are bummers. When you buy an option, you're probably down by 5 percent immediately just because of the transaction costs. Do this often enough, and you'll be left with a dry hole.

## Hedging, Smedging

Leave hedging to market makers, who have to do it. They make their living from the spreads. To make sure they stay in business, they rid themselves of as much market risk as possible because the market is as much of a mystery to them as it is to the rest of us. Whatever inventory they hold, they hedge the risk.

You can't beat investment professionals at their game. But you don't have to. You *want* long-term market risk. That's the path to future riches. In the long run, stock prices rise.

## Day Trading

Some day, especially after the market has been rising for a while, you may get the urge to quit your job, sit at your computer during the trading day, and trade stocks.

Resist the urge.

It's easy to confuse genius with a bull market. But even during the last bull market in the late 1990s, over three-quarters of day traders lost money. When the bear market arrived in 2001, most of the rest lost their money too.

Being a consistent winner as a day trader in all kinds of markets requires rare talent. You can lose a great deal of money while discovering that you don't happen to be one of the few who are blessed with the requisite aptitude.

Just in case you can't resist the urge to become a day trader, I offer the suggestions that follow.* All of them are expressed in terms that traders use, and they incorporate notions that traders believe in. Some of the suggestions seem sensible to me, but many don't. I present them anyway in hopes that they may help you to lose all of your money in, say, two years instead of just one:

- Start slowly.
- Formulate your own rules and stick to them.
- The biggest moves tend to occur at the opening and at the close.
- Use limit orders to avoid giving up the spread.
- Trade stocks and ETFs that are volatile, particularly the ones whose average daily range is at least five times the spread.

---

*From Archie Richards, Jr., *All About Exchange-Traded Funds* (New York: McGraw-Hill, 2003).

- A market that grinds slowly higher is a good buy. A market that grinds slowly lower is a good sell.
- Don't be deceived by big rate-of-return numbers. Let's say a trader is down 50 percent one year and up 80 percent the next. Another trader is down 10 percent one year and up 25 percent the next. Which one ends up with more? (The first one ends up down 10 percent; the second is up 12 percent.)
- When you lose 20 percent of your equity, do not take ridiculous shots to recapture the money you lost. Instead, get out, pull yourself together emotionally, regroup, and revise your trading tactics.
- If an ETF doesn't act right, leave it alone. If you can't tell what's wrong, you don't know where it's going.
- A price is never too high to begin buying and never too low to begin selling.
- Do not prefer a bull market to a bear market or a bear market to a bull market. Just keep focused on being right.
- Getting angry at the market is counterproductive. Oh, you can *feel* anything you like. Feelings bubble up whether you want them or not. But the market couldn't care less what you feel. Do not act out in anger. Stick to your normal style.
- When the stocks that have been market leaders in a bull market falter, be prepared for a bear market, even if the rest of the market continues to rise.
- Beware of buying a stock that refuses to follow the group leader.
- Remove the monthly profits you make from your trading account and invest those funds more conservatively.
- Trade only one security at a time. Your options positions should represent only a small portion of your entire portfolio.
- Learning how to trade means learning how not to lose money.
- Limit the number of indicators you watch.
- Stay close to the market.
- When the market turns choppy, shorten your trading horizon.
- Never trade with money you need to live on.
- Don't go for windfalls. Try for consistent small trades. The market continually serves up new opportunities.
- Have a reason for every trade you enter, where you're reasonably certain you have an edge.

- Before entering a trade, always plan your exit strategy, covering both a profit and a loss.
- Don't try to time the market perfectly.
- At the day's end, go flat.
- If you rely on tips from other people, you lose your autonomy. You might as well work for the other person. Good tips are given to only a few. Bad tips are ubiquitous.
- Reward yourself by buying things you want or vacations you want. But don't reward yourself by taking bigger risks.
- No doubt you've heard the maxim, "You'll never go broke by taking a profit." This is true, but the advice is nevertheless unhelpful. Instead, cover your losses quickly and let your profits run.
- Go short as well as long. But since bear markets last only about one-third of the time, expect to be long more often than short.
- Avoid following the crowd. The crowd is often wrong.
- The best trades are profitable right from the start.
- Use the two-order rule: When you enter any order, enter a stop order too, to protect against a significant loss. As the price moves in your direction, keep raising the stop (or lowering the stop on a short).
- When a position becomes profitable, the losing trader takes a profit. The winning trader tries to determine whether the position will continue to show more profit and lets it runs its course.
- On a short-term basis, anticipating which direction the market will move is hard enough. How far it will move, and for how long, is even harder.
- To alleviate stress, some traders drink, smoke, or do drugs. Not helpful. Better to find another vocation.
- Today's leaders may be tomorrow's losers.
- Trade issues that have consistently high volume. They have narrower spreads and greater liquidity. Liquidity means that when you want to buy, there's likely to be a seller, and when you want to sell, there's likely to be a buyer.
- Trade online and do not use a broker. If you cannot rely exclusively on your own judgment, you can't be a trader.
- The smarter you are, the more likely your mind will wander while you're trading. A bored trader is often a poor trader. If you're

really smart, you might find a way to have a job and arrange your trades on off hours.

- Don't for a moment think you can *will* the market to go your way. You're no more than a swimmer in the ocean surf. When big waves start hitting shore, get yourself onto dry land.
- If iShares GS Semiconductor (IGW) is up by 2 percent during the day, for example, while Spiders are up only 1 percent, IGW has good relative strength. You might buy IGW and sell Spiders short.
- To a trader, news is of some importance. But how the news compares with what investors were expecting and what their positions were just prior to the news are crucial. You're not just forming your own opinions; you're trying to determine other people's opinions as well. Judge markets by observing how others react to news.
- Some people believe that you haven't suffered a loss until you sell. This is nonsense. If the price has gone against you, you have *already* incurred the loss. The appropriate question is, "What investment will gain the fastest from here, the one I'm in, or another?"
- Did I mention this? Before entering a trade, always plan your exit strategy, covering both a profit and a loss. Without this, you're a dead duck.

## Back to Reality

Okay, this is the real me again. Some of the foregoing I consider fiction. For example, when a stock breaks through "resistance" on the upside, it does *not* have a good chance of becoming a profitable trade. On the contrary, the approach will probably fail as often as it succeeds.

Sometimes, market leaders correctly anticipate bear markets. Sometimes they don't. If predicting bear markets were that easy, traders would succeed at it consistently.

A market that seems "choppy" has no predictive value whatsoever. It may go up; it may go down; it may continue to chop—no one knows.

The notion of a stock's "acting right" has no meaning. When the price of a stock rises consistently enough for you to identify that it's acting right and you buy it, the stock then has a 50-50 chance of starting to act wrong.

Specialists love stop orders. Say you buy a stock at 40 and place a stop order at 39.69. To the extent the specialist can, he'll pull the market down, pick up your stock at 39.69, and let the market float back up for a profitable sale at 40. You're better off buying at 40 and holding for the rest of your life.

# 13

# Pretty Good ETF Strategies

Investment strategies that are likely to fail outnumber the ones that are likely to succeed. This chapter presents strategies that are in between. I wouldn't use them, but they do bear mentioning. At the chapter's end, I cast doubt about the strategies inherent in many new exchange-traded funds.

We begin with short selling. The short interest of exchange-traded funds is considerably higher than those of individual stocks, because financial institutions use ETFs as short-sale hedges against stock positions they hold long. The short interests of individual stocks, for example, are generally about 1 to 2 percent. The short interests of ETFs are 15 to 25 percent and sometimes more.

Market makers for ETFs usually hold big inventories. For them, lending out shares for shorting purposes is a source of income.

Remember that short selling is not permitted in IRAs, 401(k) plans, or other qualified retirement programs.

## A Feasible Short Sale, Sort of

Some people suggest going short to reduce the risk of overexposure to the industry in which you work. Let's say you're employed by a pharmaceutical company, and you're investing $20,000 in the iShares Russell 3000 Index Fund (IWV). Let's assume that pharmaceuticals compose 8 percent of the index.

It's risky enough that your job depends on the pharmaceutical industry. You don't want your investments to depend on it as well. To cut the risk, you might sell short $1,600 of iShares DJ US Pharmaceuticals (IHE), this amount being 8 percent of $20,000.

Remember that you must pay the dividends on short sales. Since this kind of short sale is intended to last a long time, you'll go on paying and paying. Meanwhile, you won't notice the dividends paid by the pharmaceutical companies included in iShares Russell 3000 Index Fund, because they're received at the *fund* level. You'll be aware of only the aggregate of dividends paid to your brokerage account from all of the fund's stocks. The dividends received from pharmaceutical companies will roughly match the ones you pay, but you'll only be aware of the payment side, which will prove bothersome.

Also, the IRS considers the profits and losses on all short sales to be short term, no matter how long the short is held.

Always bear in mind that Ms. Market goes out of her way to disappoint in the short term. If you short the pharmaceuticals fund to reduce your exposure to the industry in which you work, Ms. Market is likely to spend a few months pushing pharmaceutical prices up until the short sale is so unprofitable you can no longer stand it. You cover your short. *Then* she'll let 'em fall.

I wouldn't engage in short selling to reduce your exposure to the industry of your employment. To be a successful investor, you don't need to work that hard.

Do not, however, acquire much of the stock of the company in which you work. Counting on the success of a single company for your future income as well as your present income is a risk you can and should avoid.

# Wash Sales

The **wash sale rule** pertains to whether you can take a tax loss on a security sale. You cannot take the loss if, within 30 days before or after the sale of the security (61 days total), you buy another security that is "substantially identical."

If it's a wash sale, your loss is not immediately recognized. Instead, the disallowed loss is added to the cost basis of the new security and recognized when that security is sold. For example, if you sell General Motors at a loss and within 30 days before or after the sale you purchase GM stock again, you have engaged in a wash sale.

But ETFs can be used as temporary substitutes. Let's say you sell Chevron (CVX) but want to retain exposure to the oil industry. You might immediately acquire the Energy Select Sector SPDR ETF (XLE), of which Chevron constitutes approximately 13 percent. Thirty-one days later, you sell the XLE and move back into Chevron. With this maneuver, you pass muster with the wash sale rule.

But in my humble opinion, you're better off buying the Energy Select Sector fund in the first place and staying there. The pay is better with diversification and minimum trading.

# Sector Rotations

At a given time, you may consider some sectors to be overvalued and others to be undervalued. This is no easy thing to do when individual stocks are all one has to work with. You must buy or sell whole aggregations of stocks to reflect an entire sector. But with ETFs, it's a piece of cake. An ETF representing an entire sector can be bought or sold easily. For example, you might anticipate that Ben Bernanke, the Federal Reserve chairman, will not fail in his effort to bring inflation under control. You might further believe that rising productivity all over the world will unleash a flood of goods that, combined with prosperity and modest money-supply growth, draw inflation down to zero.

You might further note that gold and gold shares have enjoyed price increases lasting many years and that bonds have fallen victim to the fed's anti-inflation efforts and gone down in price for more than a year.

If you want to act on this sort of thing, you would sell (or sell short) iShares COMEX Gold Trust (IAU) or streetTRACKS Gold Shares (GLD) in anticipation of price declines. You might also buy iShares Lehman Aggregate Bond Fund (AGG) in anticipation of an advance. Just a few minutes time, and it's done. (I don't recommend such moves, but they're available if you're so inclined.)

### All Kinds of Sectors

Let's say you anticipate that stocks are generally undervalued in relation to bonds and you're looking for a sharp increase in prices. You note that for over half a decade, value stocks have performed well, especially small value stocks. During the same period, growth stocks have done poorly, especially the big ones.

Bingo, you could sell iShares Russell 2000 Value Index Fund (IWN) and acquire iShares Russell 1000 Growth Index Fund (IWF). If you're partial to technology, you could acquire Qubes instead.

Let's say you expect most foreign stocks to rise. But you think that less developed nations (emerging markets) show more promise than some of the traditional European nations, such as France, for example, which has inflexible labor policies, great difficulty in absorbing Muslim minorities, and potentially a declining population, You would short iShares MSCI France (EWQ) and buy iShares MSCI Emerging Index Fund (EEM). Both securities might rise in price, but if emerging markets move up faster, you'd have a net profit.

### Comparing Sectors

You might want to narrow your vision and make allocations within a limited environment. Take, for example, the Select Sector SPDR funds. The stocks in all nine of these funds are drawn from the famous S&P 500 Index. Every one of the 500 stocks in the S&P 500 is allocated to one and only one of the Select Sector Indexes. They're industry sectors, such as consumer staples, finance, and industrial.

The total number of stocks in the nine sector funds add up to 500. They're the same stocks that make up the S&P 500—no more and no less.

Let's say you like the idea of allocating among these sectors, but you'd prefer to receive a higher level of dividend income than the S&P 500 alone provides. In www.sectorspdrs.com, you can find out the dividend yield of the various nine sectors and purchase relatively more of the ones, such as utilities, that have higher yields.

Also in www.sectorspdrs.com, you can find out which sectors have outperformed and which have not and change your allocations accordingly. (I wouldn't know whether to sell the sectors that have done well or buy more of them. Perhaps you know. If you try this kind of active-trading approach and it doesn't work, be sure to stop. You might then read this book again throughout, perhaps a couple of times, to find a more reliable approach.)

## Foreign Stocks

Exchange-traded funds have been lifesavers for those who take interest in foreign stocks. Corporate information is far more available and reliable in a country like the United States than it is in, say, Malaysia. ETFs bridge the gap, making it safer to purchase foreign securities. Documents and other information provided by the foreign companies to the funds (or the indexes on which they're based) are written in English. On behalf of the iShares MSCI group of ETFs, for example, Barclays Global Investor, the sponsor, certifies the authenticity of the documents. Buyers of individual foreign stocks don't have nearly the same access.

## You Want a Hobby?

For those of you who choose to work especially hard at your investments, ETFs of the stocks of individual foreign nations offer an opportunity. After you've read Chapter 15, you may come to believe, as I do, that government economic policies create the framework for business. The less that the government interferes with the normal forces of supply and demand, the more likely the stock prices of that nation will rise.

If you can keep informed about the details of foreign national politics, you may be able to sense that a recent change of leadership is likely to improve the conditions for business. Buying one of the iShares MSCI funds of individual foreign nations would enable you to profit from those impressions.

I don't believe it's possible to profit consistently from trying to anticipate which industry or industrial sector will outperform other industries or other industrial sectors. Stock prices have already discounted any such anticipations. But politics are a different story. They set the conditions for business to a degree that most investors are unaware of. In my opinion, investors generally don't realize, for example, the positive and long-lasting effects of reducing income tax rates. If you can become reliably informed about the details of national politics of the nations covered by the iShares MSCI funds, you could enjoy substantial profits.

I'm not saying this is easy. Your sources of information about the details of foreign politics must be reliable. Most American media are not reliable, and European media are worse. In both cases, the executives and personnel generally approve of, and report on, policies that are not favorable for business. They do not approve of, nor report on, policies that *are* favorable for business.

If you endeavor to follow this strategy, do not trade in and out of the MSCI funds. If you detect positive political changes coming, buy the appropriate fund and expect to hold for several years. When government economic policies improve, the effects, as I say, are long lasting.

You run the risk, of course, that investors will *become* aware of the importance of national politics in setting the conditions for business. If they do, this strategy will no longer work because the expectations will be properly discounted.

## Need Dividend Income?

Some of the more recent sponsors of ETFs, including PowerShares and WisdomTree, design their own indexes. Those are not based on capitalization, with companies that have larger market values occupying larger positions in the fund. Instead, the stocks are chosen according to a fundamental measurement, such as sales or dividends.

The iShares Dow Jones Select Dividend Index Fund (DVY) was the first ETF to be based on fundamental factors. It tracks the Dow Jones U.S. Select Dividend Index, which in turn is drawn from the Dow Jones U.S. Total Market Index (excluding REITs). To be included in the dividend index, a stock must have the following characteristics:

- A flat to positive dividend-per-share growth rate for each of the last five years
- An average five-year dividend payout ratio of 60 percent or less (assuring enough earnings to support the dividend)
- A minimum of 200,000 average daily trading volume over the last three months

The dividend index consists of the top 100 stocks that meet these criteria, ranked by yield. The index is reconstituted annually.

As described in the appendixes, many other ETFs based on dividends have come to the market.

Dividends are a more reliable standard than sales and much more reliable than earnings. Financial statements are subject to manipulation, even with regard to sales. Dividends cannot be misinterpreted. They're cash in hand—the only fundamental factor that's completely objective.

## Changes and Controversy

Some ETFs are based on other fundamental factors, such as price/earnings ratios or price-to-book ratios. These terms are explained in Figure 13-1.

The ETFs that use these fundamental approaches, including dividends, do not use traditional security analysis, trying to guess what the future holds. Instead, they react to what has already happened and are periodically rebalanced. If the price of the stock has fallen, for example, but the fundamental factors on which the ranking of stocks remain the same, more shares are acquired. If the price has risen but the fundamental has remained level, shares are sold.

---

### Valuations

Clothes you buy for yourself you can see and touch. They're tangible. You can tell whether you received value for your money.

Stocks are intangible. Oh, you can travel to the company headquarters and walk around the place as far the security personnel will allow. But the business *potential* is out of reach. How can you estimate the company's value?

Stock analysts have many methods. None of them are perfect, to be sure. Here are two that many analysts use (the numbers referred to here can be found in company statements):

- The **price/earnings (P/E) ratio** is based on how many times the stock price exceeds the annual earnings per share. If the price is 20 and the earnings are 1 per share, the P/E is 20. If the earnings stay the same (which they usually don't), you have to wait 20 years for the cumulative earnings to equal the price paid up front.
- The price-to-book ratio is based on how many times the price exceeds the company's book value per share. To determine the book value, accountants start with the company's assets, valued as of the time they were acquired, deduct liabilities, and divide by the number of shares of common stock outstanding. If the price is 20 and the book value is 4, the price-to-book ratio is 5.

---

**Figure 13-1**

# Wisdom

Finance professor Dr. Jeremy J. Siegel is a member of the three-person board of directors of WisdomTree, a sponsor of ETFs. In a June 14, 2006, article in the *Wall Street Journal*, Dr. Siegel stated that dividend-weighted indexes have outperformed capitalization-weighted indexes and have been particularly valuable in resisting bear markets.

From the bull market peak of March 2000 to the October 2002 low, the Russell 3000 Index (a capitalization-weighted index), Siegel explained, lost almost half of its value. But a total market index weighted for *dividends* lost nothing during that same period (although, to be sure, it suffered a decline of 20 percent in the interim).

By June 2006, the dividend-weighted index was about 40 percent above where it stood in March 2000, while the Russell 3000 and S&P 500 were not nearly back to even.

Dr. Siegel found similar comparisons in other bear markets. Indeed, he wrote, "From 1964 through 2005, a total market dividend-weighted index of all U.S. stocks outperformed a capitalization-weighted total market index by 123 basis points a year and did so with lower volatility."

## Other Similar Approaches

Others have heralded similar fundamental approaches. Eugene Fama and Kenneth French, for example, suggested that higher returns can be obtained using an index of stocks with small capitalizations and low price-to-book-value ratios. Robert Arnott has favored weighting the stocks in an index using sales, earnings, book values, or other fundamental factors. Still others have pointed out that when the stock market reaches a peak, the stocks most overvalued will tend to have the largest capitalizations. A capitalization-weighted fund will therefore have too much concentration in overvalued stocks at peaks and too little concentration in undervalued stocks at bottoms.

All of these analysts have argued that fundamentally weighted indexes represent the "new paradigm" for index-fund investing. They make persuasive cases.

## More Wisdom

But not persuasive enough.

Two weeks after Dr. Siegel's WSJ article was published, an article on a related subject appeared in the *Wall Street Journal* on June 27, 2006, this one written by John C. Bogle, founder of Vanguard, and Burton G. Malkiel, professor at Princeton and author of *A Random Walk Down Wall Street*. Their ideas were intended to apply to index mutual funds using fundamental approaches, but the arguments apply just as well to ETFs that use fundamental approaches.

First of all, they point out, fundamental ETFs generally have higher operating costs.

Second, fundamental ETFs are bound to trade more frequently. Let's say the fund tracks an index based on dividend levels. Assume that one of the companies in the index doubles its dividend. The "dividend weight" of that company has increased. The fund manager must therefore double the number of shares of that company. But the dividend weights of all the *other* stocks in the index have thereby been reduced, requiring a few shares of each to be sold. All fundamentally weighted indexes incur reasonably high turnover to align the portfolio weights with the changing fundamental factors.

For a capitalization-weighted fund, such adjustments are unnecessary. If the price of one stock rises and the price of another falls, the capitalization of each one changes. But the fund itself is *weighted* by capitalization. The changes in price take care of the adjustment automatically. No buying and selling is needed.

It's true that when a buyout or a spin-off occurs, the capital-weighted portfolio must adjust the portfolio with corresponding purchases or sales. But fundamentally weighted portfolios must do the same.

## Bias toward the Small

Fundamental weighting results in portfolios whose stocks have low prices in relation to earnings, book value, and dividends. They tend not to be companies with high capitalizations; they're smaller stocks. Fundamental indexing tends to perform well in periods when small-cap stocks shine.

Such has been the case since 2000. The last six years have been among the best periods in history for the relative returns of small, dividend-paying, value stocks. No wonder funds with fundamental weighting are multiplying like rabbits! People are climbing onto an investment bandwagon.

## Growth versus Value

Finally, John Bogle and Burton Malkiel say, "We are impressed by the inexorable tendency for reversion to the mean in security returns.... We never know when reversion to the mean will come to the various

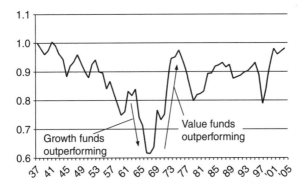

**Figure 13-2    Reversion to the Mean: Growth versus Value Funds, 1937 to June 2005**
Used with permission of John Bogle and Burton Malkiel.

sectors of the stock market, but we do know that such changes in style invariably occur."

As evidence, they present the chart in Figure 13-2, showing the relative performance of growth funds and value funds.

Notice that value funds reached their peak performance in 1942, after a long economic depression and when things looked bad for the good guys during World War II. But then growth funds began to outperform, reaching a peak in 1968.

Since 1968, value stocks have generally outperformed (except for short periods in the late 1970s and the late 1990s). By May 2006, the relative performance of value funds reached close to the levels of 1942. For all these reasons, I recommend staying away from the fundamental-weighted ETFs now coming to the market in such numbers. Despite almost 40 years of success behind them, even sophisticated bandwagons like these are best avoided.

# But ...

I'll say this for fundamentally based ETFs: They'll probably beat equivalent, actively managed mutual funds.

The rules of some ETFs are proprietary and not disclosed. (Not so of dividend ETFs; their methodologies are spelled out clearly.) But at least the managers of even the proprietary funds are likely to stick to their own rules. Actively managed mutual funds, on the other hand, fly by the seat of the manager's pants. In addition, fundamentally based ETFs generally have lower operating costs and lower turnover than actively managed funds.

## Stealthy

One of the fundamentally based ETFs intrigues me: the Claymore/Sabrient Stealth Fund. At this writing, the fund is in registration with the SEC, with the symbol and operating costs yet to be determined.

The fund consists of about 150 stocks, mostly small or micro-cap (under $1 billion), having superior risk-return profiles, but *little or no analyst coverage*. That last phrase turns me on. The stocks analysts focus on often get whipped by the ones they don't notice—the stocks that fly under Wall Street's radar.

# 14

# The Ins and Outs of Brokerage Accounts

When you open a brokerage account, you may be asked nosy questions about your investment experience, employment, income, and net worth. No one checks on the answers. But regulators require brokers to know their customers, with the idea that investments may be avoided which the broker deems inappropriate for you.

## Paying for and Transferring Securities

After you buy or sell a security, details of the transactions are sent to you on the day after the trade. These are called **confirmations**, and they should be retained.

On a purchase, the firm probably won't enter the order until the money is on hand and cleared. It wants to be sure the money will be cleared by the **settlement date**, which is three business days after the trade.

When you acquire an investment, do not make your check payable to the individual broker. Naïve investors have lost a great deal of money doing this. Make the check payable to the institution, such as a brokerage firm, a mutual fund, or a bank. It's safer.

If you lose money because your stocks or ETFs move against you, sorry, no one insures against the loss. But if the brokerage firm loses your money because of fraud or accounting errors or because other customers fail to pay for securities purchased, protection is provided to some extent by the **Securities Investor Protection Corporation**, better known as **SIPC**, which is a nonprofit corporation funded by its member broker-dealers. Most brokerage firms also provide additional insurance coverage. Your account is probably protected up to millions of dollars.

## How Most Brokers Get Paid

A brokerage house serves as a **principal** if it acts with its own money on the opposite side of a transaction with a customer—that is, if it buys a security with its own money or sells a security from its own inventory. (A brokerage house is the same as a brokerage firm.) In that situation, no commission is assessed, and the fact that the firm is serving as a principal is reported on the confirmation. The confirmation does not reveal the company's profit or loss. After all, when you buy a sweater at a department store, the store doesn't reveal what it paid for the sweater. The same applies to a brokerage firm.

When a brokerage house is not acting with its own money on the opposite side of a transaction, it's functioning as an **agent**. In this case, the firm serves as an intermediary between the buyer and seller, like a real estate agent. A **commission** is charged, which is added to the cost if you're buying and subtracted from the proceeds if you're selling. Commission amounts vary from one firm to another, depending on how much personal service is performed. Online brokers generally charge the lowest commissions because their costs are low. On the purchase of a stock, you don't write a separate check for the commission. The confirmation shows the total amount due, including the commission. On a sale, the firm deducts the commission and sends a check (or credits your account) for the net amount. Remember that the commission reduces the amount of money you invest in a security on a purchase and *also* reduces the amount of the proceeds you receive on the subsequent sale.

**Dividend reinvestment plans (DRIPs)** are good ways to let compounding do the work. In most cases, you purchase stock, obtain a stock certificate in your name, send the certificate to the company, and arrange for dividends thereafter to be reinvested in additional fractional shares of stock at the then-current stock price, at little or no cost. Some brokerage firms offer automatic reinvestments of dividends, but this is probably more costly than setting up a DRIP with the company itself.

Remember, however, that purchasing just a few individual stocks increases specific risk—the kind of risk for which you are not paid. Unfortunately, no exchange-traded fund has set up a dividend reinvestment plan.

# Orders

The basic order for buying or selling a stock or ETF is a **market order**. If you place a market order to buy, you want the order executed right away at the lowest ask price offered by market makers. A "market order to sell" means you want the order executed right away at the highest bid price offered by market makers.

(An ETF probably has several market makers who are in competition with one another. A specialist has no competition on the exchange, but the security may also be traded elsewhere.)

Since ETFs are less volatile, people are more inclined to use market orders with ETFs than they are with individual stocks. I recommend you do the same.

## Limit Orders

If you wanted to buy securities at a price lower than the current ask price, you would use a **limit order to buy**. Say the current ask price is 24. If you don't want to pay more than 23.5, you'd enter a limit order at that lower price. Only when the ask price falls to 23.5 would the trade be executed.

If you wanted to sell at a price higher than the current bid price, you would use a **limit order to sell**. Say the current big price is 24. If you don't want to sell for less than 24.5, you'd enter a limit order at that higher price. Only when the bid prices rises to 24.5 would the trade be executed.

Limit orders may not be executed at all. If the ask price fails to fall to 23.5 while the limit order to buy remains in effect, you're out of luck; the order is not executed.

If you're buying ETFs you intend to hold for decades, forget about limit orders. Limit orders are used less frequently with ETFs than they are with individual stocks. Buy ETFs at market.

Do not forget about your limit orders, especially on purchases. The brokerage house informs you about open orders in its monthly statement. But unless you keep track, an unexpected buy order may be executed when you no longer have the money to pay for it. You might, for example, buy the stock at market and forget about an open limit order you previously placed for the same stock. If the broker is busy, he or she may not remember either. It's not his or her responsibility anyway; it's yours.

### Stop Orders

Assume that you bought an ETF for 24. It's now 44, and you hate to lose your profit. You might enter a **stop order to sell** at, say, 41. If the price falls to 41, the order converts to a market order to sell.

On the New York Stock Exchange, the stop order might be executed higher or lower than 41. On the American Stock Exchange, if the price hits 41, it becomes a *limit* order to sell at 41 or higher. If the price passes quickly through 41 on the downside, it could continue on down and not be sold. Stop orders are accepted only by exchange specialists, not by OTC market makers.

A stop order to sell, then, is an order to sell at a price lower than the current price, usually in an effort to limit loss. Stop orders to sell, as I've said earlier, are generally not a good idea. The specialist sees the order sitting there like a ripe plum. To the extent that he or she can control the price (the greater the volume of trading, the less control the specialist has), he or she might endeavor to pull the price down, pick up the stock, bring the price back up again, and sell the stock for a quick profit. (Sorry about that. Helping mankind is not the primary aim of most people in the investment business. Without them, however, advanced civilization would not exist.)

If an ETF isn't for you, sell it at market. Better yet, hold it for years and let it season.

Consider another scenario: Say the price of a stock you do *not* own is 10. You anticipate a favorable news item that would reduce the risk of owning the stock. If and when favorable news comes out, you expect the price to rise to 13. With the risk lessened, you're willing to pay the higher price. In case you're unavailable when the news is announced, you would enter a **stop order to buy** at 13. When this price is hit, the order (on the NYSE) becomes a market order. A stop order to buy, then, is an order to purchase a stock at a price higher than the current price.

A limit or stop order that remains effective until it's canceled or executed is referred to as a **good-til-canceled (GTC) order**. More formally, it's described as an **open order**.

A limit or stop order that automatically expires at the end of the trading day on which it is entered is called a **day order**. Any order on which GTC instructions are omitted is automatically treated as a day order.

When a limit or a stop order is placed at a certain price and a dividend is paid while the order remains in effect, the price specified in the order is automatically reduced by the amount of the dividend unless the order is marked **DNR**, meaning **do not reduce**.

If you fail to pay for a security you have purchased, it is sold at market. If a profit results, you do not receive it (the brokerage firm does). But you are required to pay for any loss. If you cannot do so, the broker is required to pay from his or her personal funds. If the broker cannot pay, the brokerage firm pays. If the loss is huge and neither the broker nor the firm can pay, insurance kicks in.

Orders to brokers are given verbally. The broker is trained to repeat back the orders. If he or she fails to do so, insist on it.

# Markets

A **bear market** is a market in which the prices have generally been falling or are expected to fall. Those who think stock prices will go down are considered "bearish." A **bull market** is a market in which the prices have generally been rising or are expected to rise.

---

**Bulls and Bears**

In the early eighteenth century in England, the old proverb "Don't sell the bearskin before the bear is caught" began being applied as a warning to short sellers. (*Short selling* is a speculative technique that enables a person to profit when the price of stock goes down. I warn about short selling too in Chapter 12.)

Bullbaiting and bearbaiting were popular English sports in which a tethered animal was set upon by a pack of dogs. These sports being violent and frenetic, the phrase "bulls and bears" caught on as a description of the frenzied atmosphere of stock trading. By the middle of the eighteenth century, a person trading in anticipation of a rising market came to be known as a "bull," the opposite of a "bear."

In the nineteenth century, the names took on different associations, namely, that bears bring their victims down to the ground, whereas bulls spear their victims upward. Either way, a good time is had by all.

---

**Figure 14-1**

Those who think stock prices will rise are considered "bullish." (see Figure 14-1).

Whether the market is a bull or a bear market depends on the eye of the beholder. Let's say the stock market has generally been rising for five years and is considered to be a bull market. It reaches a certain level on a Wednesday. On the next day, Thursday, it declines by 1 percent. Since the market has been jiggling up and down by 1 percent and so during the entire five years, investors make little of the decline; the bull market is thought to be intact. But several months later, it becomes apparent that the Wednesday peak was the top of the bull market and that the subsequent 1 percent drop was the start of a bear market. In retrospect, the 1 percent decline is redefined. Except possibly for panic sell-offs, price trends can seldom be characterized with any certainty until after the fact.

U.S. stock markets are usually open from 9:30 a.m. to 4:00 p.m., Eastern time. After-hours trading exists, however. Within a few years, trading may take place 24 hours a day.

# Spin-Offs

Let's say that Company A owns Company B, but A decides that its shareholders would be better off if the ownership were separated. It arranges a **spin-off**.

A distributes the stock of B to the shareholders of A. The more shares of A a person owns, the more shares of B she receives. The shareholders are not required to pay anything. After the spin-off, they own the two companies separately, each one having its own price.

A spin-off is one of the things the publisher of an index must respond to quickly, without waiting for an annual rebalancing. For example, say Company A, a member of the S&P 500 Index, decides to spin off a large division as a separate company. After the spin-off, both A and B are large enough to qualify for the S&P 500 Index. Another smaller stock must therefore be removed from the index. This triggers sales by the index funds and ETFs that track the S&P 500 Index.

# When Dividends and Capital Gains Are Taxable

Dividends are taxed in the year in which they're received. The dividends from **real estate investment trusts (REITs)**, which are mutual funds of real estate, are taxed as ordinary income, that is, at the same rate as your salary. The dividends from ETFs of bonds are also taxed as ordinary income. (Although they're called "dividends," the payouts from bond funds are actually interest.) Most other dividends are federally taxed at no higher than 15 percent.

Capital gains are taxable in the year in which the item is sold. The gain or loss is then **realized**. Until the sale, the gain or loss is **unrealized** and remains untaxed. Gains on securities held for a year or less are **short-term capital gains**, taxed at the rate of your salary income. The gains on securities held for at least a year and a day are **long-term capital gains**, federally taxed at no higher than 15 percent.

## An Excellent Brokerage Firm for ETFs

The best brokerage firm I've found for the purchase of ETFs is Folio*fn*. It was founded in 1998 by Steven Wallman, a former commissioner on the Securities and Exchange Commission who despaired at how few brokerage firms made it easy for people to regularly add small amounts to investment funds that are held for long periods. That's exactly what I suggest for you: Regularly add small amounts to investment funds (or large amounts, of course) and hold them for long periods.

Folio*fn* has a number of commission arrangements. Here are the pertinent ones:

- For individual trades, the firm charges $4 or $5.95, depending on the item's overall volume of trading. These rates are remarkably low. If you're adding small amounts to the account on a regular basis, accumulate your funds in the bank until it aggregates, say, $500. This keeps the commission down to only about 1 percent.
- Whenever appropriate, you might adopt Folio*fn*'s "Bronze" plan and pay a flat annual fee of $199. This enables you to make up to 200 online trades a month, which is way more than you need, even if you're adding money every month to the nine funds I suggest (see Chapters 16 and 17). Since the $199 fee remains constant, it has less and less impact as the account grows. No fees are charged for inactivity.

With Folio*fn*, you don't have to fiddle with the number of shares. Instead, use the firm's "Window Trades." You tell the firm the amount of *money* you want to buy or sell of each security. Twice a day, the purchases and sales of all Window-Trade customers are pooled, with the orders executed as a group. Folio*fn* allocates fractional shares, making the transactions come out to the penny. You can't pick the exact time of day to trade. But if you hold your securities for many years, as you should, the time of day you bought them won't matter at all.

As with all brokerage firms, Folio*fn* handles IRAs as well as regular accounts. Visit www.foliofn.com or call 888-973-7890.

# 15

# Fear Not the Purchase of Stocks

Short-term market projections are foolhardy. But despite what I may have said earlier in this book, I think long-term projections are indeed feasible.

For the last 80 years, since 1926, the S&P 500 Index has compounded at approximately 12 percent a year. I expect the market to continue at that pace for the next 20 years or so. Remember that the last 80 years has included an agonizing worldwide depression with U.S. unemployment reaching 25 percent, a gigantic world war, the cold war, and a long bear market from the late 1960s to the early 1980s. My prediction that the market will continue rising at the same rate in the next 20 years isn't really that outrageous, is it?

Well, okay, I'll cut the prediction to 10 percent a year.

The purpose of this chapter is to make clear why my projection is not just a wild guess. Any overriding fear of stocks you may have please cast aside. Stocks are an essential part of a successful investment program. There's no need to put *all* your money in stocks, of course. In the next chapter, I will suggest a combination of exchange-traded funds that I believe will achieve an excellent return with only moderate risk. But ETFs of stocks are the dominant portion.

## The Framework

The framework for business is set by government. It's the overriding force. When government interferes too much in the economy, these are results:

* Inflation rises.
* Interest rates rise.
* Stock prices go down.
* Price/earnings ratios fall.

Limited government is essential. The following functions are those that government must fulfill. Without these, it's back to the stone age with just a few million people worldwide scraping out a living:

* Protect property rights.
* Enforce contracts.
* Keep people from directly hurting fellow citizens by force or fraud.
* Defend the nation.

No government has done as little as this. It's a matter of degree. At one end is pie-in-the-sky, very limited governments. At the other end are totalitarian governments like those of Stalin, Hitler, and Mao Tse-tung, who, between them, killed something like 170 million of their own citizens.

When government stays out of the way of economic life, the natural order of things takes hold. People work to support themselves and their families. They also create more wealth than they expend, causing the general level of wealth to rise.

Unimpeded by government, technological advances create a flood of goods and services. The economy grows, inflation lessens, and interest rates fall, while both stock prices and price/earnings ratios rise. Growing economies are natural. Weak economies are unnatural. They're brought on by bad government policies.

# The United States

Including villages, towns, cities, counties, and states, the United States has thousands of government entities. Over time, they have performed the minimum functions pretty well—an important reason why America has thrived.

U.S. governments also perform many—lordy, so many—other functions that generally do more harm than good. But at present, anyway, they're not doing this in such a way as to kill the economy. Federal economic policies, in fact, have improved markedly over the last 80 years.

U.S. economic policies are still far from ideal. Government expenditures have grown too rapidly, and regulations remain too damaging. The worst way to raise government revenues is progressive income taxation with withholding—the very system we contend with. An IRS code 60,000 pages long makes the tax system all the worse. Nevertheless, today's policies are not nearly as harmful as those that caused the two major bear markets of the twentieth century, as detailed below.

# The Great Depression

During the Great Depression of the 1930s, tariffs were raised sharply, cutting international trade by two-thirds and impairing the world economy. (In anticipation of the higher tariffs, the market plummeted in October 1929.) Top income tax rates were lifted from 25 to 70 percent and later to 90 percent. (When the affluent are heavily taxed, they're unable to supply the capital needed to equip workers. This increases unemployment.)

Federal expenditures in the 1930s grew much faster than the economy. The money supply was cut sharply, starving the economy for cash and forcing price levels down by a third. In a misguided attempt to halt deflation, the federal government urged businesses to keep labor costs high. Employees who retained their job lived well, because their expenses fell more than their income. But because employers were paying too much for the employees they retained, they had to lay off other people by the millions. Unemployment rose to literally 25 percent—a level unthinkable today.

Since federal government income tax revenues were disappointing, excise taxes were imposed on everyday things like fruit juice, phone calls, cigarettes, movie tickets, radios, electricity, and cars. These taxes hit the poor hard. The government also forced prices above their natural levels. Jacob Maged, a Jersey City immigrant, for example, was jailed for three months because he pressed a suit for 35 cents instead of 40 cents.

Unlike Wal-Mart today, chain stores were prevented in the 1930s from passing on to customers the savings from big-volume purchases. The federal government brought 150 antitrust lawsuits, losing virtually all of them but severely disrupting the economy.

In general, businesses in the 1930s were told how much to pay employees, how much to charge, how much to produce, and where to sell. All in all, faulty government policies caused, lengthened, and intensified the Great Depression. The Dow Jones Industrial Average plummeted from 381 to 41, and misery reigned in America.

Compare this with the recession that struck America after World War I. President Warren Harding interrupted his card games to cut federal spending and reduce tax rates. The economy rebounded within a year.

It's unfortunate that some of our subsequent presidents haven't spent more time playing cards.

## The 1970s

The wretched economy and stock market of the 1970s also stemmed from faulty economic policies. Federal expenditures grew enormously.

Capital gains taxes were subject to a top rate of 70 percent.

The phone industry was a government-imposed monopoly, raising consumer costs significantly.

The prices charged by railroads, airlines, and natural gas companies were all set by government. A trucker who brought a load of tomatoes from the country to the city, for example, couldn't return to the country with a load of furniture. Regulators forced him to return empty. In general, regulators endeavored to keep costs high to prevent new companies from entering the business, thereby protecting the established trucking companies.

The federal government also imposed generalized wage and price controls. With products unrealistically cheap, demand was stimulated. But the artificially low prices caused companies to cut production, resulting in shortages. When the price controls were lifted, prices shot higher than they would have had the controls not been imposed in the first place.

With the economy under stress, the Federal Reserve created an excess of money, causing inflation and high interest rates. But the fed also imposed ceilings on the interest rates banks could pay for deposits. High inflation pushed rates higher than the ceilings. People therefore withdrew billions of dollars from banks, leaving the banking system short of cash and squeezing the economy dry.

These damaging policies produced high inflation, high interest rates, and a severe bear market in stocks. The Dow fell from 1067 to 570. The U.S. rate of unemployment swelled to 9 percent, and the price/earnings ratio of the Dow stocks fell to only 7.

## Current Policies

The policies of today are far better than before. Top tax rates, for example, have been much reduced from 70 to 35 percent, with long-term gains and most dividends taxed at only 15 percent—all enormously helpful. Removing the pernicious policies of former years and replacing them with others that are less damaging is a huge improvement. Movement is building toward repeal of the estate tax and reducing the impact of runaway tort law. The popularity of conservative talk shows is one indication that Americans want government to be less intrusive. Time and again, the people have rejected referendums proposing higher tax rates. Today, more than 50 percent of households are outright owners of stocks, up from only 17 percent in 1980. More than two-thirds of voters in the 2004 election owned stocks outright. These trends bode well for favorable economic policies.

According to polls, a substantial majority of Americans want legislative terms to be limited. I expect term limits eventually to be imposed, introducing greater intellectual diversity to legislatures and bringing back citizen control of government. With greater turnover in the legislature, the pace of favorable changes will quicken.

The pernicious economic policies described above prevailed during more than two decades of the last 80 years. Yet during the entire 80 years, stocks gained at 12 percent a year, as mentioned. With economic policies now so much improved, it seems entirely reasonable to project that a rate of advance of 10 to 12 percent should persist, at least for the next several decades.

For the foreseeable future, barring a physical disaster, such as a cataclysmic explosion of the hotspot under Yellowstone Park, bear markets like those of the 1930s and the 1970s will not return.

## And Abroad

Government policies are also improving throughout the world. Legislatures that once squabbled about how much to raise tax rates now squabble about how much to cut them. From nations that impose excessive tax rates, capital quickly departs by wire transfer. The release of billions of people from communism was a joyous occurrence.

Ever more nations are becoming democracies. Democracies don't fight with one another; they talk. Warfare is beginning to resemble international police work, reducing killing, costs, and destruction. Liberty pays off in economic growth, and growth anywhere helps everyone. Ultimately, citizens determine the character of their government. It's a learning process, and the people of the world are learning fast.

With relatively free trade, prosperity anywhere helps everyone.

## Technology

People have two means of creating wealth: their brawn and their brains. Throughout most of human history, brawn predominated. Lately, brains have come to the fore. For some of us, the only brawn we exercise at work is to push "Enter," directing the computer to get busy.

Technological change started slowly. About 2.5 million years ago, someone discovered that if he chipped the edge of a stone on one side, it became more useful. This development lasted about a million years until some smart cookie realized that if he chipped the edge on *both* sides, it became even more useful.

The pace of advance has quickened, to say the least. In 2003, for example, Hewlett-Packard introduced 158 new products in a single day. Advances in the first 20 years of the twenty-first century will be as consequential as all of the advances made in the entire twentieth century. A whirlwind of changes will affect us enormously. Here are a few indications:

- A single fiber-optic cable carries 1,000 times more data per second than was carried by the telecommunications system of the *entire world* only a few years ago, in 1997.
- Nanotechnology makes possible the manipulation of individual atoms. Scientists have built a guitar only the length of a human blood cell. Each of its six strings is only 100 atoms wide—500 millionths of a meter. Imagine placing individual atoms in precise locations!
- The Internet puts us in touch with people who know what we want to know. It enables people to work together without being together. The Web empowers individuals, which in turn weakens governments. The revolutionary effects of the Web have barely started.
- Computers and robots will dominate factory floors. Such developments have already caused enormous increases in productivity (output per hour of the average U.S. worker). Assembling a car, for example, now requires only about 24 worker hours of labor. Recessions once caused productivity to fall. But during the recession of 2001, productivity started *climbing* at over 3 percent, and it has continued at about that pace since. Of all the technological developments mentioned here, higher productivity will have the greatest economic effect.
- Medical advances will be revolutionary. To test your health, you will simply spit into a paper cup. Analysis of your saliva might indicate you have cancer. A drug is quickly produced just for you. Meshing neatly with your DNA, it kills the cancer.
- Disabilities will become mere inconveniences. The blind will carry a device that bypasses the eye and transmits images directly to the brain. Hearing devices bypassing the ear will enable the deaf to hear. Prosthetics will enable the immobile to walk.

- Most automobiles will probably continue being powered by gasoline combustion engines. But subsidiary systems, like the brakes, shocks, carburetor, cooling and antipollution systems, now controlled mechanically will be controlled by computers. Cars will run better and safer, with lower cost and improved gas mileage.
- Most toxic wastes result from manufacturing processes operating at high temperatures. In the future, some manufacturing will utilize biological, not mechanical, functions. These will run at normal temperatures, reducing toxic wastes.
- Computers will converse in idiomatic English and in many other languages. You'll be able to talk with almost anyone in the world, with real-time translations provided by the Web.
- Human brains generally perform at the rate of about 20 million billion calculations per second. By about 2010, supercomputers will equal this speed. By about 2020, computers costing less than $1,000 in today's money will operate as fast as human brains.

Technological advances have expanded corporate profits in the past and will continue doing so in the future. Improvements in productivity will elicit an outpouring of goods and services.

## The Likely Future

Since 1980, improved government policies and advancing technology have brought about a rapidly growing economy, lower inflation, lower interest rates, higher personal income, higher price/earnings ratios, and higher stock prices.

All of these trends will continue. With the economy not under stress, the Fed will have no need to create excessive money. Inflation will therefore turn negative, and the general price level will fall. Economists will proclaim this as a new trend. But in fact it will be a continuation of the trend that began in 1981, when inflation and interest rates topped out. Unlike the 1930s, deflation this time will not be accompanied by widespread liquidation of debt. Real personal income will rise. The deflation will be benign.

Long-term interest rates may continue rising temporarily. But in the long run, they will resume falling. Eventually, short-term rates on low-risk money will turn negative. Instead of receiving interest from money market funds, we will instead pay the institution for keeping our money safe and readily accessible.

## All This Has Happened Before

For over eight decades in the nineteenth century, many of the trends discussed in this chapter prevailed in the United Kingdom. Beginning in 1815, after the Napoleonic Wars, British economic policies improved significantly, especially with sharp reductions of tariffs. The resulting technological advances, referred to as the "industrial revolution," caused an outpouring of manufactured goods. Until 1897, England enjoyed stable consumer prices, falling interest rates, higher personal income, and higher stock prices.

In the 1930s and 1940s, U.S. intellectuals fervently approved of large and intrusive government. Now, except in the fanciful towers of academia, intellectuals are much more inclined to favor free markets and limited government. But during the same period, federal, state, and local governments have become larger and more intrusive. Opinion about government has moved one way; government itself has moved the other. This will change. In a democracy, discrepancies of such magnitude cannot continue forever. The practice of government will catch up with the opinion. After legislators become subject to term limits, the changes will occur even faster. More and more, resources will be allocated by free markets rather than governmental force.

Good times approach, worldwide. Take advantage. Businesses should feel comfortable about investing in the future. You should acquire a broad spectrum of exchange-traded funds, with a preponderance of those that hold U.S. and foreign stocks.

C  H  A  P  T  E  R

# 16

# Approaching a Promising Investment Strategy

Stocks add volatility and risk to a portfolio of bonds, right?

No, they don't, not in modest amounts. The addition of approximately 30 percent stocks to a bond portfolio *cuts* the risk. This assertion is supported by a study of prominent stock and bond indexes by Ibbotson Associates of Chicago, Illinois, covering the period from January 1973 to December 2005. This 33-year period includes the horrific decline of stock prices in 1974—the worst since the Great Depression.

The stock index used by Ibbotson is the S&P 500 Index. The bond index is the Lehman Brothers Long-Term Government Bond Index. Dividends and interest are assumed to be reinvested in the portfolios from which they came. The percentages of stocks and bonds are fixed at the beginning and not rebalanced thereafter.*

---

* Ibbotson Associates performed the study specifically for this book. The author is very grateful.

The study contains 11 hypothetical portfolios, ranging from 100 percent bonds to 100 percent stocks. The other 9 portfolios hold the following combinations:

- 10 percent stocks and 90 percent bonds
- 20 percent stocks and 80 percent bonds
- 30 percent stocks and 70 percent bonds
- And so on. In successive segments, the percentage of stocks increases and the percentage of bonds falls, with the final segment 100 percent stocks and no bonds.

Since stocks outperform bonds, the average annual returns grows as the percentage of stocks increase from one portfolio to another:

- With 100 percent bonds, the average annual return for the 33 years was 9.7 percent.
- With 100 percent stocks, the annual return was considerably higher: 12.5 percent. As the percentage of stocks rose, the returns steadily increased.

## But the Losses?

Now, how about the largest annual losses? The answer might surprise you:

- With 100 percent bonds, the largest loss during any of the 33 years was 8.7 percent.
- With 90 percent bonds and 10 percent stocks, the largest annual loss was 6.6 percent.
- With 80 percent bonds and 20 percent stocks, the largest annual loss was 5.5 percent.
- With 70 percent bonds and 30 percent stocks, the largest annual loss was only 4.6 percent.

With 30 percent stocks, the volatility and risk were the lowest of all—considerably less than with a portfolio of 100 percent bonds.

Yet the average annual return grew from 9.7 percent with all bonds to 10.3 percent with 30 percent stocks.

Higher returns. Lower risk. Is that a good deal or what?

Stocks, mind you, are generally more volatile than bonds. But this study shows that when the percentage of stocks is increased from zero to 30 percent, the largest annual loss of the combined portfolio falls significantly. Why? Because stocks and bonds don't move up and down together. To some extent, the cycles offset one another. When bonds are falling, stocks might be rising, softening the blow.

## Lack of Correlation

Lack of correlation is the key. When stocks are trending one way, bonds may move opposite. The trends are not exactly opposite, of course, but any noncorrelation helps reduce the volatility of the entire portfolio. As mentioned, excessive volatility hurts overall returns. If a stock you own falls by 80 percent from 100 to 20, it has to gain by 500 percent just to regain where it started.

## Those Pesky Emotions

Even more importantly, limiting the volatility of the entire portfolio enables us to avoid selling in bear markets. All of us feel bad news more intensely than good news. As mentioned earlier, the discomfort we feel from a 25 percent loss in the portfolio is about 2½ times more intense than the pleasure we feel from a 25 percent gain.

When stock prices fall for an extended period, we feel shame and disappointment. The price declines are always accompanied by bad news, and we cannot help but be affected by it. The more the prices decline, the more we expect them to *continue* declining. We want the shame and disappointment to stop. We want *out!*

*The bad news is overwhelming,* you say to yourself. *Other bear markets may have ended while the news was still bad, but this one is different. The prices are going to continue falling. I can't stand this pain and uncertainty. I've got to sell.*

In the maelstrom of bad feelings, we forget that the stocks at lower prices are better buys than they were at higher prices.

## Pendulum

Prices do not continue falling. Human affairs have a pendulum effect. Trends never continue indefinitely, especially in nations whose citizens are relatively free of government control. In a democracy, the glass is always half full. More promising factors come into play. Unexpectedly, prices start rising. It's always a surprise.

For a successful long-term investment program, it is absolutely essential that you not sell and go to cash when the news is bad (Figure 16-1). Stock prices often rise most rapidly when they bounce off a bear market bottom. The best example of this occurred in 1932, right at the bottom of the Great Depression. From July to November 1932, stock prices doubled. In only four months, the Dow Jones Industrial Average rose from 42 to 84—the fastest rise in American history. People who had been so enthusiastic about owning stocks at the top in 1929 didn't want to touch them in 1932. (Well, in 1929 they had money; in 1932 they didn't.)

The major benefit of diversification into various asset classes is to limit the volatility of the entire portfolio. This relieves anxiety and makes it easier to avoid selling when stock prices decline.

Buy when you get the money. Except for annual rebalancing, don't sell.

## Not Even in Retirement

Some investors feel they should reduce their exposure to stocks when they retire. This is nonsense, for two reasons:

- People these days are retiring earlier and dying later. With more time in retirement, it's essential to continue holding the main growth element in a portfolio. The main growth element is stocks.
- As discussed in Chapter 15, the prospects for stocks in the next couple of decades are very favorable.

## Don't Be an Investment Groupie*

Here's what can happen to a groupie: You buy stocks. Over a couple of years, the market rises. Your friends say, "It can't go on like this." You take heed and sell.

The market continues rising. Your friends say, "Golly, the economy is strong, and earnings are terrific. Maybe this bull market is for real." Figuring that you were a fool to sell, you buy.

Immediately, the market begins to fall. But Rome wasn't built in a day, right? You have to take the bad with the good. Having been wrong before, you'd feel stupid selling at a loss now. You'll just ride it out.

The market falls in earnest. *Oh God*, you say to yourself, *I'm no good at this game.* But you hang on.

The market is now down 20 percent. You've lost your previous gains, and you're behind. Your friends are warning you to get out, get out, get out. "There's no telling how far this thing can fall," they say.

They're right; it falls further. One afternoon, the market falls hugely on enormous volume. Just that morning, you could hardly look at yourself in the mirror without thinking how stupid you are. The additional selling you just can't accept. You sell.

Five minutes later, prices hit bottom and start rising. By the end of the day, the market has recovered half of the day's losses. The whole thing makes you sick.

Several months later, the market is higher. But the economic news is dreadful. Corporate earnings have fallen through the floor, and lay-offs are big news. You and your friends agree that the market can't stay up in the face of all this. You're glad your money is safely in money markets funds.

But the market doesn't fall. It continues to rise. After a few months, the news improves.

*Never mind,* you say to yourself. *The record's clear. Investing isn't my bag. I'll have a less fulfilling retirement, maybe. But that's okay. At least I'll have money when I get there.*

But the market goes even higher than it did at the beginning. The news is wonderful. Your friends say, "Why pay ordinary income taxes

---

*From *All About Exchange-Traded Funds*, by yours truly (New York: McGraw-Hill, 2003).

*(Continued)*

on the interest from that money market fund when you could earn capital gains in the stock market, capped at only 15 percent? Things look great. What do you say, man? How about buying stocks?"

You pull your money out of the money market fund and buy stocks.

And just a few weeks later ...

One of your friends, who stays quiet about her investments, put about the same amount into the market as you did at first. When the market turned sour and the economic news was poor, she found it unpleasant, of course, but she stopped checking the stock prices, turned off the business shows, stopped reading the business pages, and kept assuring herself that she was no fool for having bought stocks. She knew that the work performed by the people of the world would eventually carry the day and that the bad news wouldn't last. Except for rebalancing (as we'll describe later), she did whatever was needed to avoid selling in the bear market. Now, her investments are worth far more than yours.

**Figure 16-1**

Expect to live a good long time in retirement; plan on the younger of you and your spouse living to at least 100. Forfeiting the growth of stocks during that time is foolhardy.

## Double Diversity

But why limit yourself to just two contrasting asset classes? I recommend nine—all ETFs. This limits your risk all the more and makes it easier to avoid selling during bear markets.

The idea is to achieve double diversity. For the first level of diversity, each ETF contains at least scores of stocks and in some cases over a hundred. For the second level of diversity, you'll have nine ETFs. Each is a separate asset class that, to one degree or another, doesn't correlate with the others.

## The Main Engine of Growth

Buy a preponderance of stocks. As mentioned earlier, there has never been a 10-year period in American history when, after adjusting for inflation, a broad portfolio of stocks didn't return more than bonds. Even in the *losing* 10-year periods, stocks lost less than bonds. During every 20-year period in U.S. history, stocks haven't lost even once, but bonds have. I want you to invest 60 percent in stocks, half American and half foreign.

## Who's the Greatest Around Here?

*Half foreign! The USA is the greatest country in the world, right?*
    Right.
    *So why not just stick to U.S. stocks?*
    For two reasons:

- The prospects for foreign stocks are even better than for stocks of the United States.
- The more diversity, the better. Foreign stocks often don't correlate with U.S. stocks. Lately, the correlation has been pretty close. But this hasn't always been the case. Things change. No doubt foreign stocks will once again move differently from those in the United States.

### Foreign Risks

In 1980, the value of U.S. stocks represented about 70 percent of the value of stocks of the entire world. American investors saw every reason to buy America. But those numbers are now almost reversed. The market value of foreign stocks now exceeds that of U.S. stocks. And why not? Americans represent only about 6 percent of the world's population. It seems natural that the stocks of other nations should represent more than half the total world capitalization. I welcome the advance of the others. The wealthier the rest of the world becomes, the more people Americans can sell to and the fewer wars we need to fight.

A prominent investment professional once said to me, "Stay away from the stocks of foreign nations. The political risks are higher than they are in the United States."

He was right. The political risks are indeed higher—considerably higher in some nations. But he was wrong about avoiding foreign investments because known risks are generally discounted by the stock prices.

Let's say you have two companies of about the same size and the same earnings. One is in the United States and the other in a nation where the government's economic policies are poor.

The price of the foreign company will probably be lower in relation to the earnings. In other words, the P/E ratio will be lower. Later, if the nation becomes a democracy, the growth potential of the foreign company would probably increase.

Besides, investing in the stocks of *many* nations reduces risk. When one country is undergoing difficulties, another might be enjoying a spurt of prosperity.

### Foreign Potential

Most foreign nations, especially in the less developed, "emerging" nations like India, China, Indonesia, and Brazil, have a long way to go to match where the United States is now. (By the time they do, the United States will probably have moved further ahead. Maybe the others will catch up; maybe they won't.)

But to equal where the United States stands now, foreign nations don't need to develop the technology. Developed nations have already borne the enormous cost. Other nations need only buy the technology and in some cases receive it for free. In either case, the cost is far lower than development would have been.

During the 15 years prior to 1994, foreign stocks beat U.S. stocks in every single year. To suppose they'll never do so again is absurd. In 2004 and 2005, in fact, foreign stocks outstripped U.S. stocks. I expect this trend to continue.

Okay, invest 30 percent in U.S. stocks and 30 percent in foreign stocks.

Be careful about global ETFs, which hold both U.S. and foreign stocks in a single fund. As mentioned before, when foreign stocks constitute less than half of the portfolio, as tends to be the case with global funds, the investor can only *deduct* the payment of foreign taxes. By purchasing ETFs that specialize in foreign stocks, the investor can take the foreign tax as credits, which are more favorable.

# REITs

Place a portion of your money in an ETF that tracks an index of real estate investment trusts (REITs).

REITs are portfolios of real estate. About 40 years ago, the real estate industry pointed out to the government that the investment industry was allowed to create nontaxable corporations called "mutual funds" for investment in stocks and bonds. As long as the fund paid out its net returns to investors, the corporation itself was not taxed. The taxes were passed through to the shareholders of the fund.

The real estate industry complained: "We want the same tax rules for portfolios of real estate."

The government said okay. It stipulated that as long as the REIT pays out 95 percent of the income to the fund shareholders, the REIT itself is not subject to corporate income taxes. Any tax ramifications are passed through to the REIT shareholders.

Real estate is of course an essential part of the economy. We all have to be somewhere, and most of us (except in American academia) have our feet on or in real estate most of the time. REITs pay relatively high income. They also provide a modest hedge against the possibility of inflation.

### Different Flavors

Real estate investment trusts come in a wide variety. Some are developers and builders. Others buy completed properties and hold them for income. Some specialize in office buildings, hotels, apartment dwellings, or homes. There are about 100 of them in the United States. With an ETF that acquires literally all of the REITs available, you can own 'em all.

REITs pay income to shareholders at higher rates than stock funds. Because of depreciation rules, a little of the income is nontaxable and treated as a return of capital.

### Forget the Higher Taxes

As mentioned previously, the dividend income from REITs does not qualify for the maximum tax rate of 15 percent that applies to most dividends. It's taxable at full rates, up to 35 percent. Do not take this as a reason to avoid investing in REITs. The advantage of the diversification outweighs the disadvantage of the higher tax.

For example, say your total portfolio is $500,000. You put 20 percent into an index of REITs—that's $100,000.

Assume that the dividend income is 6 percent. That's $6,000.

You're subject to the maximum federal tax bracket of 35 percent. Your tax comes to $2,100.

If REITs qualified for the 15 percent maximum tax rate, your tax would be $900 (15 percent of $6,000).

You would pay an extra $1,200 in tax ($2,100 less $900).

$1,200 is only a quarter of 1 percent of your total portfolio of $500,000—a tiny percentage of cost. I cannot quantify the investment benefit of diversifying into REITs, but I assure you that it is far greater than a quarter of 1 percent.

### How about a More Common Tax Bracket?

But the chances are, you're not subject to the highest tax rate of 35 percent. If you're filing jointly, your taxable income would have to exceed $336,550. Let's say that you and your spouse file jointly, and your joint taxable income falls between $61,300 and $123,700. Your income is taxed at a maximum of 25 percent.

Again, your portfolio is $500,000, with $100,000 in REITs. The 6 percent dividend income is $6,000. It's subject to 25 percent tax ($1,500) instead of the 15 percent tax that applies to stocks ($900). The extra tax costs you $600 ($1,500 less $900).

No one likes to pay tax, of course. But $600 is only about one-tenth of 1 percent of your $500,000 portfolio. This is minuscule—way less than the advantage of the diversification. We're looking at a fine example of not allowing tax savings to control your investment choices. Choose your investments based on their economic benefit and let the taxes fall as they may.

(By the way, the dividends on even *non*-REIT stocks are subject to ordinary income tax rates if you hold the stock for less than 61 days. This is another reason to avoid being a trader—you preserve the 15 percent rate.)

## Go for Long-Term Gains

While we're at it, let's reiterate that you should always hold your ETFs for at least a year and a day, to gain the benefit of long-term capital gains. Here, you're accommodating to a tax requirement. But it's in your interest to do so for investment reasons as well as tax reasons. Be a multiyear investor.

You do have to adjust your portfolio. It's called *rebalancing*; we'll get to that shortly. But many professionals call for rebalancing the portfolio quarterly or—yikes—even monthly. This is ridiculous. Such frequent rebalancing burns up too many commissions and spreads. Most importantly, it subjects you to tax on short-term capital gains. Rebalance no more often than every year and a day. If you make your investments on June 5, 2007, mark your calendar to rebalance on June 6, 2008.

Back to REITs. Some financial advisors count REITs as stocks and advise limiting the stock portion of a portfolio to 60 percent *including* the REITs.

Technically, those advisors may be correct: REITs are indeed stocks. But from a diversification point of view, the advisors are dead wrong because REITs don't act like other stocks. Here's evidence:

- From 1998 to 2000, stocks went up big. REITs went down.
- During the killer years from 2000 to 2003, stocks went down big. REITs went up modestly.
- From 2003 to 2006, stocks went up modestly. REITs went up big.

In every period, REITs acted differently from stocks. That's exactly what you want: asset classes whose price trends don't match, limiting the volatility of the whole.

## Long or Short Bonds?

As explained in Chapter 3, bond prices move opposite to the direction of changes in interest rates. The longer the bond's maturity, the greater the price volatility. Even though the interest rates on short bonds are usually lower than those of the long ones, many investors favor bonds with relatively short maturities in an effort to cut volatility.

As earlier sections of this book have made clear, it's essential to reduce volatility. Nevertheless, avoiding long-term bonds is not a good idea. Here's why:

The best way to reduce volatility while sacrificing little growth is to hold various asset classes whose up-and-down price trends don't match. The price trends, as academics put it, don't correlate. Stocks are the main engine of growth, but it's important to hold other asset classes that are noncorrelating. REITs are one; bonds are another. I suggest 20 percent in each.

### Get a Move On

But you want the noncorrelating groups to *move*. As long as they move differently from stocks to one degree or another, they're doing their job.

Let's say you have two portfolios of 80 percent stocks and 20 percent Treasury securities. In one portfolio, the debt portion consists of Treasury bills continually changed so that the ones you have are always due in just a few weeks. (We disregard commissions.) Their prices remain virtually unchanged.

In the other portfolio, the debt portion consists of 30-year bonds, whose prices fluctuate a lot. But when stock prices move down, the bond prices tend to move up.

Which portfolio has the lesser volatility (not just the bonds—I mean the volatility of the entire portfolio)?

You've got it: the one with the long-term bonds. Even though the long-termers by themselves are more volatile, their combination with stocks makes the whole portfolio less volatile.

Forget short-term debt; buy an exchange-traded fund of long-term bonds, preferably Treasury bonds, which are not callable. There aren't many bond ETFs, but iShares Lehman 20+ Yr Treasuries (TLT) holds Treasury bonds that mature in at least 20 years. That's the best one.

Keep focusing on using double diversity to limit the volatility of the whole portfolio. Doing so helps you avoid selling your stocks in bear markets.

## Tailoring

Financial planners jump through hoops to find out the degree to which their clients are willing to accept price volatility (otherwise known as "investment risk"). As best they can, the planners calibrate the client's inclinations and design a portfolio to fit.

Well, this may be okay for some people. But since you have the gumption to read this book, I say, "Baloney." Don't try to design a portfolio to fit your inclinations about Ms. Market. Instead, adjust your inclinations to fit Ms. Market. In the short term, Ms. Market is a lioness—all powerful and unpredictable. But in the long term, she turns into a pussy cat. As the creation of wealth by the people of the world rises, she grows in value right along with that wealth.

I want you to adjust to the market's short-term vagaries by assuming that no matter what you do, you're going to be wrong in the short term. No matter what happens in the short term, it's not your fault. When prices go down and the news is bad, turn off the tube. Avoid picking individual stocks and don't try to time the market. Use double diversity, whereby each fund holds many securities, and the funds you choose represent different asset classes whose price trends, to one degree or another, do not correlate. Rebalance once a year and otherwise hold for life.

## Judgment

I have hotly maintained that the less often you exercise investment judgment, the better your results will be. As explained earlier, stock prices generally anticipate news that won't become known to anyone for four to six months. During that period, investment judgments are likely to be wrong. If you make three judgments a year concerning your entire portfolio, you're likely to be wrong most of the time.

But in determining your choice of funds, somebody's judgment must be relied on—either yours or someone else's. Thereafter, you can proceed with the exercise of little or no judgment, even in rebalancing.

Here are my judgments in constructing an optimal portfolio. Do not assume right off the bat that they won't work for you. Try these selections for a few years:

## 60-40

The most important determination is the choice of 60 percent stocks. This is a common determination among investment advisors. I generally hate to go along with the crowd, but in this case, the judgment is correct.

Years ago, I heard of a financial planner who said, "I don't care what the question is, the answer is 60 percent stocks and 40 percent bonds." An overstatement, perhaps, but he was essentially correct. (To gain additional diversification, however, change the 40 percent portion to 20 percent bonds and 20 percent REITs.)

## Half and Half

The next most important determination is to split the stock portion into 30 percent U.S. and 30 percent foreign stocks. As mentioned previously, buying stocks only where we happen to live is too limiting. Economic growth is springing up all over the world. Spread your money worldwide. The more diversification, the better.

## Foreign Regions

Here is how the market values of all publicly held foreign stocks are currently divided among the three major regions:

| | |
|---|---|
| Europe | 58% |
| Pacific | 28% |
| Emerging markets | 14% |
| | 100% |

In my judgment, developing nations have the greatest growth potential. The European economy, strangled by faulty economic policies, has less. I therefore suggest beefing up emerging markets and cutting down on Europe, leaving Pacific nations essentially the same. This makes 33.3 percent each. But since foreign stocks compose a total of 30 percent of the portfolio, make that 10 percent each.

## U.S. Stocks

The Russell 3000 Index consists of the 3,000 largest publicly held U.S. stocks. These constitute approximately 98 percent of the value of all publicly held U.S. stocks. An additional 12,000 stocks compose the remaining 2 percent.

The top 1,000 (big-cap) stocks represent about 90 percent of the market value of the aforementioned 3,000 stocks. The next 2,000 stocks (small caps) represent 10 percent.

Over time, small-cap stocks outperform the big-caps. In originally designing my suggested portfolio, I therefore beefed up the small caps as follows:

| | |
|---|---|
| Big growth | 10% |
| Big value | 10% |
| Small growth | 5% |
| Small value | 5% |
| | 30% |

# Horrors! A Prediction

I have hotly maintained in this book that's it's impossible for anyone to predict market trends. But, sorry, I make such predictions myself, although they're long term and I don't make them often.

On December 6, 1999, shortly before the market topped out in early 2000, I published a newspaper column recommending the purchase of small-cap stocks. (Sorry, the archive of columns in my Web site www.archierichards.com doesn't extend back to 1999. In case you were wondering, I did not anticipate the bear market of 2000 to 2003.)

In my column, I pointed out that the P/E ratios of small caps are usually about 10 percent higher than those of big caps, ranging from 25 percent higher in 1983 to 15 percent lower in 1990. I noted that at the time of the column in December 1999, the P/E ratios of small caps had plunged to 30 percent lower than those of the big caps, and I suggested their purchase.

In Figure 16-2, the chart of the Russell 2000 Index shows that the prediction has worked out well. The chart values assume that dividends

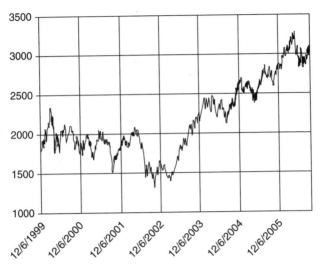

**Figure 16-2    Russell 2000 Index**
The Russell 2000® Index is a registered trademark of Frank Russell Company. Used by permission.

are reinvested. Indexes, I am required to tell you are unmanaged and cannot be invested in directly.

The ETF that tracks this index, the iShares Russell 2000 Index Fund (IWM), began trading on May 22, 2000. With its dividends reinvested in a timely manner, the fund tracks the index closely.

## What's with This Guy? Another Prediction!

My, how things have changed! The P/Es of small caps are now about 40 percent higher than those of the big caps.[†] I predict that during the next several years, big-cap stocks will outdo the small caps.

But before we nail down an adjustment to the 30 percent U.S.-stock portion of the portfolio, note an additional price trend over the

---

[†] At this writing, the P/E ratio for the MSCI US Prime Market 750 Index is 17.1. The P/E ratio for the MSCI US Small Cap 1750 Index is 24.1.

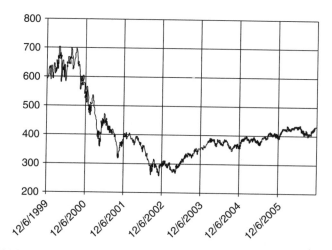

**Figure 16-3    Russell 1000 Growth Index**

The Russell 1000® Growth Index is a registered trademark of Frank Russell Company. Used by permission.

last six years. Yes, I know, historic price trends have no predictive value, right? Over short periods they certainly don't. But six years is quite a long time.

Six years ago, at about the top of the market, most people thought big-cap growth stocks were heading out into the solar system. As Figure 16-3 illustrates, the Russell 1000 Growth Index, representing big-cap growth stocks, has stayed right here on earth and proved very disappointing indeed.

In contrast, small-cap value stocks were out of favor in 2000. As Figure 16-4 illustrates in the chart of the Russell 2000 Value Index, they have since performed well.

Since 2000, big growth stocks have gotten killed, and small value stocks have risen substantially. I predict that over the next several years, these trends will reverse.

## Why?

The reason has to do with the banking system. The core business of banks is to take in short-term money at low rates and lend out long-term money at high rates. For example, banks accept checking

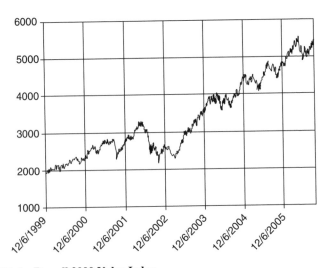

**Figure 16-4    Russell 2000 Value Index**

The Russell 2000® Value Index is a registered trademark of Frank Russell Company. Used by permission.

account money from you and me, for which they pay little or no interest (they do incur teller costs and other costs). The banks lend this money to homeowners and small businesses at relatively high rates of interest.

This is profitable most of the time because the yield curve is usually positive; long-term rates are usually higher than short-term rates.

But when the Federal Reserve Bank grapples with inflation, short-term interest rates rise faster than long-term rates. When the two are equal, the **yield curve** is said to be **flat**. When short rates exceed long rates, the yield curve is said to be **inverted**. During such times, it's no longer profitable for banks to borrow short and lend long, and they cut back their lending.

The yield curve went flat in the fall of 2005 and has generally stayed that way since.

Some 9 to 12 months after the yield curve goes flat, big growth stocks usually start performing better than small value stocks. The reason is, many big growth companies don't need bank loans. Companies like Microsoft and General Electric, for example, generally fund their own growth. But small value companies do indeed need bank loans.

But with the yield curve flat, they have less opportunity to obtain such loans.

Maybe the strategy won't work this time. But with small value stocks having done well and big growth stocks having done poorly, I think it's worth a shot. I therefore recommend that the 30 percent U.S.-stock section be adjusted to the following:

| | |
|---|---|
| Big growth | 15% |
| Big value | 5% |
| Small growth | 7% |
| Small value | 3% |
| | 30% |

Actually, I made the above recommendations in a column dated November 28, 2005 (that one *is* in the archives). Since then, small value stocks have continued to rise and big growth stocks have faltered. My prediction was premature. Why I didn't wait for the 9- to 12-month delay I do not know. Just dumb, I guess.

## The Complete Rundown

Here's my recommended asset classes in full:

| | |
|---|---|
| Big growth | 15% |
| Big value | 5% |
| Small growth | 7% |
| Small value | 3% |
| Europe | 10% |
| Pacific | 10% |
| Emerging markets | 10% |
| REITs | 20% |
| Long bonds | 20% |
| | 100% |

That's nine funds, with the smallest at only 3 percent. If you have substantial funds, you might make room among the U.S. stocks for growth and value mid-caps. But for most people, nine funds is enough. I want your investing to be as simple as possible, so that you may pay as little attention to it as possible.

### Trade-Offs

I can hear you say, *Okay, the stocks have the best growth potential. But you also want REITs and bonds to go down when stocks are going up. Don't these noncorrelating asset classes reduce the overall potential for growth?*

Excellent question. The answer is, you'd be surprised at how little the growth potential is reduced. The volatility is cut down a lot, but the growth potential is reduced only a little. The trade-off is well worth it because it keeps in check your emotional reactions to bear markets. If, just once, you go to cash in a bear market and later go back in at higher prices, you'd be amazed how much your long-term performance would be diminished.

### A Missing Ingredient

An important asset class is missing from the above recommendations: commodities and gold. They're omitted because I feel it's too late for inflation hedges. The inclusion of REITs is sufficient.

As explained earlier, I expect inflation to disappear. Over the next decade or so, I look for gold to fall to $200 an ounce or below.

When I first put these ideas together several years ago, I was certainly wrong to omit, say, 5 percent in commodities and gold. Gold, for example, has since gone up from under $300 to over $700 an ounce.

But even though commodities and gold don't correlate with stocks, I just can't bear to include them in the portfolio now. The possibility of inflation is much in the news. Investors have been scrambling for investments in TIPS, energy, and precious metals. The airways are filled with advertisements for the purchase of gold, supported by people boasting about how much money they've made. No investment should be bought under such conditions. Maybe I'll add commodities and gold later. But not now.

# Rebalancing

It's vital to review your portfolio every year and a day. In between, you may not be able to resist seeing how it's doing. But it's better if you don't. The more often you check the values, the more likely you are to trade. One is especially inclined to get out when prices are going down.

Do not go to cash after prices have fallen and the news is bad. Nothing will more surely ruin your long-term investment success.

You should, however, make necessary adjustments every year and a day. Mark your calendar. If you buy on March 10, 2008, make adjustments on March 11, 2009. The reason for the timing, of course, is to avoid short-term capital gains. You're going to be selling a portion of funds that have gone up a lot and buying funds that have gone down a lot. By selling only after a year and a day, you're assured of long-term gains.

Make the adjustments according to the calendar, as I say, and not according to what the market is doing. You're not trying to time the market. You're just selling high and buying low; after all, that's the whole idea.

Avoid being a groupie and talking about investments with friends. The types of stocks of which you're selling portions are the very ones your friends are boasting about *buying*. Therefore, stay quiet about what you're doing. Don't disagree with them openly or try to persuade them to sell along with you. You will fail, because your friends are acting according to the prevailing widespread sentiment and you are not. The chances are, they would instead convert you from a seller to a buyer.

If your friends boast about making a ton of money by jumping on the latest bandwagon, don't succumb to their pleadings to do the same. If you blame yourself for not keeping up and join the bandwagon party, you'll ruin your long-term results. Genius (on the part of your friends) should never be confused with bull markets. Rapidly rising bull markets often apply to only one asset class. In the late 1990s, it was big growth stocks that prevailed. But before too long, they got creamed—you may have noticed. No matter what others are doing, retain your double diversity with rebalancing and stay quiet about it.

### It's Automatic

Rebalancing is an automatic method of selling high and buying low. The exercise of investment judgment isn't required. You have to know your way around percentages, but otherwise, the rebalancing is automatic.

Rebalancing isn't always necessary, even annually. Don't bother with it unless an asset class has moved up a lot. In my judgment, 30 percent is the proper test. Now, I don't mean that the fund must have moved up by at least 30 percent. I do mean that the fund must have moved up by at least 30 percent *as a percentage of the entire portfolio.*

For example, let's say your ETF of REITs starts at 20 percent of the portfolio. A year later, if the ETF is 26 percent of the portfolio, leave it alone; that's a 30 percent increase in the percentage. But if it's 26.1 percent, bingo, it's over the 30 percent line. Sell enough of the fund to bring it back to 20 percent and add the proceeds to asset classes that have been weak.

As another example, if the small value stocks have risen from 3 to 4 percent of the portfolio, sell 1 percent.

Figure 16-5 gives the recommended portfolio again, showing to what extent each asset class can rise as a percentage of the entire portfolio without triggering a partial sale.

If the percentage of one fund has gone down by more than 30 percent but no fund has gone up by more than 30 percent, sell a portion of the funds that have gone up, even though they haven't hit the 30 percent limit. Money to add to weak funds has to come from somewhere.

But the money may come from the money market fund. Remember that the dividends from exchange-traded funds are not automatically reinvested in the fund from which they came. In setting up the account at Folio*fn*, arrange for them to be deposited automatically in the money market fund. That money is available for rebalancing to the weaker funds.

By the way, make sure that the money market fund you use in your investment account is different from the one in which you're storing money you know you're going to use within five years. The *investment* money market fund should be emptied regularly. Do not

| Original Percentage | Asset Class | Maximum Percentage without Selling |
|---|---|---|
| 15% | Big growth | 19.5% |
| 5% | Big value | 6.5% |
| 7% | Small growth | 9.1% |
| 3% | Small growth | 3.9% |
| 10% | Europe | 13.0% |
| 10% | Pacific | 13.0% |
| 10% | Emerging markets | 13.0% |
| 20% | REITs | 26.0% |
| 20% | Long-term bonds | 26.0% |

**Figure 16-5   The Recommended Portfolio Showing to What Extent Each Asset Class Can Rise As a Percentage of the Entire Portfolio without Triggering a Partial Sale**

hold money there in anticipation of buying investments later at a lower price. That effort will consistently fail. Investment tactics that don't work consistently shouldn't be undertaken at all.

### Buy the Weak Ones

Experienced investors who acquire *individual* stocks caution that a person should keep the ones that rise and sell the ones that fall. Individual stocks can of course fall to zero. Following one of those suckers all the way down is bad for financial health.

But asset classes do not fall to zero. Assuming that *all* big value stocks will go busted is simply unrealistic. Industries do come and go—witness the buggy whip industry of a century ago. But industries are not asset classes. The concepts of big, small, growth, and value will never die.

An asset class may remain weak for years, to be sure. Beginning in 1997 and for six years thereafter, foreign stocks performed worse than U.S. stocks. One should have continued to plow money into them. It's called "buying low." Eventually they come back, as the foreign stocks did with a vengeance in 2005 and 2006. Without the exercise of judgment, rebalancing enables you to buy low when they're weak and sell high when they're strong.

The sponsors of ETFs are required by the SEC to reveal ETF's historic returns in the prospectuses. Pay no attention to these records. The historic record of an asset class has no predictive value whatever.

## Rebalancing Miscellanea

From www.archierichards.com > Suggested Portfolios, you can download a spreadsheet that enables you to manage your portfolio, including the initial allocations and the rebalancing. The spreadsheet takes into account the 30 percent factor.

Annual rebalancing requires remarkably little time and attention. Give time for your investments to season.

The more boring your investments, the better. Between annual rebalancings, you needn't do anything except move your eyeballs to look at your monthly statements. It's better if you don't even do that. The less often you see how things are going, the less likely you are to trade. If investing has been your hobby, get a new hobby.

An investment professional probably isn't necessary. If you have a hard time with percentages, pay a bookkeeper to do the job for you. He is not providing investment advice; he is just calculating percentages. Better yet, he will save his time and save your cost by implementing the spreadsheet from my Web site www.archierichards.com.

### Regular Additions

If you're adding money regularly to the account, arrange for it to be credited to the money market fund. Then, monthly or quarterly, allocate the funds to the investment accounts. Under these circumstances, additional annual rebalancing is unnecessary. The spreadsheet from www.archierichards.com > Suggested Portfolio will automatically funnel the new money into the funds that have been weak.

### Regular Withdrawals

If you're making regular withdrawals from your portfolio, remove only what's in the money market fund during three quarters of the year. In the final quarter, take out a higher amount if necessary, but only in the course of your annual rebalancing. This avoids short-term capital gains as much as possible.

To avoid depleting the portfolio over time, remove just 4 to 6 percent of the *current* value each year. (Well, if the portfolio has performed satisfactorily for years, you might take out 7 percent, but only during the first year or two of retirement, when you're especially active.)

# 17

# A Superior Portfolio of Exchange-Traded Funds

I have an admission to make: I'm biased. I'm nuts about the Vanguard Group.

I love the company's low costs and low turnover rates. I admire its long-term interest in indexing. I like the way it handles rebalancing: When an index fund announces it will sell a component of an index and buy another, Vanguard may not participate in the flood of trading at the appointed time. It makes the change before or after, to avoid the crowd and the unfavorable prices.

I admire how Vanguard sometimes performs better than the index it's tracking, even after operating expenses. I applaud the consistency with which it holds its stocks for at least 61 days, achieving the 15 percent tax rate on its non-REIT dividends. I like the simplicity of Vanguard's written materials. Most importantly, I like the overall performance of its funds.

## Trouble

But all of Vanguard's exchange-traded funds have a potential problem. They share a single portfolio with an associated index mutual fund. Vanguard's Growth ETF (VUG), for example, participates in the same portfolio as Vanguard's Growth Index Fund (VIGRX).

You may recall earlier discussions in which I lauded the ability of ETFs to avoid nearly all capital gains taxes. When an authorized participant redeems shares, for example, the ETF passes out an equivalent value of stock. Because this is a tax-free exchange, the ETF gets rid of its low-cost stock, leaving high-cost stock behind. Later, when a stock is removed from the index because of a merger or spin-off, the sale by the fund results in no capital gains.

This normal treatment of ETFs is quite different from that of mutual funds, including index mutual funds. When a shareholder of an index fund redeems shares, the fund passes out cash. If the fund doesn't have the cash, it must sell stock to provide it. To minimize tax, most funds sell their high-cost stock, leaving low-cost stock behind. Later, when a stock is removed from the index, the sale by the fund does indeed result in capital gains.

By combining an ETF with a corresponding index fund, Vanguard runs the risk that the sales of portfolio stocks by the index fund will cause capital gains to be passed out to the associated ETF.

This is especially true in that the Vanguard index funds are considerably larger than their associated ETFs and therefore dominate the tax conditions. Vanguard's first ETF, the Total Stock Market ETF (VTI), for example, currently has a net asset value of $5.6 billion. The net asset value of the Total Stock Market Index Fund (VTSMX), not counting the share occupied by the ETF, is 12 times larger—$67.5 billion. As a result, the shareholders of VTI may suffer adverse tax consequences created by the larger index fund.

## Why?

In a conversation with George U. Sauter (commonly known as "Gus"), Vanguard's chief investment officer, I learned the reasons why Vanguard adopted the single-fund structure for its ETFs, as follows:

- Using the single-fund approach cut costs.

- The ETF could be started with little money and still have low costs.
- To the extent the index funds were already using complete replication, the associated ETF would do the same right off the bat, resulting in more accurate tracking of the underlying index.
- The associated index funds having been in existence for some time, the ETFs had long and favorable records to promulgate.

Gus Sauter pointed out mitigating features of the Vanguard index funds that have minimized the passing out of capital gains to shareholders:

- With institutional investors who redeemed shares of index funds, Vanguard sometimes has the opportunity to pass out stock instead of cash. This enables the fund to get rid of low-cost stock.
- Every day, net cash flows into Vanguard. Its index funds and their associated ETFs continually have the opportunity to add to their portfolios at current prices. In rising markets, this gives the funds high costs.
- The bear market of 2000 to 2003 gave Vanguard the opportunity to "harvest" substantial losses that could be carried forward until something like 2009. When a stock must later be sold because it's been removed from the underlying index, Vanguard has losses to offset the gains.
- Vanguard has discovered that high-cost accounting reduces taxes more than average-cost accounting. The firm is a step ahead of most other funds in this regard. Most of the others continue using average costing.

All in all, Vanguard funds have passed out very few capital gains to shareholders. The firm regularly performs "stress tests" to check the potential for capital gains. Here are examples:

- At the market bottom in December 2002, literally the entire Total Stock Market Index Fund could have been sold without incurring capital gains.
- At the top of the market in early 2000, 34 percent of the Total Stock Market Index Fund could have been sold without realizing gains.

- Even though Vanguard's Emerging Markets Index Fund tripled in value from 2003 to 2006, a Vanguard study in May 2006 revealed that 41 percent of the fund could have been sold without realizing gains.

## The Risk

But here's the risk: Let's say that (1) over the next 5 to 10 years, the world stock markets rise substantially (as I expect), (2) Vanguard's losses are used up, (3) its index funds remain substantially larger than the associated ETFs, and (4) the quality of Vanguard's management weakens, causing sources of new money to dry up. Under these circumstances, taxable gains might then be incurred by the Vanguard ETFs that would not have been incurred had the ETFs been set up as separate funds.

## A Bird in Hand ...

The tax costs I just envisioned will be incurred mostly in the future. Meanwhile, we can enjoy savings from Vanguard's low expense ratios and low turnover rates. (A check of the expense ratios in Appendix A shows that Vanguard's costs are invariably the lowest.)

We're faced with certain advantages now, as opposed to uncertain disadvantages in the future. I prefer the former. On this basis, I recommend the Vanguard funds listed in Figure 17-1.

If you have sufficient money for only one fund, begin with Vanguard's Total Stock Market ETF (VTI) and bring in iShares MSCI EAFE Index Fund (EFA) as soon as you can. Later, as your funds accumulate, bring in 20 percent each of the REIT fund (VNQ) and long-term Treasuries (TLT). Still later, when the low percentages of commissions and taxes allow it, adopt a full range of double diversity by selling VTI and EFA and acquiring the first seven funds shown in Figure 17-1.

If you have sufficient money for 11 funds, add the Vanguard Mid Cap Growth and Value Funds (VOT and VOE) and reduce the other U.S. funds accordingly.

| Original Percentage | Mostly Vanguard ETFs | Maximum Percentage without Selling |
|---|---|---|
| 15% | Growth (VUG) | 19.5% |
| 5% | Value (VTV) | 6.5% |
| 7% | Small-Cap Growth (VBK) | 9.1% |
| 3% | Small-Cap Value (VBR) | 3.9% |
| 10% | European (VGK) | 13.0% |
| 10% | Pacific (VPL) | 13.0% |
| 10% | Emerging Market (VWO) | 13.0% |
| 20% | REIT (VNQ) | 26.0% |
| 20% | iShares Lehman 20+ Year Treasuries (TLT) | 26.0% |

**Figure 17-1     Recommended Vanguard ETF Funds**

# If the Above Won't Do

If the tax-savings idea sticks in your craw, I present a fine alternative portfolio in Figure 17-2. (The Vanguard Pacific Fund appears again in this portfolio. So far, no other capitalization-weighted fund covers the Pacific in breadth, including Japanese stocks.)

Either approach will work well. I prefer Vanguard. But then, I'm biased.

# The Right Program

Over long periods, these portfolios will provide outstanding results with low volatility. The more boring your investments, the better.

| Original Percentage | Alternative ETFs | Maximum Percentage without Selling |
|---|---|---|
| 15% | streetTRACKS DJ Wilshire Large Cap Growth (ELG) | 19.5% |
| 5% | streetTRACKS DJ Wilshire Large Cap Value (ELV) | 6.5% |
| 7% | streetTRACKS DJ Wilshire Small Cap Growth (DSG) | 9.1% |
| 3% | streetTRACKS DJ Wilshire Small Cap Value (DSV) | 3.9% |
| 10% | iShares S&P Europe 350 (IEV) | 13.0% |
| 10% | Vanguard Pacific (VPL) | 13.0% |
| 10% | iShares MSCI Emerging Markets (EEM) | 13.0% |
| 20% | streetTRACKS DJ Wilshire REIT (RWR) | 26.0% |
| 20% | iShares Lehman 20+ Year Treasuries (TLT) | 26.0% |

**Figure 17-2    An Alternative Portfolio**

Give them time. Let the creation of wealth throughout the world carry you aloft.

APPENDIX A

# Current U.S. Exchange-Traded Funds

ETFs are multiplying fast. This listing includes 318 U.S. exchange-traded funds. A few of these are in registration with the Securities and Exchange Commission and are expected to begin trading by the time this book is published. Many more ETFs not listed here are also in registration, and this doesn't count numerous ETFs available abroad.

Some day, there may be too many ETFs. With an annual fee of 0.35 percent, a fund with net assets of $20 million brings in annual gross revenues of only $70,000, which could hardly be profitable.

To save space in this listing, words like "Index," "Sector," and "Fund" may be omitted from the ETF name. With the exception of the Diamonds (DIA), a State Street fund, the first word or service mark of each ETF identifies the sponsor. Information about each sponsor is given in Appendix B. In some cases, such as the Rydex funds, the sponsor's name is not included in the ETF's name. I insert the name anyway, to tie you in to Appendix B.

The ETFs are divided into four categories, as follows:

1. *Nonfundamental ETFs.*   Unless the description identifies the fund as weighted equally, assume that it's weighted by capitalization. Diamonds are the only price-weighted fund.
2. *Fundamental ETFs.*   The stocks are weighted according to the degree to which they meet the fundamental standards.
3. *Short sellers.*
4. *Commodities and foreign currencies.*

The ETFs are arranged by type and style. Each listing provides the following information:

- The stock symbol appears in parentheses after the name.
- Then comes the operating expenses, expressed as a percentage of the fund's net asset value (the lower the better).
- The average daily volume of trading for the last three months is shown. (Higher volume generally means a tighter spread between bid and ask prices.)
- The last number is the net assets in the fund, in millions or billions, as the case may be.* (Huge funds of small stocks can result in very unfavorable prices when the components are reconstituted annually.)
- Then comes distinguishing information about each fund.

## Nonfundamental ETFs

|  | Expense Ratio | Average Daily Vol. *(thousands)* | Net Assets, $ *(millions)* |
|---|---|---|---|
| **Total Market** | | | |
| iShares DJ US Total Market (IYY) | 0.20 percent | 31 | 486 |
| All companies in the Dow Jones large-cap, mid-cap, and small-cap indexes. | | | |

---

*In most cases, the average daily volume for the last three months and the net assets are found in Yahoo Finance. Some ETFs are too new for information to be available. HOLDRs are not new, but the net assets of most of them are not disclosed either on Yahoo or on the Merrill Lynch or HOLDRs Web sites. Since the volume of trading is high, the net assets are probably substantial.

| | Expense Ratio | Average Daily Vol. (thousands) | Net Assets, $ (millions) |
|---|---|---|---|
| iShares NYSE Composite (NYC) | 0.25 percent | 11 | 57 |

The index measures the performance of all common stocks, American Depositary Receipts (of foreign stocks), REITs, and tracking stocks listed on the New York Stock Exchange.

| | | | |
|---|---|---|---|
| iShares Russell 3000 (IWV) | 0.20 percent | 227 | 2.2B |

The Russell 3000 Index represents about 98 percent of the capitalization of all U.S. equities.

| | | | |
|---|---|---|---|
| iShares Russell 3000 Growth (IWZ) | 0.25 percent | 33 | 225 |

About half of the 3000 Index; companies with relatively high price-to-book ratios and higher forecasted growth.

| | | | |
|---|---|---|---|
| iShares Russell 3000 Value (IWW) | 0.25 percent | 34 | 448 |

The other half; companies with relatively low price-to-book ratios and lower forecasted growth.

| | | | |
|---|---|---|---|
| iShares S&P 1500 (ISI) | 0.20 percent | 18 | 153 |

The S&P 500, MidCap 400, and SmallCap 600 Indexes combined.

| | | | |
|---|---|---|---|
| streetTRACKS DJ Wilshire Total Market (TMW) | 0.20 percent | 4 | 96 |

The Dow Jones Wilshire Index contains more than 5,000 stocks. To reduce costs and portfolio turnover, the fund contains only 915 stocks. It uses quantitative analysis to find a representative sample.

| | | | |
|---|---|---|---|
| Vanguard Total Stock Market ETF (VTI) | 0.07 percent | 224 | 5.6B |

About 1,250 stocks representing about 95 percent of U.S. listed stocks. See Appendix B.

**Large Caps**

| | | | |
|---|---|---|---|
| Diamonds Trust Series I (DIA) | 0.18 percent | 7,492 | 6.3B |

Holds an equal number of shares of each of the 30 Dow Industrial stocks. Price weighted.

| | | | |
|---|---|---|---|
| Fidelity Nasdaq Composite Index (ONEQ) | 0.30 percent | 43 | 99 |

Tracks the 3,000 stocks traded on Nasdaq.

| | | | |
|---|---|---|---|
| First Trust Nasdaq-100 Equal Weight (QQEW) | 0.60 percent | 25 | 20 |

Unlike the Qubes (QQQQ), listed below, which is weighted by capitalization, the stocks in this fund (QQEW) are weighted equally, giving more impact to smaller companies.

| | | | |
|---|---|---|---|
| iShares Morningstar Large Core (JKD) | 0.20 percent | 7 | 95 |

See Appendix B re Morningstar.

| | | | |
|---|---|---|---|
| iShares Morningstar Large Growth (JKE) | 0.25 percent | 25 | 201 |

See Appendix B re Morningstar.

| | Expense Ratio | Average Daily Vol. (thousands) | Net Assets, $ (millions) |
|---|---|---|---|
| iShares Morningstar Large Value Index (JKF) | 0.25 percent | 59 | 237 |

See Appendix B re Morningstar.

| | | | |
|---|---|---|---|
| iShares NYSE 100 (NY) | 0.20 percent | 83 | 318 |

The index measures the performance of the 100 largest U.S. companies listed on the New York Stock Exchange.

| | | | |
|---|---|---|---|
| iShares Russell 1000 (IWB) | 0.15 percent | 225 | 2.7B |

The 1,000 largest companies in the Russell 3000 Index, representing 92 percent of the capitalization of all publicly traded U.S. equities.

| | | | |
|---|---|---|---|
| iShares Russell 1000 Growth (IWF) | 0.20 percent | 840 | 5.4B |

About half of the 1,000 index; companies with higher price-to-book ratios and higher forecasted growth.

| | | | |
|---|---|---|---|
| iShares Russell 1000 Value (IWD) | 0.20 percent | 897 | 6.9B |

The other half; companies with lower price-to-book ratios and lower forecasted growth.

| | | | |
|---|---|---|---|
| iShares S&P 500 (IVV) | 0.09 percent | 1,074 | 16.9B |

Like Spiders, this fund tracks the S&P 500 Index. Unlike Spiders, it uses a representative strategy and has lower operating fees.

| | | | |
|---|---|---|---|
| iShares S&P 500 Growth (IVW) | 0.18 percent | 283 | 3.4B |

Companies in the S&P 500 with the highest price-to-book ratios. This fund represents about half of the capitalization of the S&P 500 Index.

| | | | |
|---|---|---|---|
| iShares S&P 500 Value (IVE) | 0.18 percent | 299 | 3.4B |

The other half of the S&P 500—that is, the companies with the lowest price-to-book ratios.

| | | | |
|---|---|---|---|
| iShares S&P 100 (OEF) | 0.20 percent | 486 | 1.7B |

Tracks the 100 largest companies in the S&P 500 Index.

| | | | |
|---|---|---|---|
| Merrill Lynch Market 2000+ HOLDRs (MKH) | n/a | 1 | — |

As of July 7, 2000, when this HOLDR was launched, it contained the 50 largest U.S. companies. The fund now has 55 issues. See Appendix B.

| | | | |
|---|---|---|---|
| Nasdaq-100 Index Tracking Stock (QQQQ) | 0.20 percent | 122,041 | 17.4B |

The world's most actively traded security. It tracks Nasdaq's 100 largest nonfinancial stocks.

| | | | |
|---|---|---|---|
| ProShares Ultra Dow 30 (DDM) | 0.95 percent | 119 | — |

The Dow 30 stocks with twice the leverage. If the Dow falls by 3 percent, the fund falls by 6 percent.

| | Expense Ratio | Average Daily Vol. *(thousands)* | Net Assets, $ *(millions)* |
|---|---|---|---|
| ProShares Ultra QQQ (QLD) | 0.95 percent | 247 | — |
| Qubes with twice the leverage. | | | |
| ProShares Ultra S&P 500 (SSO) | 0.95 percent | 107 | — |
| The S&P 500 with twice the leverage. | | | |
| Rydex Russell Top 50 (XLG) | 0.20 percent | 28 | 158 |
| The 50 largest U.S. companies, weighted by capitalization. | | | |
| Rydex S&P Equal Weight Trust (RSP) | 0.40 percent | 437 | 1.6B |
| The S&P 500 stocks, weighted equally and rebalanced quarterly. | | | |
| Rydex S&P 500 Pure Growth (RPG) | 0.35 percent | 6 | 16 |
| About 140 growth stocks from the S&P 500 Index. | | | |
| Rydex S&P 500 Pure Value (RPV) | 0.35 percent | 8 | 14 |
| About 150 value stocks from the S&P 500 Index. | | | |
| SPDR Trust Series I (SPY) | 0.10 percent | 82,357 | 56.5B |
| The first ETF, called "Spiders," and described at length in Chapter 6. Tracks the famous S&P 500 Index. | | | |
| streetTRACKS DJ Wilshire Large Cap (ELR) | 0.20 percent | 4 | 6 |
| Out of the 5,000 stocks in the DJ Wilshire Total Market Index, this index and the fund itself both hold about 750 stocks, which are considered large cap. | | | |
| streetTRACKS DJ Wilshire Large Cap Growth (ELG) | 0.20 percent | 17 | 140 |
| The breakdown between growth and value is based on the projected P/E ratios, projected earnings growth, price-to-book ratios, dividend yield, trailing revenues, and trailing earnings growth. | | | |
| streetTRACKS DJ Wilshire Large Cap Value (ELV) | 0.20 percent | 8 | 105 |
| See the growth segment just above. | | | |
| Vanguard Large-Cap ETF (VV) | 0.07 percent | 51 | 379 |
| Tracks the MSCI US Prime Market 750 Index of large stocks. See Appendix B. | | | |
| Vanguard Growth ETF (VUG) | 0.11 percent | 76 | 688 |
| Tracks the MSCI US Prime Market Growth Index of large growth stocks. See Appendix B. | | | |
| Vanguard Value ETF (VTV) | 0.11 percent | 64 | 902 |
| Tracks the MSCI US Prime Market Value Index of large value stocks. See Appendix B. | | | |

| | Expense Ratio | Average Daily Vol. *(thousands)* | Net Assets, $ *(millions)* |
|---|---|---|---|
| **Mid-Caps** | | | |
| iShares Morningstar Mid Core (JKG) | 0.25 percent | 9 | 98 |
| See Morningstar in Appendix B. | | | |
| iShares Morningstar Mid Growth (JKH) | 0.30 percent | 31 | 172 |
| See Morningstar in Appendix B. | | | |
| iShares Morningstar Mid Value (JKI) | 0.30 percent | 6 | 105 |
| See Morningstar in Appendix B. | | | |
| iShares Russell MidCap (IWR) | 0.20 percent | 167 | 2.2B |
| The 800 smallest companies in the Russell 1000 Index, representing 29 percent of the capitalization thereof. | | | |
| iShares Russell MidCap Growth (IWP) | 0.25 percent | 115 | 1.3B |
| Approximately 42 percent of the capitalization of the Russell Midcap Index; companies with higher price-to-book ratios and higher forecasted growth. | | | |
| iShares Russell MidCap Value (IWS) | 0.25 percent | 136 | 2.2B |
| Approximately 58 percent of the capitalization of the Russell Midcap Index; companies with lower price-to-book ratios and lower forecasted growth. | | | |
| iShares S&P MidCap 400 (IJH) | 0.20 percent | 326 | 3.7B |
| The 400 mid-cap companies among U.S. equities. | | | |
| iShares S&P MidCap 400 Growth (IJK) | 0.25 percent | 208 | 1.6B |
| About half of the 400 Index—companies with the highest price-to-book ratios. | | | |
| iShares S&P MidCap 400 Value (IJJ) | 0.25 percent | 200 | 2.3B |
| The other half—companies with the lowest price-to-book ratios. | | | |
| ProShares Ultra MidCap 400 (MVV) | 0.95 percent | 63 | — |
| The S&P MidCap 400 with double the leverage. If the index falls by 5 percent, the fund would fall by 10 percent. | | | |
| Rydex S&P MidCap 400 Pure Growth (RFG) | 0.35 percent | 3 | 21 |
| About 100 growth stocks from the S&P MidCap 400. | | | |

|  | Expense Ratio | Average Daily Vol. (thousands) | Net Assets, $ (millions) |
|---|---|---|---|
| Rydex S&P MidCap 400 Pure Value (RPV) | 0.35 percent | 8 | 14 |
| About 110 value stocks from the S&P 500 Index. | | | |
| SPDR MidCap Trust Series I (MDY) | 0.25 percent | 3,086 | 8.6B |
| Tracks the S&P MidCap 400 Index. Both the index and the fund contain 400 stocks. | | | |
| streetTRACKS DJ Wilshire Mid Cap (EMM) | 0.25 percent | 3 | 15 |
| Out of 5,000 stocks in the Wilshire Composite Index, stocks ranked 500 to 1,000 in capitalization are considered mid-caps. | | | |
| streetTRACKS DJ Wilshire Mid Cap Growth (EMG) | 0.25 percent | 814 | 19.5B |
| The 500 mid-caps are divided about equally between growth and value. See the Wilshire DJ Large Cap Growth (ELG) above for the six factors in making the division. | | | |
| streetTRACKS DJ Wilshire Mid Cap Value (EMV) | 0.25 percent | 1 | 8.1B |
| See the Mid-Cap Growth just above. | | | |
| Vanguard Extended Market ETF (VXF) | 0.08 percent | 40 | 443 |
| About 1,200 U.S.-listed stocks except the S&P 500 Index stocks. Small and midsized stocks. See Appendix B. | | | |
| Vanguard Mid-Cap ETF (VO) | 0.13 percent | 70 | 1.3B |
| Tracks the MSCI US Mid Cap 450 Index. See Appendix B. | | | |
| Vanguard Mid-Cap Growth ETF (VOT) | 0.13 percent | 4 | — |
| Tracks the MSCI US Mid Cap Growth Index. Started August 2006. See Appendix B. | | | |
| Vanguard Mid-Cap Value ETF (VOE) | 0.13 percent | 7 | — |
| Tracks the MSCI US Mid Cap Value Index. Started August 2006. See Appendix B. | | | |

## Small Caps

| | | | |
|---|---|---|---|
| iShares Morningstar Small Core (JKJ) | 0.25 percent | 23 | 100 |
| See Morningstar in Appendix B. | | | |

|  | Expense Ratio | Average Daily Vol. (*thousands*) | Net Assets, $ (*millions*) |
|---|---|---|---|
| iShares Morningstar Small Growth (JKK) | 0.30 percent | 19 | 50 |

See Morningstar in Appendix B.

| iShares Morningstar Small Value (JKL) | 0.30 percent | 15 | 81 |
|---|---|---|---|

See Morningstar in Appendix B.

| iShares Russell 2000 (IWM) | 0.20 percent | 61,050 | 10.3B |
|---|---|---|---|

The 2,000 smallest companies in the Russell 3000 Index, representing about 8 percent of the capitalization thereof. Reconstituted annually. See toward the end of Chapter 6.

| iShares Russell 2000 Growth (IWO) | 0.25 percent | 2,120 | 2.5B |
|---|---|---|---|

About half of the 2000 Index; companies with higher price-to-book ratios and higher forecasted growth.

| iShares Russell 2000 Value (IWN) | 0.25 percent | 1,288 | 3.4B |
|---|---|---|---|

The other half; companies with lower price-to-book ratios and lower forecasted growth.

| iShares S&P SmallCap 600 (IJR) | 0.20 percent | 1,451 | 4.7B |
|---|---|---|---|

600 small-cap stocks.

| iShares SmallCap 600 Growth (IJT) | 0.25 percent | 103 | 1.3B |
|---|---|---|---|

About half of the 600 Index—companies with the higher price-to-book ratios.

| iShares SmallCap 600 Value (IJS) | 0.25 percent | 177 | 1.7B |
|---|---|---|---|

The other half—companies with the lowest price-to-book ratios.

| Rydex S&P SmallCap 600 Pure Growth (RZG) | 0.35 percent | 5 | 4 |
|---|---|---|---|

About 140 growth stocks from the S&P Small Cap 600 index.

| Rydex S and P SmallCap 600 Pure Value (RZV) | 0.35 percent | 2 | 6 |
|---|---|---|---|

About 180 value stocks from the S&P Small Cap 600 index.

| streetTRACKS DJ Wilshire SmallCap (DSC) | 0.25 percent | 9 | 25 |
|---|---|---|---|

Out of the 5,000 stocks in the Wilshire Composite, the 1,750 ranked in size from 751 to 2,500 are considered small caps. Both the index and the fund contain approximately that number. They are reconstituted quarterly.

| streetTRACKS DJ Wilshire SmallCap Growth (DSG) | 0.25 percent | 11 | 20 |
|---|---|---|---|

See the Wilshire big cap breakdown between growth and value for the factors in making the division.

| | Expense Ratio | Average Daily Vol. *(thousands)* | Net Assets, $ *(millions)* |
|---|---|---|---|
| streetTRACKS DJ Wilshire SmallCap Value (DSV) | 0.25 percent | 12 | 99 |

See the Wilshire big-cap breakdown between growth and value for the factors in making the division.

| | | | |
|---|---|---|---|
| Vanguard Small-Cap ETF (VB) | 0.10 percent | 68 | 492 |

Tracks the MSCI US Small Cap 1750 Index. See Appendix B.

| | | | |
|---|---|---|---|
| Vanguard Small-Cap Growth ETF (VBK) | 0.12 percent | 65 | 394 |

Tracks the MSCI US Small Cap Growth Index of small growth stocks. See Appendix B.

| | | | |
|---|---|---|---|
| Vanguard Small-Cap Value ETF (VBR) | 0.12 percent | 33 | 306 |

Tracks the MSCI US Small Cap Value Index of small value stocks. See Appendix B.

## Micro-Caps

| | | | |
|---|---|---|---|
| First Trust Dow Jones Select MicroCap (FDM) | 0.60 percent | 45 | 19 |

Selects U.S. micro-capitalization companies from all common stocks traded on the NYSE, Amex, and Nasdaq that are comparatively liquid and have relatively strong fundamentals. The prospectus spells out the rules.

| | | | |
|---|---|---|---|
| iShares Russell Microcap (IWC) | 0.60 percent | 122 | 219 |

Securities having the highest historical trading volumes among the companies included in the Russell Microcap Index. Capitalizations currently range from $50 million to $550 million.

## Social

| | | | |
|---|---|---|---|
| iShares KLD Select Social Index (KLD) | 0.50 percent | 29 | 107 |

Large-cap companies from the Russell 1000 and S&P 500 Indexes are scored by KLD as to their positive social and environmental characteristics. Companies with higher scores have greater representation in the index. Tobacco companies are excluded altogether.

## Aerospace and Defense

| | | | |
|---|---|---|---|
| iShares DJ U.S. Aerospace and Defense (ITA) | 0.48 percent | 30 | 66 |

Measures the performance of the aerospace and defense sector of the U.S. equity market.

| | | | |
|---|---|---|---|
| SPDR Aerospace and Defense (XAR) | 0.35 percent | — | — |

The stocks are weighted equally and rebalanced quarterly.

|  | Expense Ratio | Average Daily Vol. (thousands) | Net Assets, $ (millions) |
|---|---|---|---|

## Biotech

iShares Nasdaq Biotechnology (IBB)  0.48 percent  1,446  1.6B

The Nasdaq Biotechnology Index is one of 8 subindexes of the Nasdaq Composite, which measures all common stocks listed on the the Nasdaq Stock Market.

Merrill Lynch Biotech
HOLDRs (BBH)  n/a  478  —

18 companies. See Appendix B.

SPDR Biotech (XBI)  0.35 percent  17  43

The stocks are weighted equally and rebalanced quarterly.

## Broker-Dealers

iShares DJ U.S. Broker-
Dealers (IAI)  0.48 percent  149  45

The investment services sector of U.S. equities.

## Construction

iShares DJ US Home
Construction (ITB)  0.48 percent  44  30

Constructors of residential homes, including mobile and prefabricated homes.

SPDR Homebuilders (XHB)  0.35 percent  796  151

The stocks are weighted equally and rebalanced quarterly.

## Consumer

iShares DJ US ConsumerGoods
Sector (IYK)  0.48 percent  42  318

Includes automobiles and parts, beverages, food producers, household goods, leisure goods, personal goods, and tobacco.

iShares DJ US ConsumerServices
Sector (IYC)  0.48 percent  46  209

Includes food, drug, and general retailers, media, and travel and leisure.

Merrill Lynch Retail HOLDRs (RTH)  n/a  3,089  —

18 companies. See Appendix B.

Select Sector SPDR—Consumer
Discretion (XLY)  0.25 percent  1,111  490

Autos and components, household durables, apparel, hotels, restaurants, leisure, media, and retailing.

| | Expense Ratio | Average Daily Vol. (thousands) | Net Assets, $ (millions) |
|---|---|---|---|
| Select Sector SPDR—Consumer Staples (XLP) | 0.25 percent | 1,778 | 1.3B |
| Food and staples retailing, beverages, foods, tobacco, household and personal products. | | | |
| SPDR Retail (XRT) | 0.35 percent | 296 | 25 |
| Weighted equally and rebalanced quarterly. | | | |
| Vanguard Consumer Discretionary ETF (VCR) | 0.26 percent | 6 | 41 |
| Companies that tend to be the most sensitive to economic cycles. See Appendix B. | | | |
| Vanguard Consumer Staples ETF (VDC) | 0.26 percent | 27 | 155 |
| Companies that tend to be less sensitive to economic cycles. See Appendix B. | | | |

**Energy**

| | Expense Ratio | Average Daily Vol. (thousands) | Net Assets, $ (millions) |
|---|---|---|---|
| iShares DJ US Energy Sector (IYE) | 0.48 percent | 88 | 1.0B |
| Corresponds to the Dow Jones U.S. Oil and Gas Index. | | | |
| iShares DJ US Oil Equipment and Services (IEZ) | 0.48 percent | 15 | 24 |
| Suppliers of equipment or services to oil fields and offshore platforms. | | | |
| iShares DJ US Oil and Gas Exploration and Production (IEO) | 0.48 percent | 18 | 34 |
| Exploration, extraction, production, refining, and supply of oil and gas products. | | | |
| Merrill Lynch Market Oil Service HOLDRs (OIH) | n/a | 11,102 | n/a |
| 19 companies. See Appendix B. | | | |
| Select Sector SPDR Fund—Energy (XLE) | 0.24 percent | 22,023 | 4.3B |
| Oil, gas, and consumable fuels. Energy equipment and services. | | | |
| SPDR Oil and Gas Equipment and Services (XES) | 0.35 percent | 18 | 14 |
| Weighted equally and rebalanced quarterly. | | | |
| SPDR Oil and Gas Exploration and Production (XOP) | 0.35 percent | 24 | 20 |
| Weighted equally and rebalanced quarterly. | | | |
| Vanguard Energy ETF (VDE) | 0.26 percent | 42 | 347 |
| Energy-related equipment and services, especially for oil and gas. See Appendix B. | | | |

| | Expense Ratio | Average Daily Vol. (thousands) | Net Assets, $ (millions) |
|---|---|---|---|

**Finance**

iShares DJ US Financial Sector (IYF)    0.48 percent    24    419
Includes banks, insurance, real estate, and general finance.

iShares DJ US Financial Services Sector (IYG)    0.48 percent    12    224
Includes real estate and general finance.

iShares DJ US Regional Banks (IAT)    0.48 percent    12    37
Generally, banks whose three-year average of total assets are less than 5 percent of the three-year average of total assets held by all banks in the Dow Jones U.S. Bank Index.

Merrill Lynch Regional Bank HOLDRs (RKH)    n/a    586    —
20 companies. See Appendix B.

Select Sector SPDR Fund—Financial (XLF)    0.25 percent    8,041    2.1B
Commercial banks, capital markets, diversified financial services, insurance, and real estate.

SPDR KBW Mortgage Finance (KMF)    0.35 percent    —    —
Weighted equally and rebalanced quarterly.

StreetTRACKS KBW Regional Banking (KRE)    0.35 percent    257    49
Weighted equally and rebalanced quarterly.

streetTRACKS KBW Bank (KBE)    0.35 percent    193    86
Geographically diverse national money center and regional banks—24 in number.

streetTRACKS KBW Capital Markets (KCE)    0.35 percent    79    60
Broker-dealers, asset managers, trust and custody banks, and a stock exchange—24 stocks.

Vanguard Financials ETF (VFH)    0.26 percent    18    118
A full range of financial companies, including banks, brokers, insurance, and REITs. See Appendix B.

**Health**

First Trust Amex Biotechnology (FBT)    0.60 percent    20    30
An equal-weighted index of approximately 20 biotech companies, rebalanced quarterly.

| | Expense Ratio | Average Daily Vol. *(thousands)* | Net Assets, $ *(millions)* |
|---|---|---|---|
| iShares DJ US Healthcare Providers (IHF) | 0.48 percent | 28 | 35 |
| HMOs, hospitals, clinics, dentists, opticians, nursing homes, rehabilitation clinics, and retirement centers. | | | |
| iShares DJ US Healthcare Sector (IYH) | 0.48 percent | 109 | 1.2B |
| Health-care equipment and services, pharmaceuticals, and biotechnology. | | | |
| iShares DJ US Medical Devices (IHI) | 0.48 percent | 14 | 23 |
| Manufacturers and distributors of nondisposable medical devices. | | | |
| iShares DJ US Pharmaceuticals (IHE) | 0.48 percent | 11 | 37 |
| Manufacturers of prescription or over-the-counter drugs or vaccines, but excluding producers of vitamins. | | | |
| Merrill Lynch Pharmaceutical HOLDRs (PPH) | n/a | 713 | — |
| 20 companies. See Appendix B. | | | |
| Select Sector SPDR Fund— Health Care (XLV) | 0.24 percent | 1,051 | 1.9B |
| Health-care equipment and supplies, providers and services, biotechnology, and pharmaceuticals. | | | |
| SPDR Health Care Equipment (XHE) | 0.35 percent | — | — |
| Weighted equally and rebalanced quarterly. | | | |
| SPDR Health Care Services (XHS) | 0.35 percent | — | — |
| Weighted equally and rebalanced quarterly. | | | |
| SPDR Pharmaceuticals (XPH) | 0.35 percent | 11 | 16 |
| Weighted equally and rebalanced quarterly. | | | |
| Vanguard Health Care ETF (VHT) | 0.26 percent | 33 | 332 |
| Manufacturers and suppliers of health-care products and services, health-care facilities, pharmaceuticals, and biotech. See Appendix B. | | | |

## Industrial

| | Expense Ratio | Average Daily Vol. *(thousands)* | Net Assets, $ *(millions)* |
|---|---|---|---|
| iShares DJ US Industrial Sector (IYJ) | 0.48 percent | 40 | 306 |
| Construction and materials, aerospace and defense, general industrials, electronic and electrical equipment, industrial engineering, industrial transportation, and support services. | | | |

| | Expense Ratio | Average Daily Vol. (thousands) | Net Assets, $ (millions) |
|---|---|---|---|
| Select Sector SPDR Fund—Industrial (XLI) | 0.24 percent | 1,890 | 1.1B |

Aerospace and defense, building products, construction and engineering, electrical equipment, industrial conglomerates, machinery, commercial services and supplies, air frieight and logistics, airlines, road and rail and transportation infrastructure.

| | | | |
|---|---|---|---|
| Vanguard Industrials ETF (VIS) | 0.26 percent | 20 | 118 |

Providers of capital goods, commercial services and supplies, and transportation services. See Appendix B.

## Insurance

| | | | |
|---|---|---|---|
| iShares DJ US Insurance (IAK) | 0.48 percent | 9 | 24 |

Full-line insurance, brokers, property and casualty insurance, reinsurance, and life insurance.

| | | | |
|---|---|---|---|
| streetTRACKS KBW Insurance (KIE) | 0.35 percent | 63 | 41 |

24 stocks, representing all types of insurance companies.

## Materials

| | | | |
|---|---|---|---|
| iShares DJ US Basic Materials Sector (IYM) | 0.48 percent | 128 | 484 |

Includes chemicals, forestry and paper, industrial metals, and mining.

| | | | |
|---|---|---|---|
| Select Sector SPDR Fund—Materials (XLB) | 0.25 percent | 4,310 | 908 |

Chemicals, construction materials, containers and packaging, metals and mining, paper and forest products.

| | | | |
|---|---|---|---|
| Vanguard Materials (ETF) (VAW) | 0.26 percent | 12 | 93 |

Chemicals, construction materials, glass, paper, forest products, metals, minerals, mining, and steel. See Appendix B.

## Mining and Natural Resources

| | | | |
|---|---|---|---|
| iShares GoldmanSachs Natl Resource (IGE) | 0.48 percent | 101 | 1.5B |

U.S.-traded natural resource stocks, including mining, energy, timber, pulp and paper, and plantations.

| | | | |
|---|---|---|---|
| SPDR Metals and Mining (XME) | 0.35 percent | 28 | 27 |

Weighted equally and rebalanced quarterly.

|  | Expense Ratio | Average Daily Vol. *(thousands)* | Net Assets, $ *(millions)* |
|---|---|---|---|

## Precious Metals

### iShares COMEX Gold Trust (IAU) — 0.40 percent — 191 — 857

COMEX stands for the Commodity Exchange in New York, where gold futures contracts are traded. The ETF is priced at roughly 1/10 of the price of gold. The NAV is valued on the basis of the COMEX settlement price for the futures contract closest to maturity. Authorized participants who redeem shares receive gold in exchange. Operating costs are covered by the sale of gold. See Appendix B.

### iShares Silver Trust (SLV) — 0.50 percent — 421 — 1.1B

The NAV is based on the price of silver at the latest London Fix. Realized gains are taxed as "collectibles," subject to the maximum rate of 28 percent if held over a year.

### streetTRACKS Gold Shares (GLD) — 0.40 percent — 6,615 — 7.8B

Similar to IAU (two items above), except that the gold is valued according to the London PM Gold Fix. See Appendix B. Realized gains are taxed as "collectibles," subject to the maximum rate of 28 percent if held for more than a year.

## Real Estate

### iShares Cohen and Steers Realty Majors (ICF) — 0.35 percent — 240 — 2.3B

Relatively large and liquid REITs that may benefit from future consolidation and securitization of the U.S. real estate industry.

### iShares DJ US Real Estate (IYR) — 0.48 percent — 2,091 — 1.8B

Real estate holding and development companies and REITs.

### streetTRACKS DJ Wilshire REIT (RWR) — 0.25 percent — 87 — 1.1B

Virtually all publicly traded REITs that own and operate commercial real estate.

### Vanguard REIT ETF (VNQ) — 0.12 percent — 85 — 1.4B

The MSCI REIT Index represents a broadly diversified range of property types. See Appendix B.

## Technology

### First Trust Dow Jones Internet (FDN) — 0.60 percent — 11 — 28

Currently about 40 stocks drawn from the Dow Jones U.S. Index whose revenues are at least 50 percent derived from Internet commerce or services.

### First Trust Nasdaq-100 Technology Sector (QTEC) — 0.60 percent — 8 — —

From the Nasdaq-100 Index (the basis for Qubes), only the technology stocks are selected. In the index used here, the stocks are weighted equally, giving more importance to the smaller stocks.

|  | Expense Ratio | Average Daily Vol. (*thousands*) | Net Assets, $ (*millions*) |
|---|---|---|---|
| iShares DJ US Technology Sector (IYW) | 0.48 percent | 61 | 486 |

Software and computer services and technology hardware and equipment.

| iShares GoldmanSachs Networking (IGN) | 0.48 percent | 199 | 158 |
|---|---|---|---|

U.S.-traded multimedia networking stocks.

| iShares GoldmanSachs Semiconductor (IGW) | 0.48 percent | 166 | 264 |
|---|---|---|---|

U.S.-traded semiconductor stocks.

| iShares GoldmanSachs Software (IGV) | 0.48 percent | 82 | 81 |
|---|---|---|---|

U.S.-traded producers of software.

| iShares GoldmanSachs Technology (IGM) | 0.48 percent | 72 | 201 |
|---|---|---|---|

U.S.-traded technology stocks.

| Merrill Lynch B2B Internet HOLDRs (BHH) | — | 48 | — |
|---|---|---|---|

Six companies. ("B2B" means "business-to-business.") At the peak in 2000, the price reached 112. Two years later it was only 1.30 and is now 1.99. So much for investment fads. See Appendix B.

| Merrill Lynch Broadband HOLDRs (BDH) | — | 73 | — |
|---|---|---|---|

22 companies. See Appendix B.

| Merrill Lynch Internet Architecture HOLDRs (IAH) | — | 20 | — |
|---|---|---|---|

20 companies. See Appendix B.

| Merrill Lynch Internet HOLDRs (HHH) | — | 258 | — |
|---|---|---|---|

12 companies. See Appendix B.

| Merrill Lynch Internet Infrastructure HOLDRs (IIH) | — | 137 | — |
|---|---|---|---|

11 companies. See Appendix B.

| Merrill Lynch Semiconductors HOLDRs (SMH) | — | 15,928 | — |
|---|---|---|---|

20 companies. See Appendix B.

|  | Expense Ratio | Average Daily Vol. *(thousands)* | Net Assets, $ *(millions)* |
|---|---|---|---|
| Merrill Lynch Software HOLDRs (SWH) | — | 161 | — |
| 14 companies. See Appendix B. | | | |
| Select Sector SPDR Fund—Technology (XLK) | 0.25 percent | 1,442 | 1.4B |
| Internet software and services, IT services, software, communications equipment, computers and peripherals, electronic equipment and instruments, office electronics, semiconductors and semiconductor equipment, diversified telecommunications services, and wireless telecommunications services. | | | |
| SPDR Computer Hardware (XHW) | 0.35 percent | — | — |
| Weighted equally and rebalanced quarterly. | | | |
| SPDR Computer Software (STW) | 0.35 percent | — | — |
| Weighted equally and rebalanced quarterly. | | | |
| SPDR Outsourcing and IT Consulting (XOT) | 0.35 percent | — | — |
| Outsourcing and information technology consulting. The stocks are weighted equally. | | | |
| SPDR Semiconductor (XSD) | 0.35 percent | 58 | 51 |
| Weighted equally and rebalanced quarterly. | | | |
| streetTRACKS Morgan Stanley Technology (MTK) | 0.50 percent | 59 | 135 |
| Computer software and hardware, semiconductors, communications, data processing, and other technologies. | | | |
| Vanguard Information Technology ETF (VGT) | 0.26 percent | 24 | 151 |
| A broad range, including software and services, technology hardware and equipment, and semiconductors. See Appendix B. | | | |

**Telecommunications**

| | | | |
|---|---|---|---|
| iShares DJ US Telecommunications (IYZ) | 0.48 percent | 315 | 705 |
| Fixed-line and mobile telecommunications. | | | |
| Merrill Lynch Telecom HOLDRs (TTH) | — | 212 | — |
| 12 companies. See Appendix B. | | | |

| | Expense Ratio | Average Daily Vol. *(thousands)* | Net Assets, $ *(millions)* |
|---|---|---|---|
| Merrill Lynch Wireless HOLDRs (WMH) | — | 15 | — |
| 18 companies. See Appendix B. | | | |
| SPDR Telecom (XTL) | 0.35 percent | — | — |
| Weighted equally and rebalanced quarterly. | | | |
| Vanguard Telecommunications ETF (VOX) | 0.26 percent | 43 | 108 |
| Communications services via fixed-line, cellular, wireless, high-bandwidth, fiber-optic cables. See Appendix B. | | | |

**Transportation**

| | | | |
|---|---|---|---|
| iShares DJ Transportion Average (IYT) | 0.48 percent | 857 | 441 |
| Corresponds to the price and yield performace of the Dow Jones Transportation Average. | | | |
| SPDR Transportation (XTN) | 0.35 percent | — | — |
| Weighted equally and rebalanced quarterly. | | | |

**Utilities**

| | | | |
|---|---|---|---|
| iShares DJ US Utilities Sector (IDU) | 0.48 percent | 87 | 704 |
| Electricity and gas, water, and multiutilities. | | | |
| Merrill Lynch Utilities HOLDRs (UTH) | — | 284 | — |
| 19 companies. See Appendix B. | | | |
| Select Sector SPDR Fund—Utilities (XLU) | 0.25 percent | 3,477 | 2.7B |
| Electric and gas utilities, multiutilities, and independent power producers and energy traders. | | | |
| Vanguard Utilities ETF (VPU) | 0.26 percent | 22 | 121 |
| Electricity, gas, and water. See Appendix B. | | | |

**Global (U.S. and Foreign Stocks Combined)**

| | | | |
|---|---|---|---|
| iShares S&P Global 100 (IOO) | 0.40 percent | 30 | 512 |
| The world's 100 largest multinational businesses, screened for sector representation, liquidity, and size. Adjusted to reflect shares available to foreign investors. | | | |

| | Expense Ratio | Average Daily Vol. *(thousands)* | Net Assets, $ *(millions)* |
|---|---|---|---|
| streetTRACKS DJ Global Titans (DGT) | 0.50 percent | 11 | 90 |

Tracks the Dow Jones Global 50 Index, generally "the biggest of the big." Both the index and the fund contain 50 stocks.

## Global Industry

*(Note: All five of these ETFs are subsets of the S&P Global 1200 Index.)*

| | | | |
|---|---|---|---|
| iShares S&P Global Energy (IXC) | 0.65 percent | 30 | 753 |

Producers and refiners of oil.

| | | | |
|---|---|---|---|
| iShares S&P Global Financial (IXG) | 0.65 percent | 17 | 172 |

Banks, finance, insurance, real estate, S&Ls, and securities brokers.

| | | | |
|---|---|---|---|
| iShares S&P Global Healthcare (IXJ) | 0.65 percent | 109 | 545 |

Health-care providers, biotech, medical supplies, and pharmaceuticals.

| | | | |
|---|---|---|---|
| iShares S&P Global Info Technology (IXN) | 0.65 percent | 17 | 101 |

Development and production of technology products.

| | | | |
|---|---|---|---|
| iShares S&P Global Telecommunications (IXP) | 0.65 percent | 13 | 86 |

Communication companies and carriers.

## Foreign—Broad Based

| | | | |
|---|---|---|---|
| iShares MSCI—EAFE (EFA) | 0.35 percent | 4,049 | 29.3B |

See Appendix B re MSCI and EAFE.

| | | | |
|---|---|---|---|
| iShares MSCI—EAFE Growth (EFG) | 0.40 percent | 40 | 247 |

See Appendix B re MSCI and EAFE.

| | | | |
|---|---|---|---|
| iShares MSCI—EAFE Value (EFV) | 0.40 percent | 60 | 353 |

See Appendix B re MSCI and EAFE.

## Foreign—Regional

| | | | |
|---|---|---|---|
| BLDRS Asia 50 ADR (ADRA) | 0.30 percent | 36 | 101 |

50 actively traded Asian stocks having free-float capitalization of $5 billion to over $140 billion.

| | Expense Ratio | Average Daily Vol. *(thousands)* | Net Assets, \$ *(millions)* |
|---|---|---|---|
| **BLDRS Developed Markets 100 ADR (ADRD)** | 0.30 percent | 20 | 64 |
| 100 actively traded stocks from non-U.S. developed markets having free-float capitalization of \$10 billion to over \$260 billion. | | | |
| **BLDRS Emerging Markets 50 ADR (ADRE)** | 0.30 percent | 425 | 288 |
| 50 actively traded emerging market stocks having free-float capitalization of \$3 billion to over \$30 billion. | | | |
| **BLDRS Europe 100 ADR (ADRU)** | 0.30 percent | 13 | 24 |
| 100 actively traded European stocks having free-float capitalizations of \$5 billion to over \$260 billion. | | | |
| **Claymore/BNY Bric (n/a)** | — | — | — |
| Currently 75 U.S.-traded ADRs of companies from Brazil, Russia, India, and China. | | | |
| **iShares MSCI—Emerging Markets (EEM)** | 0.75 percent | 6,865 | 12.0B |
| Includes the stocks of 26 countries. | | | |
| **iShares MSCI—EMU (EZU)** | 0.59 percent | 110 | 1.7B |
| The European Monetary Union currently consists of 11 countries: Austria, Belgium, Finland, France, Germany, Greece, Ireland, Italy, the Netherlands, Portugal, and Spain. | | | |
| **iShares MSCI—Pacific ex-Japan (EPP)** | 0.50 percent | 147 | 2.0B |
| Australia, Hong Kong, New Zealand, and Singapore. | | | |
| **iShares S&P Europe 350 (IEV)** | 0.60 percent | 196 | 1.7B |
| 350 leading companies of Europe. | | | |
| **iShares S&P Latin America 40 (ILF)** | 0.50 percent | 319 | 1.2B |
| 40 leading companies of Mexico, Brazil, Argentina, and Chile. | | | |
| **Merrill Lynch Europe 2001 HOLDRs (EKH)** | n/a | 1 | — |
| 41 companies. See Appendix B. | | | |
| **streetTRACKS DJ STOXX 50 (FEU)** | 0.32 percent | 15 | 35 |
| 50 large stocks, pan-European. | | | |
| **streetTRACKS DJ Euro STOXX 50 (FEZ)** | 0.32 percent | 112 | 212 |
| 50 large European stocks, excluding those Denmark, Norway, Sweden, Switzerland, and the United Kingdom. | | | |

| | Expense Ratio | Average Daily Vol. *(thousands)* | Net Assets, $ *(millions)* |
|---|---|---|---|
| Vanguard European ETF (VGK) | 0.18 percent | 108 | 724 |

594 stocks from 16 European nations. See Appendix B.

| | | | |
|---|---|---|---|
| Vanguard Pacific ETF (VPL) | 0.18 percent | 60 | 575 |

546 stocks from Japan, Australia, Hong Kong, Singapore, and New Zealand. Japan is 75 percent of the capitalization and Australia 16 percent. See Appendix B.

| | | | |
|---|---|---|---|
| Vanguard Emerging Market ETF (VWO) | 0.30 percent | 188 | 1.2B |

666 stocks from 18 emerging market nations. The largest are South Korea (20 percent), Taiwan (15 percent), and Brazil (12 percent). See Appendix B.

**Foreign—Individual Countries**

| | | | |
|---|---|---|---|
| iShares FTSE/Xinhua China 25 Index (FXI) | 0.74 percent | 623 | 2.9B |

FTSE is the trademark of the London Stock Exchange and the *Financial Times*. "Xinhua" is the trademark of Xinhua Financial News Network. These companies provide the index of 25 of the largest and most liquid Chinese companies, all of which trade on the Hong Kong Stock Exchange.

(*Note*: The MSCI index for each of the following nations "corresponds generally to the price and yield performance ... of publicly-traded securities" of that nation. See Appendix B re MSCI.):

| | | | |
|---|---|---|---|
| iShares MSCI—Australia (EWA) | 0.59 percent | 373 | 671 |
| iShares MSCI—Austria (EWO) | 0.59 percent | 205 | 397 |
| iShares MSCI—Belgium (EWK) | 0.59 percent | 66 | 128 |
| iShares MSCI—Brazil (EWZ) | 0.74 percent | 4,748 | 2.3B |
| iShares MSCI—Canada (EWC) | 0.59 percent | 503 | 1.1B |
| iShares MSCI—France (EWQ) | 0.59 percent | 161 | 169 |
| iShares MSCI—Germany (EWG) | 0.59 percent | 507 | 768 |
| iShares MSCI—Hong Kong (EWH) | 0.59 percent | 1,393 | 789 |
| iShares MSCI—Italy (EWI) | 0.59 percent | 75 | 141 |
| iShares MSCI—Japan (EWJ) | 0.59 percent | 21,702 | 13.5B |
| iShares MSCI—Malaysia (EWM) | 0.59 percent | 802 | 409 |
| iShares MSCI—Mexico (EWW) | 0.59 percent | 1,693 | 757 |
| iShares MSCI—Netherlands (EWN) | 0.59 percent | 56 | 108 |

|                                        | Expense Ratio | Average Daily Vol. (thousands) | Net Assets, $ (millions) |
|----------------------------------------|---------------|--------------------------------|--------------------------|
| iShares MSCI—Singapore (EWS)           | 0.59 percent  | 781                            | 577                      |
| iShares MSCI—South Africa (EZA)        | 0.74 percent  | 109                            | 298                      |
| iShares MSCI—South Korea (EWY)         | 0.74 percent  | 1,212                          | 1,614                    |
| iShares MSCI—Spain (EWP)               | 0.59 percent  | 58                             | 156                      |
| iShares MSCI—Sweden (EWD)              | 0.59 percent  | 101                            | 148                      |
| iShares MSCI—Switzerland (EWL)         | 0.59 percent  | 97                             | 186                      |
| iShares MSCI—Taiwan (EWT)              | 0.74 percent  | 2,682                          | 1,871                    |
| iShares MSCI—United Kingdom (EWU)      | 0.59 percent  | 311                            | 861                      |
| iShares S&P TOPIX 150 (ITF)            | 0.50 percent  | 25                             | 305                      |

150 companies that make up 70 percent of the Japanese market. "TOPIX" stands for the Tokyo Stock Price Index.

| Merrill Lynch Canada CP HOLDRs (HCH)   | —             | 723                            | —                        |

Five Canadian companies. See Appendix B.

**Fixed Income**

| iShares Lehman 1–3 Year Treasury Bonds (SHY) | 0.15 percent | 658 | 5.1B |

Currently 36 issues with remaining maturities of one to three years. See Appendix B re Lehman Brothers.

| iShares Lehman 7–10 Year Treasury Bonds (IEF) | 0.15 percent | 194 | 1.6B |

Currently 20 issues with remaining maturities of 7 to 10 years. See Appendix B.

| iShares Lehman 20+ Year Treasury Bonds (TLT) | 0.15 percent | 918 | 1.5B |

Currently 12 issues with remaining maturities of 20 years or more. See Appendix B.

| iShares Lehman TIPS Bond (TIP) | 0.20 percent | 196 | 4.2B |

See Chapter 6 re TIPS. All TIPS with remaining maturities of one year or more are held (currently 18 issues).

| iShares Lehman Aggregate Bond (AGG) | 0.20 percent | 235 | 3.9B |

A curiosity; see Appendix B.

| | Expense Ratio | Average Daily Vol. *(thousands)* | Net Assets, $ *(millions)* |
|---|---|---|---|
| iShares GS $ InvesTop Corporate Bond (LQD) | 0.15 percent | 110 | 2.5B |

The Goldman Sachs index contains 100 highly liquid corporate bonds of companies of several nations. See Appendix B re Goldman Sachs.

# Fundamental ETFs

All of the following funds are weighted by fundamentals. The most weight is given to the stocks that best meet fundamental standards, as measured by proprietary methods. "Proprietary" means the company doesn't disclose exactly how they do it.

## Total Market

| | | | |
|---|---|---|---|
| PowerShares FTSE RAFI US 1000 (PRF) | 0.60 percent | 46 | 166 |

The 1,000 largest U.S. equities, weighted by analysis of sales and earnings, book value, cash flow, and dividends. FTSI is the London Stock Exchange. RAFI is Research Affiliates, a U.S. company.

| | | | |
|---|---|---|---|
| PowerShares ValueLine Timeliness Select Portfolio (PIV) | 0.60 percent | 143 | 185 |

50 stocks with potential to outperform the U.S. equity market, weighted equally and rebalanced quarterly.

## Large Caps

| | | | |
|---|---|---|---|
| Claymore/Zacks Sector Rotation n/a | — | — | — |

About 100 stocks selected from a universe of 1,000 largest listed equities. Quantitative methodology used to overweight sectors with potentially superior risk-return profiles.

| | | | |
|---|---|---|---|
| PowerShares Dynamic Market Portfolio (PWC) | 0.60 percent | 97 | — |

100 companies selected quarterly by complex fundamental factors from the 2,000 largest U.S. stocks.

| | | | |
|---|---|---|---|
| PowerShares Dynamic OTC Portfolio (PWO) | 0.60 percent | 22 | — |

100 companies selected quarterly by fundamental factors from Nasdaq stocks.

| | Expense Ratio | Average Daily Vol. *(thousands)* | Net Assets, $ *(millions)* |
|---|---|---|---|
| PowerShares Dynamic Large Cap Growth (PWB) | 0.60 percent | 102 | 145 |
| 50 large-cap growth companies selected for appreciation potential. | | | |
| PowerShares Dynamic Large Cap Value (PWV) | 0.60 percent | 78 | 124 |
| 50 large-cap value companies selected for appreciation potential. | | | |
| WisdomTree LargeCap Dividend (DLN) | 0.28 percent | 34 | — |
| 300 dividend-paying, companies with the largest capitalizations, weighted by projected cash dividends. | | | |
| WisdomTree Top 100 (DTN) | 0.38 percent | 14 | — |
| 100 large-cap stocks weighted by dividend yields. | | | |

### Mid-Caps

| | | | |
|---|---|---|---|
| PowerShares Dynamic Mid Cap Growth (PWJ) | 0.60 percent | 36 | — |
| 75 mid-cap growth stocks, selected by their fundamentals. | | | |
| PowerShares Dynamic Mid Cap Value (PWP) | 0.60 percent | 20 | 55 |
| 75 mid-cap value stocks, selected by their fundamentals. | | | |
| WisdomTree MidCap Dividend (DON) | 0.38 percent | 8 | — |
| A dividend-weighted, mid-cap fund. REITs make up a relatively large portion. | | | |

### Small Caps

| | | | |
|---|---|---|---|
| First Trust IPOX-100 Index (FPX) | 0.60 percent | 12 | 22 |
| A rules-based, value-weighted index consisting of the 100 largest, best-performing, and most liquid IPOs from the 7th day after the IPO until the 1,000th day. As new stocks come in and others are moved out, the index is reconstituted regularly. | | | |
| PowerShares Dynamic Small Cap Growth (PWT) | 0.60 percent | 74 | — |
| 100 U.S. small-cap growth stocks selected for capital appreciation potential. | | | |
| PowerShares Dynamic Small Cap Value (PWY) | 0.60 percent | 36 | 63 |
| 100 U.S. small-cap value stocks selected for capital appreciation potential. | | | |

| | Expense Ratio | Average Daily Vol. *(thousands)* | Net Assets, $ *(millions)* |
|---|---|---|---|
| PowerShares Zacks Small Cap (PZJ) | 0.60 percent | 21 | 59 |

250 small-cap companies with superior risk-return profiles.

| | | | |
|---|---|---|---|
| WisdomTree SmallCap Dividend (DES) | 0.38 percent | 13 | — |

A dividend-weighted, small-cap fund. REITs comprise a relatively large portion.

**Micro-Caps**

| | | | |
|---|---|---|---|
| PowerShares Zacks Micro-Cap Portfolio (PZI) | 0.60 percent | 72 | — |

300 to 500 companies of approximately $58 million to $575 million, ranked high in terms of risk and reward.

**Dividend Based, General Market**

| | | | |
|---|---|---|---|
| Claymore/Zacks Yield Hog n/a | — | — | — |

125 to 150 stocks. Approximately half are in dividend-paying common stocks and ADRs. The rest are in REITs, master limited partnerships, closed-end funds, and traditional preferred stocks. Seeks high dividend yields and superior risk-return profiles to outperform the Dow Jones U.S. Select Dividend Index.

| | | | |
|---|---|---|---|
| First Trust Morningstar Dividend Leaders (FDL) | 0.45 percent | 10 | 32 |

The index consists of the top 100 stocks, based on the yield of qualified dividends, of the securities listed on NYSE, Amex, and Nasdaq, and selected by Morningstar's proprietary multistep screening process. The complex rules are spelled out in the prospectus.

| | | | |
|---|---|---|---|
| iShares DJ Select Dividend (DVY) | 0.40 percent | 336 | 6.6B |

The first dividend ETF, consisting of 100 of the highest dividend-yielding securities (excluding REITs) in the Dow Jones U.S. Total Market Index, selected according to various characteristics. See Chapter 13.

| | | | |
|---|---|---|---|
| PowerShares Dividend Achievers (PFM) | 0.50 percent | 27 | 34 |

Currently 314 stocks selected principally on their consecutive years of dividend growth.

| | | | |
|---|---|---|---|
| PowerShares HighGrowth Dividend Achievers (PHJ) | 0.50 percent | 15 | 30 |

100 stocks selected on the highest growth rate of dividends.

| | | | |
|---|---|---|---|
| PowerShares HighYield Equity Div Achievers (PEY) | 0.50 percent | 137 | — |

50 stocks selected for dividend yield and consistent growth of dividends.

| | Expense Ratio | Average Daily Vol. (thousands) | Net Assets, $ (millions) |
|---|---|---|---|
| PowerShares International Dividend Achievers (PID) | 0.50 percent | 89 | 210 |

Currently 48 non-U.S. stocks with consistent growth of dividends over the last five years.

| | | | |
|---|---|---|---|
| streetTRACKS Dividend (SDY) | 0.30 percent | 18 | 112 |

50 of the highest dividend yielding stocks from the S&P Composite 1500 that have consistently increased dividends every year for at least 25 years. Weighted by dividend yield and rebalanced annually.

| | | | |
|---|---|---|---|
| Vanguard Dividend Appreciation ETF (VIG) | 0.28 percent | 22 | 49 |

Companies that have a record of increasing dividends over time.

| | | | |
|---|---|---|---|
| WisdomTree Total Dividend (DTD) | 0.28 percent | 10 | — |

A total market index for the dividend-paying segment of the U.S. market.

| | | | |
|---|---|---|---|
| WisdomTree High-Yielding Equity (DHS) | 0.38 percent | 11 | — |

Based on a dividend-weighted, U.S. multicapitalization index.

**Specialty**

| | | | |
|---|---|---|---|
| Claymore/Sabrient Insider | n/a | — | — |

About 100 U.S.-traded stocks and ADRs with superior risk-return profiles, especially those reflecting favorable insider buying trends and Wall Street analyst upgrades. Adjusted quarterly. Equal weighting.

| | | | |
|---|---|---|---|
| Claymore/Sabrient Stealth | n/a | — | — |

About 150 stocks, mostly small or microcap (under $1 billion), having superior risk-return profiles but little or no analyst coverage. See the end of Chapter 13.

| | | | |
|---|---|---|---|
| PowerShares WilderHill Clean Energy (PBW) | 0.60 percent | 364 | — |

Companies that focus on greener, more renewable sources of energy.

**Aerospace**

| | | | |
|---|---|---|---|
| PowerShares Aerospace and Defense (PPA) | 0.60 percent | 57 | 86 |

About 57 stocks regarding warfare and homeland security. Modified market capitalization, rebalanced quarterly.

**Construction**

| | | | |
|---|---|---|---|
| PowerShares Dynamic Building and Construction (PKB) | 0.60 percent | 26 | 10 |

30 stocks in the industry with the greatest potential for capital appreciation, rebalanced quarterly.

|  | Expense Ratio | Average Daily Vol. (thousands) | Net Assets, $ (millions) |
|---|---|---|---|

## Consumer

PowerShares Dynamic Food and
Beverage (PBJ) — 0.60 percent — 40 — —

30 stocks in the industry with the greatest potential for capital appreciation, rebalanced quarterly.

PowerShares Dynamic Leisure and
Entertain (PEJ) — 0.60 percent — 11 — —

30 stocks in the industry with the greatest potential for capital appreciation, rebalanced quarterly.

PowerShares Dynamic Media (PBS) — 0.60 percent — 10 — —

30 stocks in the industry with the greatest potential for capital appreciation, rebalanced quarterly.

PowerShares Dynamic
Retail (PMR) — 0.60 percent — 16 — 7

30 stocks in the industry with the greatest potential for capital appreciation, rebalanced quarterly.

PowerShares Dyn. Hardware
and Consumer Electronics (PHW) — 0.60 percent — 12 — 10

30 stocks in the industry with the greatest potential for capital appreciation, rebalanced quarterly.

## Energy

PowerShares Dyn. Energy
Exploration and Production (PXE) — 0.60 percent — 125 — —

30 stocks in the industry with the greatest potential for capital appreciation, rebalanced quarterly.

PowerShares Oil and Gas
Services (PXJ) — 0.60 percent — 243 — 347

30 stocks in the industry with the greatest potential for capital appreciation, rebalanced quarterly.

## Health

PowerShares Dynamic
Pharmaceuticals (PJP) — 0.60 percent — 73 — —

30 stocks in the industry with the greatest potential for capital appreciation, rebalanced quarterly.

PowerShares Dyn. Biotech and
Genome Portfolio (PBE) — 0.60 percent — 153 — —

30 stocks in the industry with the greatest potential for capital appreciation, rebalanced quarterly.

| | Expense Ratio | Average Daily Vol. (thousands) | Net Assets, $ (millions) |
|---|---|---|---|
| **Insurance** | | | |
| PowerShares Dynamic Insurance (PIC) | 0.60 percent | 13 | 30 |

30 stocks in the industry with the greatest potential for capital appreciation, rebalanced quarterly.

**Technology**

| | | | |
|---|---|---|---|
| PowerShares Dynamic Networking Portfolio (PXQ) | 0.60 percent | 14 | — |

30 stocks in the industry with the greatest potential for capital appreciation, rebalanced quarterly.

| | | | |
|---|---|---|---|
| PowerShares Dynamic Semiconductor Portfolio (PSI) | 0.60 percent | 100 | — |

30 stocks in the industry with the greatest potential for capital appreciation, rebalanced quarterly.

| | | | |
|---|---|---|---|
| PowerShares Dynamic Software Portfolio (PSJ) | 0.60 percent | 41 | — |

30 stocks in the industry with the greatest potential for capital appreciation, rebalanced quarterly.

| | | | |
|---|---|---|---|
| PowerShares Lux Nanotech (PXN) | 0.60 percent | 63 | 118 |

Currently 26 stocks, invested in microscopic robots, weighted equally and rebalanced quarterly.

**Telecommunications**

| | | | |
|---|---|---|---|
| PowerShares Dyn Telecommunications and Wireless (PTE) | 0.60 percent | 13 | 30 |

30 stocks in the industry with the greatest potential for capital appreciation; rebalanced quarterly.

**Utilities**

| | | | |
|---|---|---|---|
| PowerShares Dynamic Utilities (PUI) | 0.60 percent | 45 | 35 |

30 stocks in the industry with the greatest potential for capital appreciation; rebalanced quarterly.

| | | | |
|---|---|---|---|
| PowerShares Water Resources (PHO) | 0.60 percent | 443 | 938 |

Currently 25 U.S. stocks and ADRs with revenues at least 50 percent derived from water-related activities. Equal weighted; rebalanced quarterly.

|  | Expense Ratio | Average Daily Vol. *(thousands)* | Net Assets, $ *(millions)* |
|---|---|---|---|

## Global

Claymore/Robeco Developed
World Equity n/a                          —              —              —

A global fund. Same as just below, but includes U.S. stocks.

## Foreign—Broad Based

Claymore/Robeco Developed
International Equity n/a                   —              —              —

200 to 300 stocks from developed countries (excluding U.S.), selected by Robeco USA, LLC, to have liquidity, momentum, earnings estimate revisions, and management policies that offer the greatest potential for price appreciation. Rebalanced monthly.

## Foreign—Regional

WisdomTree DIEFA (DWM)          0.48 percent         3             —

"DIEFA" stands for WisdomTree's "Dividend Index of Europe, Far East Asia, and Australasia."

WisdomTree DIEFA High-
Yielding Equity (DTH)           0.58 percent         6             —

Especially high ielding stocks in DIEFA.

WisdomTree Europe
Total Dividend (DEB)            0.48 percent         1             —

Dividend payers from 16 European nations.

WisdomTree Europe
High-Yield Equity (DEW)         0.58 percent         5             —

High-yielders from the developed nations of Europe.

WisdomTree Europe
SmallCap Dividend (DFE)         0.58 percent         3             —

Dividend-weighted, small-caps from the dividend-paying segment of Western Europe.

WisdomTree Pacific ex-Japan
Total Dividend (DND)            0.48 percent         1             —

Dividend-weighted, multicap fund for the dividend-paying companies of Hong Kong, Singapore, Australia, and New Zealand.

WisdomTree Pacific ex-Japan
High-Yield Equity (DNH)         0.58 percent         3             —

High-yielders. Otherwise, the same as just above.

| | Expense Ratio | Average Daily Vol. *(thousands)* | Net Assets, $ *(millions)* |
|---|---|---|---|
| WisdomTree International LargeCap Dividend (DOL) | 0.48 percent | 6 | — |
| Dividend-weighted, large-cap fund for non-U.S. stocks. | | | |
| WisdomTree International Dividend Top 100 (DOO) | 0.58 percent | 8 | — |
| 100 largest-cap dividend yielders among non-U.S. companies. | | | |
| WisdomTree International MidCap Dividend (DIM) | 0.58 percent | 5 | — |
| Mid-cap dividend yielders among non-U.S. companies. | | | |
| WisdomTree International SmallCap Dividend (DLS) | 0.58 percent | 7 | — |
| Small-cap dividend yielders among non-U.S. companies | | | |

**Foreign—Individual Countries**

| | Expense Ratio | Average Daily Vol. *(thousands)* | Net Assets, $ *(millions)* |
|---|---|---|---|
| PowerShares Golden Dragon Halter USX China (PGJ) | 0.60 percent | 102 | 231 |
| Currently 38 U.S.-exchange-listed stocks deriving a majority of revenues from mainland China. The fund uses a modified market-capitalization methodology. | | | |
| WisdomTree Japan Total Dividend (DXJ) | 0.48 percent | 5 | — |
| Dividend-weighted, total market fund for the dividend-paying segment of Japan. | | | |
| WisdomTree Japan High-Yielding Equity (DNL) | 0.58 percent | 3 | — |
| Dividend-weighted, multicap fund of high-yielding Japanese stocks. | | | |
| WisdomTree Japan SmallCap Dividend (DFJ) | 0.58 percent | 110 | — |
| Dividend-weighted, small-cap fund of Japanese dividend payers. | | | |

# Short Sellers

## Large Caps

| | Expense Ratio | Average Daily Vol. *(thousands)* | Net Assets, $ *(millions)* |
|---|---|---|---|
| ProShares Short Dow 30 (DOG) | 0.95 percent | 67 | — |
| An inverse ETF. As the Dow 30 falls this fund rises (and vice versa). | | | |

| | Expense Ratio | Average Daily Vol. (*thousands*) | Net Assets, $ (*millions*) |
|---|---|---|---|
| ProShares Short QQQ (PSQ) | 0.95 percent | 124 | — |
| As the Nasdaq-100 falls, PSQ goes up. | | | |
| ProShares Short S&P 500 (SH) | 0.95 percent | 72 | — |
| As the S&P 500 falls, this fund rises. | | | |
| ProShares UltraShort Dow 30 (DXD) | 0.95 percent | 95 | — |
| Twice the inverse of the Dow 30. If the Dow falls by 1 percent, the DXD rises by 2 percent. | | | |
| ProShares UltraShort QQQ (QID) | 0.95 percent | 670 | — |
| Twice the inverse of the Qubes. | | | |
| ProShares UltraShort S&P 500 (SDS) | 0.95 percent | 180 | — |
| Twice the inverse of the S&P 500. | | | |
| **Mid-Caps** | | | |
| ProShares Short MidCap 400 (MYY) | 0.95 percent | 148 | — |
| As the S&P MidCap falls, this fund rises. | | | |
| ProShares UltraShort MidCap 400 (MZZ) | 0.95 percent | 96 | — |
| Twice the inverse of the S&P MidCap. If the index rises by 10 percent, this fund falls by 20 percent. | | | |

# Commodities and Foreign Currencies

| | | | |
|---|---|---|---|
| Claymore/MACROshares Oil Up Holding Shares n/a | — | — | — |
| Based not on futures contracts but on the price of West Texas Intermediate light sweet crude oil on the New York Mercantile Exchange. | | | |
| Claymore/MACROshares Oil Down Holding Shares n/a | — | — | — |
| Based not on futures contracts but on the *inverse* of the NvYMEX price of West Texas Intermediate light sweet crude oil. | | | |
| iPath GSCI Total Return Index ETN (GSP) | 0.75 percent | — | 56 |
| See iPath Appendix B. | | | |

| | Expense Ratio | Average Daily Vol. (thousands) | Net Assets, $ (millions) |
|---|---|---|---|
| iPathDowJones-AIG Commodity Index ETN (DJP) | 0.75 percent | — | 261 |
| See iPath Appendix B. | | | |
| iPath Goldman Sachs Crude Oil IndexETN (OIL) | 0.75 percent | — | 39 |
| See iPath in Appendix B. | | | |
| PowerShares DB Commodity Index Tracking Fund (DBC) | 0.83 percent | 312 | 608 |
| Purchases futures contracts to reflect the performance of the Deutsche Bank Liquid Commodity Index, which is composed of light sweet crude, heating oil, aluminum, gold, corn, and wheat. See Appendix B re commodities. | | | |
| Rydex Euro Currency Shares (FXE) | 0.40 percent | 117 | 646 |
| Based on the value of the Euro. See Appendix B. | | | |
| Rydex Australian Dollar Shares (FXA) | 0.40 percent | 4 | — |
| Based on the value of the Australian dollar. | | | |
| Rydex British Pound Sterling Shares (FXB) | 0.40 percent | 15 | — |
| Based on the value of the British pound. | | | |
| Rydex Canadian Dollar Shares (FXC) | 0.40 percent | 13 | — |
| Based on the value of the Canadian dollar. | | | |
| Rydex Mexican Peso Shares (FXM) | 0.40 percent | 27 | — |
| Based on the value of the Mexican peso. | | | |
| Rydex Swedish Krona Shares (FXS) | 0.40 percent | 2 | — |
| Based on the value of the Swedish krona. | | | |
| Rydex Swiss Franc Shares (FXF) | 0.40 percent | 7 | — |
| Based on the value of the Swiss franc. | | | |
| United States Oil Fund, LP (USOF) | 0.50 percent | — | — |
| Based on the price of the near month oil futures contracts for West Texas Intermediate light sweet crude oil listed on the New York Mercantile Exchange. | | | |

# B

# Sponsors, Indexers, and Other Information

The sponsors of U.S. ETFs are listed here, with some of the index providers. The Web sites of sponsors are identified. If the Web site provides a phone number, it's included here.

**BNY.** The Bank of New York serves as trustee and custodian of ETFs and in some cases as the operator of indexes.

**BLDRS.** All four BLDRS funds, which are sponsored by Nasdaq, are unit investment trusts that track indexes of the stocks of foreign regions. The indexes are operated by the Bank of New York in conjunction with Dow Jones. BLDRS hold nothing but **ADRs**, a term that stands for **American Depositary Receipts**. (An ADR is issued by a U.S. custodian to serve in place of a foreign stock that is not negotiable in the United States. The ADR represents the foreign stock, is negotiable here, and pays dividends in U.S. dollars.) www.bldrsfunds.com.

**Claymore Advisors.** An Illinois investment firm whose ETFs, at this writing, are still in registration with the SEC. The company is not yet in a position to disclose the symbols or expense ratios. See *Wisdom-Tree* below. www.claymore.com. (800) 345-7999.

**Cohen & Steers Capital Management.**   Provides financial, economic, and investment information to the financial community and is strong on real estate investment trusts.

**Commodities.**   The PowerShares DB Commodity Index Tracking Fund and the United States Oil Fund are based on prices of futures contracts. When an authorized participant requests a creation or redemption, the person pays or receives cash in return, based on the current price of the relevant futures contract. The transactions are subject to tax according to rules applying to futures contracts, as follows: No matter how long the contract has been held, the gains or losses are assumed to be 60 percent long term and 40 percent short term. Contracts held at the turn of the year are valued as of the end of the year. Taxable gains or losses are calculated as of that time, even though the contracts have not been sold.

**DB Commodity Services LLC.**   A futures broker and commodity pool operator affiliated with the large German bank Deutsche Bank AG. (Commodity pool operators pool money from many investors to acquire futures contracts.) This is a PowerShares fund. See *commodities* above.

**DJ.**   Dow Jones & Company, Inc., is the publisher of the *Wall Street Journal* and other publications and media. It is also a major provider of indexes.

**EAFE.**   The MSCI EAFE Index is an equity benchmark for the performance of stocks of Europe, Australia and Asia, and the Far East. Each stock in the index is quantified as to its growth and value characteristics. Based on the two scores, a stock may be assigned to growth or value, or it may be represented by both styles in unequal proportions. A single creation unit for the EAFE Index Fund, currently worth about $35 million, is unusually large.

**First Trust Portfolios, LP.**   The sponsor of numerous closed-end mutual funds and other investments. Like Claymore Securities, an unaffiliated company, it's in Lisle, Illinois. www.ftportfolios.com. (800) 621-1675.

**Goldman Sachs (GS).**   A prominent broker-dealer and investment banker. The iShares GS $ InvesTop Corporate Bond Index Fund (LQD) tracks a Goldman Sachs index of 100 highly liquid corporate bonds. To be eligible for inclusion, the bonds (1) must be U.S. dollar-denominated, SEC registered corporate bonds issued by companies domiciled in the United States, Canada, Western Europe, or Japan; (2) must be rated investment grade; (3) must have at least $500 million of outstanding face value; (4) must be less than five years old; and (5) must have at least three years to maturity. The index is equally weighted by par value.

**HOLDRs.**   See *Merrill Lynch* below.

**iPath.**   The service mark for exchange-traded notes (ETNs), which are offered by Barclays Bank PLC (see *iShares* just below). ETNs are unleveraged debt securities, due in 2036. Although they have no NAV, each iPath does have intrinsic value, which is published regularly and linked to the performance of a specific commodity index, less fees. Creation or redemption occurs weekly, on Thursdays, in exchange for cash. Anyone can request creation or redemption but only in multiples of 50,000 units. ETNs are also listed for secondary trading on the NYSE. They can be sold short but only on an uptick. ETNs are taxed like stocks and bonds, not like futures contracts. www.ipathetn.com. (877) 764-7284.

**iShares.**   This is the service mark for Barclays Global Investors, N.A. (BGI), a subsidiary of the large British bank, Barclays Bank PLC. BGI currently sponsors more ETFs than any other company. All of its exchange-traded funds track indexes passively. www.ishares.com. (800) 474-3747.

**KBW.**   Keefe, Bruyette & Woods is an institutionally oriented broker-dealer and investment bank specializing in the North American and European financial services sectors.

**KLD.**   KLD Research & Analytics, Inc., provides social investment research, indexes, compliance, and consulting services to the investment community.

**Lehman Brothers.**   A leading financial firm that deals with corporations, governments, institutional clients, and high-net-worth individuals worldwide. iShares offers five bond indexes based on Lehman indexes. The first four are capitalization weighted, and each component must have $250 million of outstanding face value.

Three of the Lehman bond indexes just mentioned are based solely on U.S. Treasuries. As the maturities of the bonds shorten over time, they're passed from the longer-term to the shorter-term indexes and dropped altogether when the maturities fall below one year. The fourth index consists of TIPS.

Lehman's fifth index, the U.S. Aggregate, includes U.S. Treasury and other government-related bonds, investment-grade corporates, mortgage pass-through securities, commercial mortgage-backed securities, and asset-backed securities that are publicly offered for sale in the United States. State and local government series bonds and certain other bonds are excluded. This ETF is a curiosity. The Lehman AGG Index contains over 6,000 bond issues, yet the iShares fund that tracks it currently contains only 122 issues. The portfolio turnover, furthermore, is horrific—over 900 percent during the two years ending February 28, 2006, not counting the exchanges for creations and redemptions. Turnover costs, of course, are paid by shareholders. Nevertheless, it all seems to work. Even after adjusting for the 0.20 percent fee, Lehman's Aggregate Index Fund during the last three years lagged its index by only 9 basis points.

**Merrill Lynch.**   One of the world's largest broker-dealers. It sponsors HOLDRs, which, if you consider them to be ETFs at all, are quite different from the others, as follows: (1) They're not mutual funds; shareholders are treated as owners of the underlying securities and may vote the shares thereof. (2) HOLDRs do not track indexes. Instead, the component stocks, selected by Merrill Lynch, were, at the time of the HOLDR was introduced, generally the most liquid and had the largest market capitalizations of the relevant industry. Most HOLDRs were created in 2000, around the top of the market, with a few created in 1999 and in 2001. In some of the industries, such as the Internet, conditions have since changed markedly. (3) HOLDRs are never rebalanced. Except for unavoidable changes, such as splits, mergers, spin-offs, or bankruptcies, the component stocks and the number of shares remain the same. HOLDRs can hold fractional shares. (4) Anyone can request the creation or redemption of HOLDRs. Alternatively, investors can trade HOLDRs in the secondary market through any brokerage firm. All such requests and all such trading are acceptable only in round lots of 100 shares or multiples thereof. (5) In unusual cases, short sales of HOLDRs may be subject to the uptick rule (although not when the investor is undertaking an arbitrage; the uptick rule never applies to arbitrageurs).

The costs of HOLDRs are twofold: (1) When requesting creation or redemption, the Bank of New York charges the investor $10 per 100-share lot. (2) As to HOLDRs held in a brokerage account, BNY charges a custodian fee of $2.00 per quarter per 100-share lot. But this fee is reduced, if necessary, to no more than the amount of dividends received from the underlying stocks. In other words, the investor never has to pay the custodian fee from other funds. At this writing, the prices of all the HOLDRs averaged about 69. On this basis, the annual custodian fee amounts to 0.12 percent ($8.00 divided by $6,900). Merrill Lynch charges no HOLDR fees whatever.

HOLDRs offer an advantage that other ETFs do not: Since the investor owns the underlying shares, he or she can redeem the HOLDR and take delivery of the underlying stocks. He or she can then sell the ones that stand at losses with respect to when the HOLDR was acquired but hold the stocks that have gained. (I don't consider this much of an advantage. Commissions, spreads, and the excessive exercise of investment judgment make extensive trading much more costly than most people realize. I suggest you just buy broad-based ETFs, rebalance once a year, and let the taxes fall as they may. If investing is your hobby, get a new hobby.) www.holdrs.com.

**Morgan Stanley Capital International, Inc. (MSCI).** A leading supplier of indexes to investors worldwide.

**Morningstar, Inc.** A leading provider of independent investment research, offering Internet, software, and print-based products to the investment community. All nine of the iShares Morningstar index funds are subsets of the proprietary Morningstar US Market Index, a broad index representing approximately 97 percent of the market capitalization of publicly traded U.S. stocks. Stocks with relatively high valuations are designated as growth stocks; those with relatively low valuations are designated as value stocks. Stocks not considered either growth or value are designated as core securities.

Stocks forming the top 70 percent of the capitalization of Morningstar's US Market Index are considered large cap. Those between the seventieth and ninetieth percentile of the capitalization of

Morningstar's US Market Index are considered mid-cap. And those between the ninetieth and ninety-seventh percentile are considered small cap. Each of the three groups are divided into growth, value, and core, making nine iShares funds in all.

**National Association of Securities Dealers Automated Quotation system (Nasdaq).** National Association of Securities Dealers Automated Quotation system, which enables broker-dealers to trade several thousand stocks over the counter. www.nasdaq.com.

**PowerShares.** Recently acquired by Amvescap, PLC, PowerShares is the sponsor of numerous ETFs. It uses quantitative analysis in the effort to outperform benchmarks. Many of its indexes, called "Intellidexes," were designed by PowerShares. But since the company isn't permitted to track its own indexes, it has arranged for the American Stock Exchange to operate the indexes using PowerShare rules. The indexes are then followed passively by PowerShares for its ETFs. See *WisdomTree* below. www.powershares.com. (800) 843-2639 (the phone number of the American Stock Exchange).

**ProShares.** So far the only company to launch inverse ETFs, whose prices rise when the prices of the underlying securities fall (or fall when the underlying securities rise—that's the bad part). Inverse ETFs enable investors to short the market without having a margin account. ProShares is also the only company so far to introduce funds that have twice the leverage—some on the long side and others on the short side. www.amex.com. (800) 843-2639.

**Russell.** The Frank Russell Company is a prominent supplier of market indexes. The Russell 3000 Index represents about 98 percent of all publicly held U.S. stocks. The Russell 1000 consists of the 1,000 largest companies of the 3000 Index. The Russell 2000 makes up the remainder of the 3,000; its constituents are considered small cap.

**Rydex Investments.** An investment manager of mutual funds and ETFs—one of the first to specialize in index funds. Some of the Rydex ETFs hold stocks; others hold foreign currencies. Rydex's foreign currency ETFs are not based on futures contracts; they're based on the currency values in the spot markets. An authorized participant who requests the creation of ETF shares supplies the foreign currency in return. An authorized participant who requests the redemption of shares receives the foreign currency in return. These are tax-free exchanges. www.rydexfunds.com. (800) 830-0888.

**Select Sector SPDR.**   See *State Street Global Advisors* below.

**SPDR.**   See *State Street Global Advisors* below.

**streetTRACKS.**   See *State Street Global Advisors* below.

**State Street Global Advisors.**   SSgA, an affiliate of State Street Bank & Trust, is the world's largest institutional asset management firm. It sponsors three groups of exchange-traded funds, as follows:

The names of one group begin with "SPDR," which stands for "Standard & Poor's Depositary Receipts." This is the name of the first ETF and the one from which the Spider name was drawn. Most of the exchange-traded funds whose names begin with "SPDR" contain the stocks of separate industries. All of the component stocks are drawn from the Standard & Poor's Total Market Index, which tracks all U.S. common stocks listed on the NYSE, the Amex, the Nasdaq National Market, and the Nasdaq Small Cap exchanges.

The names of another group of SSgA exchange-traded funds begin with "Select Sector." All nine of these sectors are drawn from the famous S&P 500 Index. Every one of the 500 stocks in the S&P 500 is allocated to one and only one of the Select Sector Indexes, which include Consumer Staples, Finance, and Industrial. (The allocations are made by Merrill Lynch in consultation with Standard & Poor's.) The total number of stocks in the sector funds totals 500. Those are the same stocks that make up the S&P 500—no more and no less.

The names of the third group of State Street's ETFs begin with "streetTRACKS." The characteristics of these funds vary. One of them, the streetTRACKS Gold Shares (GLD), was the first ETF based on gold bullion. www.ssgafunds.com. (866) 787-2257.

**United States Oil Fund, LP.**   A limited partnership and commodity pool (see *DB Commodity* and *commodities* above). The manager and general partner is Victoria Bay Asset Management, LLC. www.amex.com. (800) 843-2639.

**Value Line.** Publisher of investment information and recommendations. One of the first companies to sponsor a stock index whose components are weighted equally.

**Vanguard.** Noted for its low operating costs and low turnover rates, Vanguard is one of the nation's leading sources of mutual funds and ETFs. With the exception of the Extended Market ETF (VXF), all of its ETFs track indexes of MSCI. As discussed in Chapters 16 and 17, Vanguard ETFs are unique in that each of them shares the portfolio of an associated index mutual fund. www.vanguard.com. (877) 662-7447.

**Wilshire.** Wilshire Associates is a leading global investment technology, investment consulting, and investment management firm. The company works jointly with Dow Jones in the operation of the DJ Wilshire Indexes.

**WisdomTree.** The sponsor of numerous ETFs that invest in dividend-yielding stocks—some domestic, some foreign. The stocks are weighted by the dividend amount or dividend yield. Chapter 13 offers an extensive discussion of the fundamental, quantitative factors, which apply to the ETFs of WisdomTree, PowerShares, Claymore, and the streetTRACKS Dividend Fund (SDY). www.wisdomtree.com. (866) 909-9473.

# Glossary

**12(b)1 charge**   A charge against a mutual fund account. Charges for advertising, sales literature, and other marketing costs cannot exceed .75 percent of the fund's average net assets per year. Charges to pay the broker-dealer associated with the account, to induce the firm and the registered representative to remain interested in servicing it, cannot exceed .25 percent of the average net assets per year. Some no-load funds and exchange-traded funds charge 12(b)1 fees at very modest levels.

**accrued interest**   The interest accrued on a bond from the last interest payments to the date of settlement. The buyer of a bond pays this amount to the seller in addition to the cost of the bond itself.

**accumulation period**   The period of an annuity policy during which funds are paid in and compounded within the policy. At the owner's request, funds may be withdrawn in whole or in part.

ADRs   See *American Depositary Receipts.*

**aftermarket**   Secondary market.

**agent**   A brokerage firm acts as an agent when it is not the opposite party in a transaction with a customer. The firm's income from the trade is derived from the commission and possibly a small shipping and handling charge.

**all or none (AON)**   The requirement by a brokerage firm that a customer acquire a security entirely or not at all. Usually applies to bond offerings.

**American Depositary Receipts (ADRs)**   An ADR is issued by a U.S. custodian to serve in place of a foreign stock that is not negotiable in the United States. The ADR represents the foreign stock, is negotiable here, and pays dividends in U.S. dollars.

**American Stock Exchange (Amex or ASE)**   America's second largest stock exchange, but the largest in the trading of exchange-traded funds. Sometimes referred to as the *Curb.*

**Amex**   See *American Stock Exchange.*

**amortize**   The systematic payment over time, not just of interest but also of the principal of a debt.

**annual costs**   The costs of operating a mutual fund, expressed as an annual percentage of the fund's total value. Each business day, a small fraction of the anticipated costs are deducted from the fund.

**annuitant**   The person to whom fixed payments are made periodically during the annuity payment period of an annuity. The annuitant is the owner or a person chosen by the owner.

**annuity**   An insurance policy within which the income and appreciation earned are not taxable until they're paid out of the policy. An annuity has two periods of life. The first is the accumulation period, during which funds are paid in, either periodically or all at once, to compound within the policy. At the owner's request, funds may also be withdrawn during the accumulation period, in whole or in part. When the owner chooses (but no later than when the annuitant reaches the advanced age specified in the policy), the policy may be switched to the second period, called the *annuity payment period.* Switching over is called *annuitizing* the policy. The policy then begins paying out funds to the annuitant automatically in accordance with one of many payout options. Once a payout option is selected and the annuity payment period begins, the payouts are fixed and are paid at the insurance company's risk. Funds may not thereafter be removed prematurely.

**annuity payment period**   The period of an annuity during which funds are paid out periodically to the annuitant in accordance with one of several formulas.

**AON**   See *all or none*.

**arbitrage**   The purchase of an item in one market and its simultaneous sale in another. An example would be the purchase of IBM stock in London and its immediate sale in New York.

**ASE**   See *American Stock Exchange.*

**ask price**   The price at which a market maker is willing to sell a security in a reasonable amount at a particular time. Also called the *public offering price* or just the *offering price*. The ask price is always higher than the bid price.

**at-the-money**   An option is at-the-money when the stock's current price is the same as the option's strike price.

**authorized but unissued stock**   Shares of stock whose existence stockholders have authorized but that have not yet been issued. Such shares may become issued in an IPO, a secondary offering, as an employee stock option, or in payment for the acquisition of another company.

**average return**   The total compound return of an investment over several periods, divided by the number of periods. Assume, for example, that 100 grows to 200 in two years. The average return is 50 percent, computed by dividing the total return by the number of periods. For a given number of periods, the average return is always higher than the compound return.

**basis point**   One-hundredth of one percent (1/100 of 1 percent). A rise of interest rates from 5.5 to 5.6 percent would be an increase of 10 basis points.

**bearer bond**   A bond for which the owner's name is not recorded on the issuer's books and not inscribed on the bond certificate. Like cash, the possessor is presumed to be the owner.

**bear market**   A stock market that has generally been falling or is considered to be falling.

**beta**   A comparison between the volatility of a stock and the volatility of the S&P 500 Index. If a stock rises or falls by 10 percent when the S&P 500 also goes up or down by 10 percent, the volatility of the stock is equal to that of the market and the beta of the stock is 1. If a stock rises or falls by 20 percent when the market goes up or down by only 10 percent, the volatility of the stock is twice that of the market and the beta of the stock is 2. If a stock's volatility is half that of the market, the beta is 0.5. A stock's beta cannot be relied upon to remain the same.

**bid price**   The price at which a market maker is willing to buy a security in a reasonable amount at a particular time. The bid price is always lower than the ask price.

**board of directors**   A group of individuals who are elected by the shareholders and are responsible for supervising the affairs of a corporation. The board appoints the corporation's senior officers. Usually, one or more of the senior officers are also members of the board.

**bond**   An IOU of relatively long duration, offered by a corporation or a government entity. The issuer is the debtor, and the bondholder is the creditor. The bond promises repayment of a certain amount of money on a certain date, with level interest payments in the interim, usually semiannually. Bonds are ordinarily denominated in units of $1,000.

**bond power**   A document containing the same provisions as the reverse side of a bond certificate. A blank bond certificate and a signed bond power may be mailed separately, thereby protecting against fraud. When the two documents come together at the brokerage firm, the security can be transferred.

**book-entry bond**   A bond for which there is no certificate. No one holds a certificate; the bond is instead recorded electronically by a bank or brokerage firm that carries the account. All Treasury securities are book-entry instruments.

**book value**   The valuation of a company by the historic costs of its assets and liabilities, not by its current market value.

**breadth**   A technical indicator, based on the number of stocks rising and the number of stocks falling each day.

**broker** An individual or brokerage firm that brings buyers and sellers together but does not take a position in the security being exchanged.

**broker-dealer** A securities firm that may serve as either broker or dealer. Most firms commonly referred to as "brokers" or "brokerage firms" are in fact broker-dealers. (*Brokerage house* is a substitute term for *brokerage firm*.)

**bull market** A stock market that has generally been rising or is considered to be rising.

**Bulletin Board stocks** The category of smaller stocks that are neither listed on exchanges nor included on the Nasdaq. They're traded on the Internet via the OTC Bulletin Board (www.otcbb.com).

**business cycle** An economic cycle of a relatively short-term nature, thought to last for six years or less.

**buy-and-sell agreement** An agreement between two or more owners of a closely held business that provides for the purchase of the interest of a withdrawing or deceased owner by the surviving owner(s). Drawn properly, the agreement sets the value of the interest for estate tax purposes.

**buy-in** When the owner of a stock that has been lent to a short seller chooses to sell the shares, the broker must borrow the stock from another owner. If no such stock is available, the short sale is covered in the open market with or without the short seller's approval. The purchase is called a *buy-in*.

**call** The redemption of a bond before maturity by the issuer after a specified date and at a specified price. If interest rates have risen since the bond was issued, the bond would probably not be called. If interest rates have fallen since the bond was issued, the issuer would probably sell a new bond at the lower rate and use the proceeds to call the older, higher-interest bond. The U.S. Treasury stopped issuing callable bonds in 1984. Many corporate bonds are callable. Virtually all municipal bonds are callable. To the bondholder (or creditor), the call feature limits the potential for gain but does not limit the potential for loss.

**call option**   An options contract in which the seller gives the buyer, in return for the payment of a premium, the right but not the obligation to buy 100 shares of a stock at a certain price by a certain time. The buyer expects the price to rise prior to expiration.

**call protection**   During the period before a bond may be called, the bondholder is considered to be protected from calls. But the upside price is limited by the expectation of a call.

**callable preferred stock**   Preferred stock in which the company has the right but not the obligation to buy back the issue at a certain price after a certain date.

**capital**
- Money needed by a business enterprise to develop, produce, and distribute products and services before the company is actually paid for them. Capital is raised by borrowing funds directly, offering shares of ownership in the enterprise, or a hybrid of the two.
- The principal of an investment from which income and/or gains are derived.

**capital gain**   The amount by which the proceeds from the sale of a security exceed the cost. The profit, derived only from the price change, is in addition to dividends or interest received.

**capital goods**   Factors of production, such as mines, factories, farm machinery, office buildings, and stores, that the public does not want to buy but that are needed to make available the goods and services the public does want to buy.

**capitalization**   The total market value of a company, calculated by multiplying the price by the number of shares of common stock outstanding. If a company has 1 billion shares outstanding and the price is 30, for example, the capitalization is $30 billion.

**capital loss**   The amount by which the cost of a security exceeds the proceeds from the sale.

**capital stock**   Shares of ownership of a corporation, including various classes of common and preferred stock.

**cash value**   The savings element of a whole life insurance policy. It is the amount the insurance company pays upon the policy's cancellation before the insured's death, less surrender charges, if any.

**CBOE**   See *Chicago Board Options Exchange.*

**CD**   See *certificate of deposit.*

**CEO**   See *chief executive officer.*

**certificate**   Paper evidence of ownership of a stock or bond. A certificate provides information about the issuer, the terms of the security, and usually the name of the owner. The back of a certificate ordinarily contains provisions enabling the security's ownership to be transferred.

**certificate of deposit (CD)**   A type of bank deposit ranging in maturity from 30 days to five years. If the money is withdrawn prior to maturity, interest for at least a portion of the period is forfeited.

**chartist**   See *technician.*

**Chicago Board Options Exchange (CBOE)**   An exchange that specializes in options contracts. Although options have existed for centuries, secondary markets for options contracts were made possible only recently by the development of computers.

**chief executive officer (CEO)**   A company's boss. In some companies, the CEO is also the president. In others, he or she may be the chairman of the board.

**circuit breaker**   The closing of all stock trading after the Dow Jones Industrial Average has declined by a substantial predetermined percentage.

**class of mutual funds**
- Some mutual fund organizations offer several classes of the same fund. The essential difference between the classes is the amount of the commissions and the manner in which they're charged. Class A funds charge the commission up front. Class B funds assess extra charges and declining redemption charges for several years. Class C funds incur extra charges indefinitely.

- Other mutual funds, notably Vanguard, have two classes of stock for the same index fund. One is a conventional, open-end index fund and the other an exchange-traded fund.

**class of stock**   A category of stock with special characteristics. Classes A and B might differ, for example, as to dividends and voting power. Most corporations have only one class of stock.

**clearing broker**   If brokerage firm A handles most of the operations for brokerage firm B, A is said to "clear" for B and is referred to as the "clearing firm." The assets are held by A, and most of the operations are performed by A. B's customers receive their confirmations and statements from the clearing firm A, with the names of A and B both displayed thereon.

**close**   The termination of exchange trading. In the United States, the close is generally at 4:00 p.m. New York time.

**closed-end mutual fund**   A mutual fund that maintains a fixed number of outstanding shares. Buyers acquire shares from other investors who wish to sell them. Sellers sell shares to other investors who wish to buy them. The stocks of closed-end funds are traded in the secondary market, many of them on the New York Stock Exchange. The prices of closed-end funds usually stand at premiums above or discounts below the fund's net asset value, ordinarily the latter.

**closing purchase transaction**   The type of order entered when the writer of an options contract subsequently buys it to exit the position prior to expiration.

**closing sale transaction**   The type of order entered when the buyer of an options contract subsequently sells it to exit the position prior to expiration.

**CMO**   See *collateralized mortgage obligation*.

**collateral**   Assets pledged to secure a loan. If the loan is defaulted, the asset may be sold and the proceeds used to repay the loan. Collateral reduces the creditor's risk and, other things being equal, makes possible a lower interest rate.

**collateralized mortgage obligation (CMO)**   The securitization of residential mortgages. Home mortgages of similar characteristics are pooled and sold to the public in various kinds of bond obligations. As homeowners pay the interest and principal, the bondholders are paid accordingly. When the mortgages are paid off or refinanced prematurely, the bonds are also paid off prematurely, giving them an element of uncertainty most other bonds do not possess.

**commercial paper**   A short-term loan made by a money market fund to a corporation.

**commission**   The compensation paid to a brokerage firm for arranging an agency transaction on the purchase or sale of a security. Aspects of the trade on which commissions are based might include the price, the number of shares, and/or the dollar value of the trade. Minimums apply.

**common stock**   A form of capital stock that has no preference as to dividend distributions or distribution of assets in bankruptcy. Common stock shareholders get what's left after creditors and preferred stockholders are paid; if the company fails, this is likely to be little or nothing. If the company is successful, the common shareholders may profit handsomely. Common shareholders may vote in corporate elections. Common stock is usually called just *stock*.

**compound return**   The rate of return of an investment or portfolio in which at least some of the income and appreciation is reinvested in the investment or in the portfolio that generated them. The return in any given period is derived not only from the original investment but also from the returns accumulated in previous periods. Assume that 100 grows to 200 in two years. The compound return is 41.4 percent. In the first year, 100 grows by 41.4 percent to 141.4. In the second year, 141.4 grows by 41.4 percent to 200.

**confirmation**   A brokerage firm's written advice to a customer showing all pertinent information about the purchase or sale of a security. Confirmations and statements should be retained for tax purposes.

**convertible debenture**   A debenture that, at the option of the holder, may be converted into the corporation's common stock, if and when the common stock reaches a specified price that is higher than the price it had at the time the convertible debenture was issued.

**convertible preferred stock**   Preferred stock that, at the holder's option, may be exchanged for another asset, generally a fixed number of shares of common stock of the same company. The conversion can be made if and when the price of the common stock reaches a specified level that is higher than the price of the common stock at the time the convertible preferred stock was issued.

**convertible securities**   Securities having characteristics of both stocks and bonds but that may eventually be converted into common stock of the same company.

**corporation**   A method of owning a business enterprise. The state grants a charter recognizing the corporation as a separate legal entity, having its own rights, privileges, assets, and liabilities distinct from those of the individuals creating the business. Corporations have unlimited lives and may enter into contracts, own property, incur liabilities, and may sue or be sued. Ownership is represented by shares of stock.

**coupon**
- A small portion of a bearer bond physically cut off by the holder and deposited in a bank. The bank mails it to the transfer agent for collection and provides the funds to the holder.
- The annualized interest paid by a bond, expressed as a percentage of the par value.

**cover**   The purchase of a stock held short.

**covered option**   The writer of a call has a covered call if the writer also owns the stock that the buyer of the call has the right to call. If the writer does not also own the underlying stock, he or she is the writer of an uncovered, or naked, call. The writer of a put has a covered put if the writer is also short the underlying stock. Without the underlying short position, the person has written a naked put.

**creation unit**   A minimum module for the creation or redemption of shares of an exchange-traded fund. The fund issues ETF shares in exchange for securities deposited in the fund by an authorized participant. The fund redeems ETF shares in exchange for securities transferred to an authorized participant. With minor exceptions, the exchanges are made in kind, not cash. The minimum number of ETF shares in a single creation unit varies from one fund to another, ranging from 25,000 to 300,000 shares.

**cumulative preferred stock**   Preferred stock in which, if one or more of the dividends are not paid because of the company's ill fortunes, all omitted dividends must be paid before any dividends may be paid to common shareholders.

**currency board**   A monetary system used by some developing nations. No new currency is issued unless the government holds a given amount of a major currency, most likely the dollar, to back it up. Citizens may exchange their currency for the major currency whenever they wish. The purpose is to reduce the rate of inflation of the nation's currency.

**current yield**   A bond's annual interest payments divided by the current price. For this calculation, maturity is irrelevant.

**cyclical**   A term applied to economic variables of a lesser, short-term nature.

**day order**   A limit or stop order that automatically expires at the end of the trading day on which it is entered.

**dealer**   A firm or individual that buys securities with its own funds and sells securities from its own inventory.

**debenture**   An unsecured corporate bond, backed only by the corporation's earning power.

**debit balance**   The amount borrowed from the brokerage firm in a margin account.

**deflation**   The creation of relative low amounts of money in relation to the supply of goods and services, causing a decline in the economy's general price level. Since the repayments of debts are made with funds whose buying power has increased, deflation is hard on debtors.

**derivative**   A market whose values are based on the values prevailing in another market. Options and futures contracts are derivatives.

Options on futures contracts are doubly derivative; they're based on the prices of futures contracts, which themselves are based on the cash prices of the underlying commodities.

**Diamond share**   An exchange-traded fund based on the 30 stocks of the Dow Jones Industrial Average. Structured as a unit investment trust, Diamond shares are listed on the American Stock Exchange. The underlying trust owns an equal number of shares of the stocks selected by Dow Jones & Company for the famous average. Diamonds were originally priced at 1/100 the value of the average, although that ratio has slowly changed over time and will continue doing so.

**dilution**   A potential increase in the number of common shares outstanding, caused by a secondary offering, the exercise of employee stock options, or the conversion into common stock of convertible preferred, convertible debentures, or warrants. Given a certain amount of earnings, an increase in the number of common shares causes the earnings per share to decline.

**discount**
- The amount by which the price of a bond is lower than the par value.
- The amount by which the price of a closed-end mutual fund is lower than the net asset value. Most closed-end mutual funds are priced at discounts most of the time.
- The amount by which the price of a futures contract is lower than the cash price of the underlying commodity or index.

**discount broker**   A broker-dealer that charges lower commissions and generally supplies less service than full-commission houses.

**disinflation**   Moderation in the creation of money, causing the rate of inflation to diminish.

**dividend**   A distribution to the shareholders of a class of stock, sometimes in the form of additional stock (called a *stock dividend*) but usually in the form of cash, generally paid quarterly. Dividends are approved by the board of directors, and the board may discontinue, lower, or raise them. The dividend is expressed as a certain amount per share. The amount received by a shareholder is proportionate to the number of shares held. Not all stocks pay dividends. Stocks with higher dividends tend to be more mature, nontechnological companies that are less volatile in price.

**dividend reinvestment plan (DRIP)**  The ongoing reinvestment of cash dividends of a corporation in shares of the company's stock at the then-current price—fractional shares, if necessary—at little or no commission cost.

**DJIA**  See *Dow Jones Industrial Average.*

**DNR**  See *do not reduce.*

**do not reduce (DNR)**  An optional addition to a limit or stop order directing that the price of the stock not be reduced on dividend ex-dates. Without this instruction, the price at which the stock is to be bought or sold is automatically reduced by the dividend amount.

**dollar cost averaging**  Investing a given amount of money periodically, on the assumption that when prices fall, you can buy more shares.

**double witching day**  A day when two of the three derivatives applying to stocks expire—namely, stock index futures, options on stock index futures, and options on individual stocks. The unwinding of such contracts can induce high volatility of stock prices on the day of expiration.

**Dow Jones Industrial Average (DJIA)**  Started in 1896, the Dow average is based on the stocks of 30 prominent NYSE companies selected and changed from time to time by Dow Jones & Co., publisher of the *Wall Street Journal.*

**downtick**  A stock is on a downtick when it trades at a price that is lower than the last different price.

**DRIP**  See *dividend reinvestment plan.*

**earned income**  Income earned from one's own labor, as distinguished from *unearned income.*

**earnings**  The net, after-tax income for a quarter or a year—that is, corporate revenues reduced by taxes and expenses for the period. Some or all of the earnings may be paid to shareholders as dividends. Any balance is reinvested to spur the company's growth.

**earnings per share (EPS)**   A corporation's net, after-tax earnings for a quarter or a year, divided by the average number of common shares outstanding during the period.

**earnings yield**   The inverse of the price/earnings ratio. For example, if a stock has a P/E ratio of 20, its earnings yield is 5 percent (1/20). The concept is useful for comparing stock valuations with bond yields.

**entrepreneur**   A person who endeavors to create wealth by developing better ways of satisfying people's needs.

**EPS**   See *earnings per share.*

**equity**
- *Common-* or *preferred-stock* ownership in a business. (Compare to *bonds.*)
- The portion of a company's capital raised from the IPOs and secondary offerings of common and preferred stock rather than from the offerings of bonds.
- The net value of an account. Assuming the investments are liquidated and the account closed, it is the net proceeds available to the account owner. The equity of a margin account is the total market value less the margin balance.

**ETF**   See *exchange-traded fund.*

**exchange**   An organization that provides for and regulates the trading of securities in a particular facility. Prominent U.S. exchanges include the New York Stock Exchange (NYSE), the American Stock Exchange (Amex or ASE), and the Chicago Board Options Exchange (CBOE). U.S. cities with regional stock exchanges include Boston, Philadelphia, Chicago, and San Francisco.

**exchange-traded fund (ETF)**   An index fund whose shares can be created or redeemed only in large blocks, by the deposit of securities to or the delivery of securities from the fund's portfolio. But lots as small as a single share may be traded in secondary markets.

**ex-date**   The day on which the stock first trades without the impending dividend. *Ex* means "from" or "without" in Latin. If you buy the stock before the ex-date, you receive the next dividend. If you buy it on or after the ex-date, you don't. All else remaining the same, the price of the stock drops on the ex-date by the amount of the dividend.

**exercise**    The purchase of a stock under the terms of a call option or the sale of a stock under the terms of a put option, at the strike price specified in the contract.

**expense ratio**    A charge against a mutual fund or ETF portfolio for investment management, custody, administration, license fees, 12(b)1 fees, and other related costs. Does not include transaction costs. Usually expressed as a percentage of net assets.

**expiration**    The date on which an option expires.

**family of mutual funds**    Several mutual funds offered by the same mutual fund organization.

**fed**    See *Federal Reserve Bank.*

**federal funds market**    A U.S. money market used by banks to lend money to one another, usually for only one business day. The rates of interest charged are taken into account by the Federal Open Market Committee in regulating the nation's money supply.

**Federal Open Market Committee (FOMC)**    A committee consisting mostly of members of the board of governors of the Federal Reserve Bank, to which the Federal Reserve Bank delegates the task of determining the money supply.

**Federal Reserve Bank**    The central bank of the United States, whose most important function is to create most of the nation's money supply. Referred to informally as the *fed.*

**fed funds**    The federal funds market.

**finance company**    A company that borrows money at low rates and makes higher-risk loans at relatively high interest rates.

**financing**    The obtaining of money by businesses and consumers who need to spend it soon from those who choose to spend it later. An individual borrows from a bank, for example, to finance the purchase of a house.

**fiscal expansion**   The expansion of government spending, tending to create or increase the federal government's deficit.

**fiscal year**   An organization's 12-month accounting period that differs from the calendar year. Corporations for which Christmas sales are significant, for example, may adopt fiscal years ending during the first quarter of the year.

**fixed annuity**   An annuity invested exclusively in bonds.

**fixed-rate capital security**   A preferred security.

**float**   The portion of outstanding stock generally available for purchase by the investing public. The term may exclude stock held by descendants of the founder, for example, who have no intention of selling.

**FOMC**   See *Federal Open Market Committee.*

**fractional reserve**   The requirement imposed on most U.S. banks whereby a portion of depositors' funds must be held on deposit at the Federal Reserve Bank at no interest.

**fundamental analysis**   An analysis of stocks based on real-world elements, such as products, competition, dividends, price/earnings ratios, earnings prospects, and public attitudes.

**futures contract**   Contracts representing agreements to buy or sell specific amounts of physical commodities or financial instruments at a certain time in the future at an agreed-upon price. The value of the contract is based on, although usually not the same as, the current cash value of the underlying asset. Most purchasers of futures do so with considerable leverage, rendering them highly speculative.

**future value (FV)**   The amount, given an assumed rate of interest, to which a series of cash flows will grow over time. The future value and the present value are linked over time by the assumed interest rate.

**FV**   See *future value.*

**good-faith deposit**   Money placed on deposit in a futures account to protect the broker against the customer's default.

**good-til-canceled order (GTC)**   Informal reference to an open order.

**GTC**   See *good-til-canceled order.*

**hedge**   Passing off investment risk to another party by the offsetting purchase or sale of a similar security in another market or by a short-against-the-box. Securities used for hedging include options, futures contracts, exchange-traded funds, or other derivatives. If the hedge is complete, the changes in price of the item owned are completely offset, except for trading costs, by the equivalent but opposite price movements of the offset.

**hedge fund**   A mutual fund with high minimum investments, many of which trade actively using high-risk investment strategies. Investor interests can generally be sold only at prescribed times.

**Holding Company Depositary Receipts (HOLDRs)**   Quasi-exchange-traded funds created by Merrill Lynch. Each HOLDR started with the 20 largest stocks of a narrow industry group. The holdings are neither managed nor rebalanced. Shareholders are treated as owners of the underlying securities. Unlike other ETFs, HOLDRs can be bought and sold only in 100-share increments. They do not have creation units, but investors may at any time exchange 100-share units for the underlying stocks.

**HOLDRs**   See *Holding Company Depositary Receipts.*

**hybrid**   An investment product having some of the characteristics of bonds and some of stocks.

**index**   A measurement of the performance of a specific group of securities, using a clearly defined set of rules that are held constant regardless of market conditions.

**index fund**   An open-end mutual fund that buys, in the correct proportions and adjusts when necessary, the specific stocks used in a market index. The best-known index fund purchases in the proper proportions all 500 of the stocks chosen by Standard & Poor's for the S&P 500 Index.

**indicative net asset value**   The market value of the assets owned by an exchange-traded fund, reduced by liabilities, and all divided by the number of outstanding shares of the ETF owned by investors. The number is promulgated every 15 seconds during the trading day.

**individual retirement account (IRA)** See *individual retirement arrangement.*

**individual retirement arrangement (IRA)** A means of holding investments to provide tax advantages, including traditional IRAs, inherited IRAs, rollover IRAs, Roth IRAs, spousal IRAs, education IRAs, SEP-IRAs, SIMPLE–IRAs, and individual retirement annuities. Each has its own tax characteristics, but all provide tax-free environments while the funds remain in the IRAs. (To the IRS, IRAs are known as "individual retirement arrangements." To most individuals, they're known as "individual retirement accounts.")

**inflation** The creation of excessive amounts of money in relation to the supply of goods and services, causing a rise in the economy's general price level. Since the repayments of debts are made with funds whose buying power has diminished since the borrowing was incurred, inflation eases the way for debtors.

**inflation-indexed bond** A bond offered by the U.S. government for which the interest payments and par value are periodically adjusted in accordance with the consumer price index. The more the dollar's buying power declines, the higher the interest payments and the more the bond pays at maturity.

**initial public offering (IPO)** A company's initial sale of its stock to the public, usually to provide capital for business expansion. Some IPOs also enable the entrepreneurs and early investors to liquidate at least some of their shares.

**interest** The earnings derived from the principal of an investment. If the interest is withdrawn when earned, it's called "simple interest." If the interest is left in and added to the principal, it is referred to as "compound interest."

**intermediary** A company, such as a bank, investment banking firm, life insurance company, money market fund, or finance company, that attracts money not needed to be spent right away and provides it to businesses, individuals, and governments that do need it.

**in-the-money** A call option is in-the-money when the stock's current price is higher than the strike price. A put option is in-the-money when the stock's current price is lower than the strike price. In either case, the degree to which the option is in-the-money is the *intrinsic value*. Any excess of the premium over the intrinsic value is the *time value*.

**intrinsic value**   A call option has intrinsic value when the stock's current price is higher than the strike price and the option is in-the-money. A put option has intrinsic value when the current price is lower than the strike price and the option is in-the-money. The degree to which an option is in-the-money is the intrinsic value.

**inverse exchange-traded fund**   An ETF whose price rises when the prices of the underlying securities fall (and vice versa). The ETF enables an investor to go short without having a margin account.

**inverted yield curve**   See *yield curve.*

**investment advisory account**   See *investment management account.*

**investment banking firm**   A brokerage firm that arranges *initial public offerings* (IPOs) and *secondary offerings* of securities.

**investment management account**   An investment account managed by a registered investment advisor for a fee. The advisor is usually given discretion to make trades without the owner's prior approval. Also called an *investment advisory account.*

**IPO**   See *initial public offering.*

**IRA**   See *individual retirement arrangement.*

**iShares ETF**   A group of exchange-traded funds managed by Barclays Global Investors. All are structured as open-end mutual funds, and most trade on the American Stock Exchange.

**junior debt**   Debt that is subordinate as to the payment of interest or principal of debt that is senior to it. The ranking of a debt is specified at the time it is incurred.

**leaps**   See *long-term anticipation securities.*

**leverage**   The acceptance of price risk in amounts exceeding the equity. Leverage increases the potential for loss as well as for profit. Margin accounts provide leverage by allowing borrowing. Options and futures contracts offer high leverage but without borrowing.

**limit order to buy**   An order to buy a security at a price that is lower than the current ask price. The customer specifies the highest price he or she is willing to pay.

**limit order to sell**   An order to sell a security at a price that is higher than the current bid price. The customer specifies the lowest price at which he or she is willing to sell.

**line of resistance**   A line drawn above successive highs on a chart of the historic prices of a stock (or of a market of stocks). The line can be level, upward sloping, or downward sloping. Technicians consider it likely that the next time the price hits the line, it will reverse trend, as occurred before, and move down.

**line of support**   A line drawn underneath successive lows on a chart of the historic prices of a stock (or of a market of stocks). The line can be level, upward sloping, or downward sloping. Technicians consider it likely that the next time the price hits the line, it will reverse trend, as occurred before, and move up.

**liquidity**   A measure of traders' ability to turn assets into cash quickly and easily, with little effect on price stability.

**listed stock**   A stock that is traded on a U.S. exchange is said to be "listed." Currently numbering about 4,000.

**load fund**   An open-end mutual fund that charges commissions or sales expenses to compensate the broker who sold the account. The compensation is shared by the fund's wholesalers, the broker-dealer, and the registered representative assigned to the account.

**long**   An investor who owns a security in expectation of the price's rising is said to be "long the security." To go long a security is to buy it. To be long is to own it. The opposite notion is to go short or be short.

**long-term anticipation securities (leaps)**   Put and call stock options of relatively long duration.

**margin**   The amount borrowed from the brokerage firm with which to purchase securities or make a cash withdrawal.

**margin account**   A brokerage account in which some of the funds are borrowed from the firm. The brokerage firm charges interest, and the loan is collateralized by the securities and/or cash held in the account. Some speculative and/or lower-priced securities are rejected for use as collateral. The amount of the loan is referred to as the *margin* (or *debit balance*). The net amount payable to the customer, if all the securities in the margin account are sold and the net proceeds are distributed, is called the *equity*. The total market value less the margin equals the equity. At present, brokerage firms cannot lend more than half the value of the securities permitted to serve as collateral.

**margin agreement**  A written agreement signed by the customer describing the terms of a margin account and permitting the broker to treat securities in the account as collateral for loans. It also permits the broker to lend the securities to others for shorting purposes and to execute buy-ins of short sales.

**margin call**  A notice from the brokerage firm to the margin account owner requiring that additional cash or securities be added to a margin account to prevent some of the securities from being sold.

**marginal tax rate**  The rate of tax that would apply to any additional dollar of taxable income a taxpayer might receive.

**market maker**  An individual, usually associated with a brokerage firm, who, to accommodate supply or demand for stock by investors, stands ready to buy or sell one or more securities on a continuous basis for the firm's account. Market makers assigned on a particular stock exchange are called *specialists*.

**market order**  An order to buy or sell a security immediately at the best price obtainable. A buyer at market wants to buy at the lowest of the (high) ask prices. A seller at market wants to sell at the highest of the (low) bid prices.

**market risk**  The possibility that the value of a portfolio of stocks will decline because the market falls. (Compare to *specific risk*.) A long-term investor is rewarded for taking market risk, but not specific risk.

**mark to market**  The calculation of values of a margin account, frequently, when necessary, to ensure that the equity does not fall below required levels.

**maturity**   The time at which a debt must be repaid. The term generally applies to debt that is not being amortized.

**monetary expansion**   The creation of additional money. If the pace of expansion is rapid, the monetary policy is said to be "loose" or "accommodating." If the pace of money expansion is slow or if the money supply is actually diminishing, the policy is considered to be "tight."

**money market fund**   An open-end mutual fund that lends money short term to corporations and government entities. Investors in the fund may withdraw their money at any time and receive interest to the day of withdrawal. The rate of interest paid by the fund fluctuates modestly every day, with the price held level at $1.00 a share.

**mortgage bond**   A corporate bond backed by specified property owned by the corporation, such as buildings or transportation equipment.

**municipal bond**   A bond issued by a state or municipal government. The interest paid by most municipal bonds is free from income tax by the federal government. The interest is also free from state taxes for residents of the state in which the bond is issued. For residents of Virginia, for example, the interest from a bond issued by Virginia or one of its municipalities is free from tax by both Virginia and the federal government.

**mutual fund**   A pooling of funds from many investors and the investment thereof by an investment company. The performance of the fund, reduced by operating costs, is shared by the investors proportionate to their ownership. Although mutual funds are corporations, they are not themselves taxed. Except for capital losses, the tax consequences flow through to investors.

**naked option**   An uncovered option. (Compare to *covered option*.)

**NASD**   See *National Association of Securities Dealers.*

**Nasdaq**   See *National Association of Security Dealers Automated Quotation System.*

**National Association of Securities Dealers (NASD)**   An association of broker-dealers who trade over the counter. Just as exchanges monitor the action of their members, the NASD regulates the over-the-counter markets.

**National Association of Securities Dealers Automated Quotation system (Nasdaq)** An electronic system that displays quotes and other market information for approximately 5,400 OTC stocks.

**NAV** See *net asset value*.

**negative divergence** When the preponderance of stocks is falling from day to day but the market, as represented by the Dow or the S&P 500, is staying level or rising, the market is said to have negative divergence, supposedly signaling that the market trend will reverse and follow the weak breadth down.

**net asset value (NAV)** The market value of the assets owned by a mutual fund, reduced by liabilities, and all divided by the number of outstanding shares of the fund owned by investors. The NAV is computed once a day at the close.

**New York Stock Exchange (NYSE)** America's largest stock exchange.

**no-load fund** An open-end mutual fund that charges no sales commissions. Investors acquire shares of such funds directly with the fund, usually without broker involvement.

**nominal return** The annualized return (or yield) on an investment without adjusting for inflation. The nominal return of a security yielding 6 percent is 6 percent.

**NYSE** See *New York Stock Exchange*.

**offering price** The price at which a load fund may be acquired. It is the net asset value increased by the up-front sales commission, if any.

**on-the-money** An option is on-the-money when the price of the stock is equal to the strike price.

**open-end mutual fund** A mutual fund whose shares are acquired directly from the fund, in a continual offering of new shares. For investors who wish to sell, the fund redeems the shares at the net asset value (NAV). The share price of an open-end fund is always equal to the NAV.

**opening purchase transaction**   The type of order entered when an option is purchased.

**opening sale transaction**   The type of order entered when an option is written.

**open order**   A limit or stop order that remains in effect until it is canceled or executed. Referred to informally as a good-til-canceled (or GTC) order.

**ordinary income**   Earned income and investment income that is subject to regular income tax rates.

**OTC**   See *over-the-counter market.*

**out-of-the-money**   A call option is out-of-the-money when the stock's current price is lower than the strike price. A put option is out-of-the-money when the stock's current price is higher than the strike price. In either case, the premium, having no intrinsic value, has time value only.

**over-the-counter (OTC) market**   The linkage of market makers and brokers for the trading of thousands of stocks electronically. When a brokerage firm has an order to sell a stock at market, for example, the firm contacts the market maker with the highest bid price. If the brokerage firm has an order to buy stock at market, it contacts the market maker with the lowest ask price. Competition among market makers tends to narrow the spreads. All government and municipal bonds and almost all corporate bonds are traded over-the-counter.

**panic sell-off**   Usually a portion of a single day's trading, when many investors feel a sense of urgency about selling stocks and prices fall precipitously on huge volume. Panic sell-offs occur infrequently, although severe bear markets may be punctuated by several of them.

**paper**   An informal substitute for the word *security*, usually referring to a debt instrument.

**par value**
- The amount paid by a bond at maturity. For a $10,000 bond, the par value is $10,000.

- Both the issue price and the price at which a preferred stock or a convertible bond may be called—usually $25 or $50 for preferred stock and $1,000 for a bond.

**P/E ratio**   See *price/earnings ratio*.

**phantom income**   A taxpayer is taxed on income he or she is prevented from receiving.

**POP**   See *public offering price*.

**positive yield curve.**   See *yield curve*.

**preferred stock**   A stock that has some characteristics of a bond. Its dividend is a fixed dollar amount. Most preferred stock dividends must be paid in full before common shareholders may receive any dividends at all. If a company is liquidated in bankruptcy, the preferred stock has a priority lower than the company's debt but higher than the common stock. Preferred stocks can be cumulative, redeemable, callable, and/or convertible.

**premium**
- The amount by which the price of a bond exceeds the par value.
- The amount by which the price of a closed-end mutual fund exceeds the net asset value.
- The amount by which the price of a futures contract exceeds the cash price of the underlying commodity or index.
- The dollar amount paid by the buyer and received by the writer of an option. The premium is expressed as a price, which changes with the fluctuations in price of the underlying stock. It consists of intrinsic value plus time value. Regardless of whether the option is exercised, the writer retains the premium.

**prerefunding**   The sale of a new municipal bond issue that enables the municipality to call an older bond issue whose interest rate is higher than that of the new issue.

**present value (PV)**   The current value of future cash flows that are discounted at an assumed rate of interest. The present value and the future value are linked over time by the assumed interest rate.

**price/earnings ratio (P/E ratio)**   The price of a stock divided by the year's net, after-tax earnings per share. The P/E ratio is a measure of the value of the stock. If a company earns $2 a share and the stock price is 40, the P/E ratio is 20 times (40 divided by 2). If you were to buy a stock selling at 20 times annual earnings and the earnings did not change, you'd have to wait 20 years for the cumulative annual earnings to equal your cost. Generally, the faster the earnings are expected to grow and the more favorably investors look upon a stock, the higher is the price/earnings ratio.

**primary market**   The market in which a company first offers its newly issued securities for sale to investors. The company issuing the security uses the proceeds to build the business and possibly to enable early investors to cash out at least some of their holdings. The first issuing of a company's stock is called an initial public offering (IPO). (Compare with *secondary market.*)

**prime rate**   The rate at which banks lend money to their most trustworthy customers.

**principal**
- The portion of an investment from which income is derived. The original amount invested. The word usually refers to loans that pay simple interest.
- A brokerage firm acts as a principal when it serves as the opposite party in a transaction with a customer—that is, when it sells to the customer a security from its own inventory or buys a security with its own funds. Other than a modest shipping and handling charge, no commission is assessed. The firm may be a market maker for that security or may simply have accumulated an inventory.

**program trading**   The simultaneous purchase or sale of at least 15 stocks with a total value of $1 million or more. Program trading is facilitated by the use of computers to buy or sell large numbers of stocks quickly. It is often used as an arbitrage, whereby the purchase or sale of individual stocks is offset by the sale or purchase of futures contracts, exchange-traded funds, or options. In its best-known form, the program trader buys or sells, in the proper proportions, all 500 stocks in the S&P 500 Index and at the same time sells or buys an offsetting derivative. When used in an arbitrage, short sales of stocks by program traders are not subject to the uptick rule. Program trading generally constitutes over half of the volume of NYSE trading.

**progressive income tax**   A system of taxation applying higher tax rates to higher levels of taxable income.

**prospectus**   Pertinent information for potential investors about an IPO, a secondary offering, mutual funds, or exchange-traded funds.

**proxy**   Proxy forms are mailed to shareholders prior to stockholders' meetings. They explain the issues to be voted on at the meeting and enable shareholders to register their preferences. Since only a small percentage of stockholders attend the stockholder meetings of publicly held corporations, most shareholder votes are cast by proxies. The votes of shareholders who fail to send in their proxies are cast by management. Important issues on which shareholders are asked to vote include the membership of the board of directors, choice of auditors, authorization of employee stock options, and authorization of the creation of new shares of stock.

**public offering price (POP)**   Another term for *offering price* and *ask price*.

**put option**   An options contract in which the seller gives the buyer, in return for payment of a premium, the right but not the obligation to sell 100 shares of a stock at a certain price by a certain time. The buyer expects the price to fall prior to expiration.

**PV**   See *present value*.

**Qubes**   An exchange-traded fund that tracks the technology-laden Nasdaq 100. The name "Qubes" is derived from the symbol QQQQ. The ETF is structured as a unit investment trust and trades on the American Stock Exchange.

**rating**   A determination by a rating organization as to the likelihood of a bond's issuer meeting all of its terms regarding the payment of interest and principal.

**real estate investment trust (REIT)**   A closed-end fund that invests in developed real estate, undeveloped real estate, and/or mortgages.

The stocks of real estate investment trusts trade in secondary markets, many of them on the New York Stock Exchange.

**realized gain or loss**   A gain or loss having tax consequence because the security has been sold.

**real return**   The annualized return on a debt security after adjusting for inflation, as usually measured by the consumer price index (CPI). If the nominal return of an investment is 5 percent and the rate of inflation is 2 percent, the real return is 3 percent. Over many decades, the real returns of long-term bonds have averaged about 3 percent. This is the return the creditors of long, risk-free bonds have received, on average, net of inflation, as compensation for postponing the expenditure of their funds.

**redeemable preferred**   Preferred stock in which the company has the right, but not the obligation, to buy back the issue at a specified price at any time.

**redemption charge**   A commission charged against money redeemed from a mutual fund within a certain number of years. Not all funds impose redemption charges.

**registered bond**   A bond that may, at the owner's option, be registered in the owner's name and held in his or her possession. Interest payments are sent directly to the owner.

**registered investment advisor (RIA)**   An individual or company that is authorized by the SEC to be paid for rendering investment advice and that ordinarily buys and sells securities for others without obtaining prior approval for each trade.

**registered representative**   An owner or representative of a brokerage firm who is licensed to sell securities.

**reinflation**   The creation of excessive money, causing the rate of inflation to increase.

**REIT**   See *real estate investment trust.*

**replication method**   The exact copying by an index fund or ETF of the underlying index. The very same stocks are acquired in the correct proportions.

**representative sampling**   The holding by an index fund or ETF of only some of the stocks in the underlying index. Used when replication requires excessive trading because the index contains too many small, illiquid stocks. The fund endeavors to match the characteristics of the entire index in terms of performance, industry weights, and market capitalization.

**return on equity (ROE)**   The annual earnings of a company as a percentage of the equity. Say a company has raised $10 million from the initial public offering and secondary offerings of its stock. If the company subsequently earns $1 million in a year, the return on equity for that year would be 10 percent ($1 million divided by $10 million).

**reverse mortgage**   A bank loan, secured by the borrower's residence, for which no repayments are required until the borrower moves or dies. The money can be received up front, in increments for a certain number of years, in increments for life, or a combination thereof. Borrowers must be at least 62 years old. Usually, the loan is repaid from the proceeds of the sale of the home. If the proceeds are insufficient to repay the loan, the bank absorbs the loss.

**reverse stock split**   A reduction in the number of shares outstanding, to bring the price of the stock up to the range in which the company believes the public would feel more comfortable buying it. Reverse stock splits usually occur after a company has suffered ill fortune. Say you own 10,000 shares of stock priced at 3, and the company declares a 1-for-10 reverse stock split. Instead of 10,000 shares at 3, valued at $30,000, you would own 1,000 shares at 30, also valued at $30,000.

**RIA**   See *registered investment advisor*.

**risk**   The possibility of the value of a security or a group of securities being lower than the owner desires at the time he or she may need the money. The more volatile the price of a security, the greater the risk. Volatility is generally higher for younger companies than for more mature companies. Stocks paying higher percentage dividend yields tend to have lower volatility and lower risk.

**ROE**   See *return on equity*.

**S&P 500**   See *Standard & Poor's 500 Index*.

**SEC**   See *Securities and Exchange Commission.*

**secondary market**   The market where previously issued securities are traded among investors using brokers/dealers as intermediaries. This contrasts with the *primary market* where newly issued securities are first sold to investors. The great majority of stock trades occur in the secondary market. Also called the *aftermarket.*

**secondary offering**   An offering of additional stock to the public by a company for which other stock has previously been sold in an initial public offering. Additional stock is sold to finance the further expansion of the business and/or to enable the entrepreneurs and early investors to liquidate some or all of their shares.

**secondary stocks**   Stocks issued by companies whose total market value is relatively low. Also called *small caps.* They tend to be more volatile and speculative. Many, but not all, are traded over the counter.

**secular**   A term applied to economic variables of an important, long-term nature.

**securities**   See *security.*

**Securities and Exchange Commission (SEC)**   The federal agency that regulates the securities industry.

**Securities Investor Protection Corporation (SIPC)**   A nonprofit, membership corporation, funded by its member broker-dealers, providing certain protections for the customers of securities firms that are unable to meet their financial obligations.

**security**   Collateral guaranteeing repayment of a debt. Also, any of the following instruments:

- Ownership of some or all of a corporation in the form of common stock.
- A creditor relationship, in the form of a bond, note, or bill.
- A traditional preferred stock, convertible bond, preferred security, or other hybrid, representing part ownership and part debt.
- An option contract, in the form of a put, call, leap, or warrant.

**seigniorage**   The profit earned by the entity that creates the nation's currency (usually the national government). The profit results from the currency's face value being worth more than the production costs. For bank deposits, which constitute the bulk of the U.S. money supply, production costs are virtually zero.

**self-directed IRA**    An IRA offered by a brokerage firm for which any or all investments permitted by IRS rules may be selected by the owner.

**senior debt**    Debt that has priority as to the payment of interest or principal over debt that is junior to it. The ranking of a debt is specified at the time it is incurred.

**settlement date**    On a purchase, it is the day on which payment for the purchase of a security must be received by the brokerage firm. On a sale, it is the day on which the proceeds become available for reinvestment or the day on which the firm mails a check for the proceeds. For stocks and bonds, settlement occurs three days after the trade. For options and government securities, settlement occurs one day after the trade.

**share**    A single unit of a class of stock ownership of a corporation. With some stocks, the shares of ownership may, at the owner's request, be represented by a stock certificate.

**share of beneficial interest**    The combination of stock and a warrant at an initial public offering.

**share price**    Stock prices, expressed in term of dollars and cents.

**shares outstanding**    The total number of shares of a company's stock held by all members of the public, including company employees.

**short against the box**    The short sale of a stock that is also owned by the short seller. The seller delivers borrowed stock rather than his or her own. If the number of shares sold short equals the number owned, the price risk is eliminated.

**short sale**    A method of profiting when the price of a security declines. The trader endeavors to buy low and sell high but does the selling first. To sell a security not already owned, it is first borrowed from the brokerage firm. A sale is made. Later, the item is bought, hopefully at a lower price, and the loan is repaid. Short selling is made possible by securities, such as stocks and bonds, being homogeneous. Shares sold short need not be bought from the same person to whom they were originally sold. The short seller is said to be "short" the security, in anticipation of the price falling. To "go short" is to take a short position. The opposite notion is to "go long" or to be "long."

**simple return**   The rate of return of an investment from which the income and/or appreciation is withdrawn.

**SIPC**   See *Securities Investor Protection Corporation.*

**soft dollars**   Originally, mutual fund payments of high commissions in return for stock research and other investment-related costs borne by the brokerage firm. The practice has expanded so that some commissions are many times the normal rates in return for non-investment-related costs borne by the brokerage firm, including administration expenses, computers, and accounting costs. In effect, the payment of soft dollars shifts costs from the mutual fund operating fees, which are disclosed, to the fund's transaction costs, which are not, enabling the income of the managers to increase at the shareholder expense.

**specialist**   A market maker on a stock exchange assigned to a particular stock or group of stocks.

**specific risk**   The possibility that, even though the stock market as a whole rises, the few stocks in which the individual is disproportionately invested fall in price. Also referred to as *unsystematic risk.* Specific risk can be diversified away by investing in many stocks, mutual funds, or ETFs. A long-term investor is rewarded for *market risk* but not for specific risk.

**Spiders**   Shares of an exchange-traded fund based on the 500 stocks included in the S&P 500 Index. Structured as a unit investment trust, Spiders are listed on the American Stock Exchange. The underlying trust owns in the proper proportions all 500 of the S&P 500 stocks. Spiders were originally priced at 1/10 the value of the index, although that ratio has slowly changed over time and will continue doing so.

**spin-off**   The distribution of the stock of a subsidiary company to the shareholders of the parent company.

**spread**   The difference between the bid and ask prices. The spread not only enables the market maker to earn a living, it also compensates him or her for holding in inventory securities whose value may fall. Generally, spreads are wider for securities that are riskier and traded less actively.

**Standard & Poor's 500 Index (S&P 500)**   An index of the stock market, based on 500 stocks selected and changed from time to time by the Standard & Poor's publishing company. The S&P 500 is the index most widely accepted by stock professionals as "the market."

**stock**   A share of ownership of a business enterprise organized as a corporation. Owners of stock are part owners of the company, proportionate to the number of shares they own.

**stock dividend**   The distribution of additional stock to shareholders in lieu of cash dividends. Say you hold 100 shares of a stock priced at 50, and a 10 percent stock dividend is paid. Instead of having 100 shares at 50, valued at $5,000, you would own 110 shares at 45.45, also valued at $5,000. (11/10 of 100 shares is 110 shares. 10/11 of 50 is 45.45.)

**stock option**   A contract in which the seller gives the buyer, in return for the payment of a premium, the right but not the obligation to buy or to sell 100 shares of a stock at a certain price by a certain time. A *call option* gives the buyer the right to buy the asset. A *put option* gives the buyer the right to sell the asset.

**stock power**   A document containing the same provisions as the reverse side of a stock certificate. A blank stock certificate and a signed stock power may be mailed separately, thereby protecting against fraud. When the two documents come together at the brokerage firm, the security can be transferred.

**stock repurchase**   A company's purchase of its own stock. The stock may be held in the company's treasury or retired. Given that the earnings remain the same, the reduction in available stock causes the earnings per share to rise.

**stock split**   An increase in the number of shares outstanding. A stock is split to bring its price down to the range at which investors feel more inclined to buy the shares. Say you hold 200 shares priced at

$60, and the stock splits three for two. Instead of 200 shares at $60, valued at $12,000, you would own 300 shares priced at $40, also valued at $12,000. (The old number of shares is multiplied by 3/2. The old price is multiplied by 2/3.) A two-for-one stock split has the same effect as a 100 percent stock dividend.

**stop order to buy**   An order to buy at a price that is higher than the current price. Stop orders are accepted only by exchange specialists, not by OTC market makers.

**stop order to sell**   An order to sell a security at a price that is lower than the current price, usually in an effort to limit loss. Stop orders are accepted only by exchange specialists, not by OTC market makers.

**street name**   The holding of a customer's security by a brokerage firm. No certificate exists. The security is recorded electronically, and the owner's signature is not required to transfer the security. Always expressed as "in street name."

**strike price**   The price to be paid upon exercise for 100 shares of the stock specified in an options contract.

**style shift**   A technique used by some actively managed mutual funds to gain a competitive advantage. Between reporting periods, the fund moves out of some of the types of stocks it's supposed to own, as described in the prospectus, and buys different types of stocks—ones that seem to have current momentum.

**subordinated debenture**   Corporate debt with a claim to corporate assets that is subordinate, or junior, to that of other more senior debt of the same corporation.

**symbol**   A brief set of characters that identifies a security on the tape. The symbols of common stocks listed on exchanges have three or fewer letters. The symbols of common stocks in the over-the-counter market or on the Bulletin Board have four or more letters.

**systematic risk**   See *market risk*.

**tape**   An automated system for reporting stock transactions. The transactions are reported electronically, but the term is left over from the days when the transactions were printed on ticker tapes.

**taxable yield equivalent**   The yield required from a taxable bond to equal, after taxes, the yield from a tax-free municipal bond. A specific tax rate is assumed, usually the top rate.

**tax bracket**   A range of taxable income subject to a specific percentage of tax.

**tax rate**   A rate of tax applicable to a specific tax bracket.

**technical analysis**   An analysis of stocks based on historic price and volume trends.

**technician**   Stock market analyst who studies the price and volume patterns of stocks in an effort to predict future prices. Also known as *chartist*.

**tender offer**   An offer to the shareholders of a company to buy their shares of the stock. The offer might be made by another company. It might also be made by the company's own management, who wish to remove the stock from public circulation and own it themselves.

**time value**   The amount by which the premium of an option exceeds its intrinsic value. If the premium has no intrinsic value, the premium has time value only. Time value declines to zero by expiration.

**TIPS**   See *Treasury Inflation-Protected Security*.

**trading collar**   The banning of program trading after the Dow Jones Industrial Average has moved down by a specific substantial amount from the previous day's close.

**trailing earnings**   A company's earnings for the last four reported quarters, not necessarily the calendar year.

**transfer**
- The recording of a change of ownership of a security on the issuer's books.
- The delivery of a security by the seller's broker to the buyer's broker.
- A change of custodian or trustee of an IRA.

**transfer agent**   A company, usually a bank, that is appointed by a firm to maintain the record of ownership of the firm's securities and to execute the transfers of such securities on the books.

**Treasury bill**   Debt of the U.S. Treasury, with the duration at the time of issue ranging from 90 days to one year.

**Treasury bond**   Debt of the U.S. Treasury, with the duration at the time of issue ranging from 10 to 30 years.

**Treasury Direct**   A method of buying Treasury securities directly from the U.S. Treasury Department without the payment of commissions.

**Treasury Inflation-Protected Security (TIPS)**   A Treasury bond for which neither the par value nor the interest payments remains level. Both are adjusted for inflation.

**Treasury note**   Debt of the U.S. Treasury, with the duration at the time of issue ranging from 1 to 10 years.

**Treasury security**   IOU sold by the U.S. Treasury Department, which can consist of a Treasury bills, notes, and bonds. Since the Treasury Department and the Federal Reserve can create whatever money is needed to enable the federal government to repay its debts, Treasury securities are considered free from the risk of default. They are not, however, free from the risk of price fluctuation or from the dollar's loss of buying power.

**treasury stock**   Shares of a corporation's stock that were once held by members of the public but which the company has bought back, usually in the open market.

**triple witching day**   A day of expiration of all three of the derivatives applying to stocks—namely, stock index futures, options on stock index futures, and options on individual stocks. The unwinding of such contracts can induce high volatility of stock prices on that day.

**turnover rate**   The annual rate of buying and selling of a mutual fund portfolio. A rate of 100 percent means that during a single year, the fund has replaced securities in amounts equal to the total value of the fund.

**UIT**   See *unit investment trust*.

**uncovered option**   The writer of a call option has an *uncovered call* if he does not own the stock he is giving the buyer the right to call. The writer of a put option has an *uncovered put* if he is not short the stock he is giving the buyer the right to put. Also called a *naked option*.

**underwriter**   An investment banking firm that buys an initial public offering or secondary offering of a security with its own money and resells it to the public. Agreed-on proceeds are guaranteed to the company. In the event the security cannot be sold at the anticipated price, the underwriter accepts the risk of loss.

**unearned income**   Income derived from investments, such as dividends, interest, capital gains, pension plan, or rental property, as distinguished from *earned income* derived from current personal labor.

**unit investment trust (UIT)**   An unmanaged, open-end mutual fund that acquires a portfolio of stocks or bonds (in most cases, bonds) and holds them unchanged for a specified period ranging from 1 to 30 years.

**unit of beneficial interest**   The combination of a bond and a warrant at an initial public offering.

**unrealized gain or loss**   A gain or loss having no tax consequence because the security has not been sold. (Tax rules differ with respect to futures.)

**unsystematic risk**   See *specific risk*.

**uptick**   A stock is on an uptick when it trades at a price that is higher than the last different price.

**uptick rule**   A rule imposed by the Securities and Exchange Commission in an effort to keep stock prices from being driven down by short selling. The rule provides that a short sale may be executed only on an uptick.

**variable annuity**   An annuity that can be invested at the owner's option in one or more stock or bond mutual funds.

**volatility**   The rate at which the price of a security moves up and down relative to the market as a whole.

**warehouse receipt**   A negotiable receipt given by a warehouse for the deposit of a specific quantity of a commodity, such as wheat.

**warrant**   A security permitting the holder to purchase from the company by a certain time a specific number of common shares at a specific price. Warrants originate as part of a secondary offering of a stock or bond issue, as an incentive for investors to buy the accompanying stocks or bonds. The combination of *stock* and a warrant at an offering is called a *share of beneficial interest*. The combination of a *bond* and a warrant at an offering is called a *unit of beneficial interest*. After the offering, the warrants trade separately. Although warrants are not traded on options exchanges, they are in fact long-term options.

**wash sale rule**   An IRS rule which provides that, on the sale of a security at a loss, you cannot deduct the loss if, within 30 days before or after the sale (61 days total), you buy another security that is substantially identical. Instead, the disallowed loss is added to the cost basis of the new security and recognized when that security is sold.

**wrap account**   An arrangement with a brokerage firm whereby the client can engage in unlimited trading for a preset annual fee. Instead of charging commissions on each trade, the firm charges fees based on a percentage of the account.

**yield**   The cash paid out by an investment during the year, divided by the current price.

**yield curve**   The graphic representation of the yields of Treasury securities of various maturities. When long-term issues have higher yields than short-term issues, the yield curve is said to be *positive*. This is the normal condition, due to the greater uncertainty of holding long-term debt. Sometimes, short-term rates exceed long-term rates. The yield curve is then said to be *inverted*.

**yield-to-call**   The annualized yield of a bond, taking into account the annual interest payments, the time remaining until a call date, and the difference between the purchase price and the call price. When the yield-to-maturity and yield-to-call differ, the salesperson offering the bond is required to quote the lower of the two.

**yield-to-maturity**   The annualized yield of a bond, taking into account the annual interest payments, the time remaining until maturity, and the difference between the purchase price and the par value.

**zero coupon bond**   A bond that, until maturity, pays neither interest nor principal.

# Bibliography

Bach, David. *The Automatic Millionaire.* New York: Broadway Books, 2004.

Bogle, John C. *John Bogle on Investing.* New York: McGraw-Hill, 2001.

Economides, Steve and Annette. *America's Cheapest Family Gets You Right on the Money.* Three Rivers Press, 2007.

Gastineau, Gary L. *The Exchange-Traded Funds Manual.* New York: Wiley, 2002.

_____. *Someone Will Make Money on Your Funds—Why Not You?* New York: Wiley, 2005.

Geist, Dr. Richard. *Investor Therapy.* New York: Crown Business, 2003.

Gibson, Roger C. *Asset Allocation.* New York: McGraw-Hill, 2000.

Hehn, Elizabeth, ed. *Exchange Traded Funds: Structure, Regulation and Application of a New Fund Class.* Berlin, Heidelberg: Springer, 2005.

Meziani, Seddik. *Exchange Traded Funds as an Investment Option (Finance and Capital Markets).* New York: Palgrave MacMillan, 2005.

Richards, Archie, Jr. *All About Exchange-Traded Funds.* New York: McGraw-Hill, 2003.

# Index

# About the Author

A BA degree from Yale University and 30 years in the investment and financial planning industries has given Archie Richards special insight about long-term market trends and a keen awareness of how to take advantage of them.

Every week, thousands of people heed Archie Richards's investment advice in his newspaper columns. Richards is the author of a previously published McGraw-Hill book, *All About Exchange-Traded Funds* (2003). He is also a dynamic public speaker.

Formerly a successful broker and certified through the Certified Financial Planner Board of Standards, Inc., Richards no longer carries on a financial planning practice. In money matters, having no conflict of interest makes a crucial difference for readers and audiences.

Visit the author's Web site at www.archierichards.com. From the section "Suggested Portfolio," you can download a spreadsheet that enables you to manage your portfolio. The downloading costs you nothing.

The Web site also enables you to contact Richards, which he encourages you to do.